D0651579

The Mediation Field Guide

The Mediation Field Guide

Transcending Litigation and Resolving Conflicts in Your Business or Organization

Barbara Ashley Phillips

JOSSEY-BASS
A Wiley Company
San Francisco

Published by

JOSSEY-BASS
A Wiley Company
350 Sansome St.
San Francisco, CA 94104-1342

www.josseybass.com

Jossey-Bass books and products are available through most bookstores. To contact Jossey-Bass directly, call (888) 378-2537, fax to (800) 605-2665, or visit our Web site at www.josseybass.com.

Substantial discounts on bulk quantities of Jossey-Bass books are available to corporations, professional associations, and other organizations. For details and discount information, contact the special sales department at Jossey-Bass.

We at Jossey-Bass strive to use the most environmentally sensitive paper stocks available to us. Our publications are printed on acid-free recycled stock whenever possible, and our paper always meets or exceeds minimum GPO and EPA requirements.

Library of Congress Cataloging-in-Publication Data

Phillips, Barbara Ashley, date.
    The mediation field guide: transcending litigation and resolving conflicts in your business or organization / Barbara Ashely Phillips.—1st ed.
       p. cm.
    Includes bibliographical references and index.
    ISBN 0–7879–5571–X (alk. paper)
    1. Conflict management. 2. Mediation. 3. Mediation and conciliation, Industrial. 4. Dispute resolution (Law) I. Title.
    HD42 .P48 2001
    658.4'053—dc21   2001002180

FIRST EDITION
HB Printing 10 9 8 7 6 5 4 3 2 1

Contents

Appendixes

This book is dedicated to the movement recognizing the truth of our interconnectedness—one with another. I know of no better legacy for my sons, John and Matt Phillips, my daughters-in-law, Denise and Erin Phillips, their children, Galen, Timothy, Nicholas, Amelia, and Roland Phillips, and for all of us.

Acknowledgments

Whenever a book is written and published, many hands, heads, and hearts have made it so. And it is almost impossible to name them all.

Many have seeded the creativity that may be found here. Chief among the most recent influences on my work is the Canadian-born teacher, John de Ruiter. Through him, I have glimpsed a way of being in the world that is neither mind-driven nor feeling-dependent. Rather, this way of being flows and is expressed through the heart when I allow it to do so. It has deepened my mediation practice and training work and afforded me a very different perspective on what divides us and what might bring us together. Most important, it has brought me a capacity for giving attention that I never knew before. As my awareness has grown, I've begun to recognize when I am working or being in old-mind ways—whether in writing this book or in my work or in other aspects of my life. You may judge for yourself the extent to which I've made room for new-mind ways. de Ruiter's work is largely oral and is available in audio tapes, videos, and his book, *Unveiling Reality* (2000), which can be obtained on the Web at http://www.johnderuiter.com.

Other influences on my work are William Isaacs's book *Dialogue and the Art of Thinking Together* and the dialogue training I've received from DIA-logos Inc., the firm Isaacs cofounded. Peter Senge, David Whyte, and David Bohm have profoundly influenced how I hear and what I now listen for. Frank Fukuyama's book *Trust: The Social Virtues and the Creation of Prosperity* (1995) spoke to me of the extraordinary importance of the intangible qualities of civil, peaceful, and prosperous societies. Steven Keeva's extraordinary book *Transforming Practices* put me in touch with parts of the holistic law movement I had not been aware of—including the International Alliance of Holistic Lawyers, the McGill Center for Creative Problem-Solving, Therapeutic Jurisprudence (inspired by David Wexler), and the Comprehensive Law Movement, of which Susan Daicoff writes so powerfully. The Restorative Justice movement is another inspiration, which includes the Victim-Offender Mediation movement, spawned at least in significant part by Marty Price. And then there are the peacemaking and sentencing circles—extraordinary models of collaborative process and vehicles for drawing citizens back into meaningful participation in their communities and vastly reducing the recidivism rate and the need for jails. All of these movements seek to achieve greater responsiveness to the needs of clients, our justice system, and those who practice, whether on the bench or at the bar. It is heartening to see so many people laboring in so many distinct fields who are willing to say, "The emperor has no clothes." The system isn't working, and it is taking a terrible toll on those who work in it or come in contact with it.

Of those who have helped with the writing, research, and editing of the book, I especially acknowledge Andrea Gietz and Jossey-Bass executive editor Alan Rinzler. Of assistance on this project have been Mary Cooney, Marie Strauss, and others too numerous to mention. Little is more priceless to an author than someone who will read the manuscript. Those who have helped me in shaping the book include Ted Phillips, San Francisco attorney, and Marg Huber, former director of the Conflict Resolution Center at the Justice Institute in British Columbia, who has pioneered training in heart-based processes. Marg has inspired me to offer workshops and training in what I'm learning and has been a great model for me. As has Chris Merchant, who inspires and leads others into a deeper understanding of our underlying interconnectedness, and William F. Lincoln, my original teacher and mentor.

Others who have inspired me in particular are Kenneth Cloke and Zena Zumeta, two colleagues who have distinguished themselves in the field and in training work and who are focused on bringing the heart more into the work of mediation. We three have supported each other for years in our efforts to mine structures and processes for the gold that is in them. It is so easy to offer a knockoff of the substance that engages the power of the heart. Who is to say which is the real thing, unless one has had experience in both the imitation and the original? These two—Cloke and Zumeta—uniquely know the difference between the two, and their continued support of my work has been immensely reassuring.

April 2001   Barbara Ashley Phillips
Edmonton, Alberta

Introduction
Mediation and Wholeness

This is a book about how conflict resolution can be done with grace and dignity and how this fits in with larger societal changes. It is written particularly for those people whose insight, passion, work, or interests lead them to seek more of mediation's potential for resolving complex, highly sensitive, or otherwise multifaceted disputes. You will learn how mediation is changing the way we do business around disputes and how to apply this simple, versatile, and powerful tool to matters touching your business, organizational, and family life. I will show you what I have learned about stumbling blocks and cultural traps, as well as how to select and use professionals such as lawyers and mediators. There are stories in this book of how mediation has touched people's lives and hearts and insight into how they allowed flow into their conflict resolution experiences. *Flow* is a dynamic that arises of its own accord and is characterized by what Martin Buber calls an "elemental togetherness." (Buber quoted in Isaacs, 1999, p. 403). Flow carries a unique fruitfulness, which brings healing and life to all who are touched by it. To taste flow is to participate in life itself. We will look at what is happening in the field of mediation from many perspectives. To me, it is an adventure.

At a conference on construction industry dispute resolution in the mid-1990s, European engineer Guenther Raberger observed, "Our civilization is like a bird with one wing, flying round and round in circles. The other wing is the Feminine. Without it, we cannot go anywhere" (G. Raberger, personal interview, Oct. 1994). What he perceived in Europe is also evident in many other places in the Western world: the end of "the way it has always been done" mentality.

"The way it has always been done" suggests a certainty that has less and less validity. It has its weaknesses; as Oliver Wendell Holmes once said, "There must be some better reason for a rule of law than that it's always been done that way." Yet at the same time, it has been a source of strength through stability. As our civilization loses its rigidity, it may lose stability until some small but critical mass of humans learns to seek mutual gain—seeing themselves as part of a community, a whole, rather than as completely separate individuals pursuing purely personal gain.

Mediation is the feminine face of dispute resolution. Mediation is not the cause but a product of significant changes in society, and it is the beneficiary of a trend away from confrontation toward problem solving and beyond to mutual respect and wider gain. There is widespread evidence that people do not lose their human characteristics when they become litigants—that they prefer processes in which they have an opportunity for choice and for significant participation, particularly a chance to tell their stories.[1] The mediation process satisfies this preference better than any other form of alternative dispute resolution (ADR), which is perhaps more aptly termed *appropriate dispute resolution*. It also has procedural integrity in the hands of dedicated practitioners. Nonetheless, the habits of *old-mind* lawyers, judges, and professional litigants have yielded slowly, so that many are unaware of the potential of mediation being trampled underfoot.

THE STRENGTH OF WEAKNESS

Mediation's strengths look like weaknesses from the point of view of *old-mind thinking,* which sees adversarial process as the norm and everything else as the alternative. For example, from the perspective of the war paradigm, it looks weak to have a broad focus and acknowledge dependence on the consent and trust of the parties. Yet these are hallmarks of mediation's strength. It is the strength of water rather than the more apparent strength of rock. Few dispute, upon reflection, that water vanquishes rock every time.

It is the strength of water rather than the more apparent strength of rock.

Understanding mediation's true potential requires engaging *new mind,* a paradigm holding that mutual gain is desirable and possible through mutual effort, even in the face of apparently insurmountable difficulties. Fortunately, it is not necessary to choose between these two approaches, the combative and the problem-solving transformative, for the choice is not lost. But it is a choice—"adversarial mediation" is a contradiction in terms. Use mediation to build enough trust so that litigants, their lawyers, and their experts may pierce the adversarial facade and confront the reality of their situation. Mediation is, by definition, facilitative.

Trust is the currency of social capital: the ability of people, groups, and organizations to work together for common purposes (Fukuyama, 1995). When trust is low, all manner of enforcement mechanisms and control mechanisms need to be in place. Imagine the collection machinery that would be required if most people in this country did not more or less willingly assess and pay their perceived fair share of taxes. Consider penitentiaries, where we house people at a cost exceeding that of putting a student through a private college. It is far easier to function in high-trust societies, such as Western democracies—to secure not only basic needs but also recognition as a respected and appreciated individual. Most of us would agree that recognition is a primary motivator of human beings in community (Bush and Folger, 1994). The prosperity and organizational structures of modern society are dependent upon this quality of recognition, of being seen (Fukuyama, 1992).

> *"Adversarial mediation" is a contradiction in terms.*

Our legal institutions are products of earlier times and served far lower-trust societies than those in Western democracies today. It is time for dispute resolution models to become appropriate to and supportive of higher-trust ways of being together in society. Social capital is a fragile thing, relatively easy to destroy and impossible to bring into being. It grows organically out of the culture, and once it is deeply impaired, it can take a very long time to regrow (Fukuyama, 1995).

THE ROLE OF COURTS

Courts that see themselves in the business of dispute resolution rather than merely in the business of litigation are seeking to develop a balanced, user-friendly, and effective system of dispute management and resolution. Our society is in desperate need of more effective and appropriate means of shepherding to their final resolution the 95 percent of filed lawsuits that will never be tried. Lawyers and disputants need more humane and effective tools for resolving disputes. What will help most is a recognition of mediation as the principal resource for dealing with the majority of civil disputes that will be settled. Mediation needs to be accepted on its own terms, not remade in an adversarial model, as happens when old mind runs the process. After that, courts need only integrate case management tools with a vision of alternative dispute resolution. What is at stake is the vast power of mediation to heal the conflict, the combatants, and the community. That requires new mind.

The advent of modern mediation is working profound changes in our social system in ways we cannot yet even imagine. Thomas Stipanowich tells us that "a quiet revolution is occurring in America and throughout the industrialized world. It has to do with the way people perceive the controversies that affect them, and their involvement in the search for solutions" (Stipanowich, 1996, p. 65). So great is the change brought about by mediation that observers struggle for words to describe it. ADR pioneer Frank Sander speaks of mediation as "the sleeping giant [of dispute resolution]" (Reuben, 1996, p. 54) and notes the differences between it and trial and arbitration (Lewis, 1995).

Societal changes of this magnitude are so large that we cannot see the pattern developing until it is pretty much fully formed. The order, symmetry, and power of the movement is hidden, as with fractals—shapes irregular and fragmented in appearance that look like nothing at all, but when viewed with high magnification, are revealed to be breathtakingly ordered and powerful—so it is with large-scale social movements such as collaborative ways of being in the world, from which mediation flows.

When people want more involvement in their search for solutions to controversies that affect them, and those controversies are perceived as problems to be solved rather than as victories to be won, the whole social underpinning of civil litigation begins to give way. This may help account for the relative decline in both filings and in civil trials over the past ten to fifteen years (Ostrom and Kauder, 1998).

As Western societies move toward more collaborative processes, there is serious question as to whether courts and lawyers will remain at the center of civil dispute resolution. Their centrality today is based on control of civil litigation, which in a rapidly increasing number of jurisdictions is the source of a large number of referrals to mediation. If courts and lawyers abandon the illusion of exclusive control, they may remain center stage in dispute resolution, although instead of occupying this space exclusively, courts will share their space with communities and provide resources to enable them to act wisely in their own behalf (Stuart, 1996). And lawyers will share the stage with people from other disciplines. If they do share the stage, both the public and the legal profession will be well served (Toben, 1996; MacNaughton, 2000b).

THE ATTRACTION OF SELF-DETERMINATION

Mediation is in one sense old as well as new. Our tendency to resolve disputes on our own is a central characteristic of our Anglo-American heritage. From the most remote antecedents of our legal system, there is evidence of procedures that gave disputants some control over their destiny (Sanchez, 1996). Blood feuds and self-help were common. And a mere legal judgment—absent a willingness to comply—had its limitations. In Anglo-Saxon England, from the seventh to the mid-eleventh centuries, the third-party decision makers often persuaded the losing party to come to terms with the winning party, thus promoting reconciliation. This occurred *after* winner-take-all judgments were announced to the parties but *before* these judgments were finalized by oath swearing. Reparation amounts for personal injury were made expressly subject to negotiation (Sanchez, 1996).

Other parts of the world have long perceived the New World—the source of the current impetus toward mediation—as a model of people's ability to work together. This is characteristic of pioneer societies. Stories of how North American pioneers built villages and communities through helping each other with fellowship, hard work, and perseverance take a back seat to the shootout at the OK corral, but they are perhaps the greater part of the Western cultural heritage. It is in this grand tradition of the new-mind way that mediation moves most comfortably.

THE SEARCH FOR JUSTICE

Civil court resolutions by themselves do not provide a satisfactory example of justice. Justice does not mean getting the same result on the same facts in all or even most instances; and despite the assumed certainty, there is more flexibility in the application of law than generally appears.[2] Nor is popular culture very helpful; it espouses a view of justice that leaves compassion and mercy out of the equation.

Justice without compassion is the kind of justice one demands for the other person—one who is not us. The *other* is not us personally and is not among those we consider our kind. Societies do things to *others* they would never tolerate for their members—enslaving them, for example. Many believe that doers of evil deeds have taken themselves out of society, so that they become others, to be killed or treated inhumanely (in ways we would not want our kind treated) because we no longer relate to them as human beings. The restorative justice movement[3] is acting on the recognition that others (those we treat as other) do not readily become productive citizens when they return to society. For our own wholeness, we need to give them a way to pay for their misdeeds that integrates them back into the mainstream, so that they have a stake in protecting it. In this way, they lose their otherness.

Archbishop Desmond Tutu has written passionately of the deep African philosophical underpinnings for the Truth & Reconciliation Commission. There is, he says,

> a central feature of the African Weltanschauung (or worldview)—
> what we know as *ubuntu* in the Nguri group of languages, or *botho*
> in the Sotho languages. What is it that constrained so many to
> choose to forgive rather than to demand retribution, to be so
> magnanimous rather than wreaking vengeance? *Ubuntu* is very
> difficult to render into a Western language. It speaks of the very
> essence of being human. When we want to give high praise to
> someone we say *'Yu, u nobuntu'* 'Hey, he or she has *ubuntu.'* This
> means they are generous, hospitable, friendly, caring, and compassionate. They share what they have. It also means my humanity is
> caught up, is inextricably bound up, in theirs.
>
> We belong in a bundle of life. We say, 'a person is a person
> through other people.' It is not 'I think therefore I am.' It says

rather: 'I am human because I belong.' I participate, I share. A person with *ubuntu* is open and available to others, affirming of others, does not feel threatened that others are able and good; for he or she has a proper self-assurance that comes from knowing that he or she belongs in a greater whole and is diminished when others are humiliated or diminished, when others are tortured or oppressed, or treated as if they were less than who they are [Tutu, 1999, p. 31].

In the great traditions of Western civilization, justice without mercy and compassion is no justice at all. Justice is symbolized by a blindfolded woman holding a scale and a sword. It is no accident that Justice is portrayed as a woman. Symbolically, the archetypal feminine speaks of whole-seeing and reason with wisdom (van der Post, 1994). Whole-seeing reads the hearts of those involved and is not limited to hearing their words. The blindfold aids this inner vision, this understanding.

Laurens van der Post spoke eloquently of our times as the period in recorded history when for the first time Sophia, the feminine archetype of wisdom, is emerging. He attributes much of the suffering of this century, particularly World War II and its antecedents, to the dominance of the Siegfried archetype, the heroic but immature masculine that disdains and rudely uses the feminine. Without Sophia, he says, we have no wisdom, and, without the feminine, no balance.

The scale of justice that Lady Justice holds represents the balancing of inner and outer powers, masculine and feminine powers, and the interests of the individual and society. The sword that Justice carries at rest represents the sword of discrimination and discernment, not the sword of vengeance (Fontana, 1993).

What does justice mean in the context of mediation? The law is only one factor that parties consider in evaluating settlement options. If mediation is about self-determination and if the affected participants reach an accommodation that works for them (absent a lack of capacity or other taint), why would a court question it?[4] Carrie Menkel-Meadow points out that "people may choose out-of-court settlement precisely because legislatively enacted legal solutions do not meet the underlying needs or interests of parties in particular cases" (1995, p. 2676).

Perhaps we are looking for justice in the wrong place. We do not speak of justice in referring to what people do to or for themselves.

Justice has meaning only in a more public context—when people are done unto or acted upon, particularly when the one acted upon is required to submit. Protection of the mediation process is far more critical to the realization of mediation's potential than to the justice of the mediated agreement in the eyes of a third party.

As relevant to institutionally fostered mediation, justice means that mediation to which the parties are committed must not only be seen as fair and just but must be so in fact. This is no invitation for courts to control the process or the providers, for fairness and justice lie in the eyes of the users. As they are given options and choices about the appropriate dispute resolution process and the provider, justice in this sense will happen automatically.

POWER

Old mind thinks of power in terms of authority and compulsion. New mind knows better. Power is the ability to get results. There are two contending definitions of power vying for prominence in our society: *power over,* which wins people's hands and uses its resources to maintain control over what people do, and *power with,* which wins people's hearts and uses its resources to carry out a common purpose. Supporters of either view do not believe that the other side of the debate refers to power at all. The principal tools of power over are fear and authority; the principal tools of power with are reasoning, dialogue, leadership, and enthusiasm.[5] Compared to power with, power over is limited, yet power with requires a more broadly defined self-interest, and many people still believe that those who seek power with are either weak or not grounded in reality.

Courts too are caught in the debate over what power means, for power is their lifeblood. Courts are constrained as long as all they can do is award money damages, order, and enjoin. For all of the social ills courts successfully have addressed, it seems they may be approaching the limit. In a society whose citizens are raising complex problems affecting relationships far beyond those before the court, the limited remedies available to courts are grossly inadequate.[6] Monetary and injunctive relief fall far short of the broad range of remedies available when the discussion broadens into a problem-solving process and the parties fashion their own solutions

(Menkel-Meadow, 1984). The answer is not broader legal remedies but more appropriate processes for addressing problems that will bring out the best in lawyers and disputants. It is no secret that the adversary system often brings out the worst in advocates and litigants. And, in fact, it can be argued that the system is *designed* to bring out the worst (Resnik, 1995).

It takes negotiators and mediators to bring power with into the equation. And there is considerable evidence that power with is assuming primacy both at home and abroad. *Soft power* attracts others to want what you want rather than using force to get them to do what they do not want to do (Jaffe, 1997). Today, soft power is in—from international affairs, to rearing children, training horses, farming, and ranching. On a global scale, the United States's soft power is replacing force, the traditional currency of clout. America's economic and cultural hegemony in the world contrasts starkly with the tiny, withered fruits of would-be conquerors (Jaffe, 1997).

The days of "come home with your shield or on it" are over. The twentieth century, for all of its wars, may have demonstrated once and for all the futility of war and conquest. At the same time, it points to the wealth that is possible with an open society and a nation of generous people. Like mediation and other collaborative processes, soft power rests on a broad sense of self-interest, visible in the remarkable post–World War II Marshall Plan and America's comparatively wide-open society, unique in recorded history. In the light of this sea change in perception of what is good and what is effective, litigation's flaws and deficits stand out starkly.

In the twenty-first century, mediation and other collaborative processes such as partnering will become the tools of choice in conflict management. Partnering is an approach to construction and other projects in which owner, contractor, subcontractors, and the design team sit down and work out an agreement in advance to provide mechanisms for early conflict management and to minimize the incentives and opportunities for disruptions. (See Chapters Thirteen and Sixteen.) Lawyers will either be on board or be swept aside (Toben, 1996). The way in which courts and the legal profession respond to mediation and other collaborative conflict management processes will determine the degree to which they participate in what is more a birthing process than a titanic struggle.

A NEW APPRECIATION OF BALANCE

The truths about the nature of the problem-solving/transformative universe are reflected in the following rules of life, expressed by Tom Frantzen at a 1998 conference on holistic management in agriculture:

1. Everything is related to everything else.
2. Water always runs downhill.
3. Nature always laughs last.

These attitudes—such as *ubuntu,* described by Archbishop Desmond Tutu—are essentially inconsistent with a zero-sum approach. When the legal community adopts them, it moves away from an adversarial system into a fertile, diverse universe like nature's own. The world of courts and lawyers becomes at once generative and highly relevant to a society of people far more willing than they may have appeared in the historical past to take responsibility for constructive resolution of conflict.

A problem-solving/transformative approach, unlike the adversarial approach, is naturally balanced. The balance required in dispute resolution is more concerned with the mutual good of the parties. Historically, the adversarial process has focused on winners and losers and assumed that one wins and the other loses. It has tended to produce more losers than winners, because of transaction costs. A wiser approach incorporates the feminine elements in the search for mutually and more broadly beneficial solutions. This too can become a self-fulfilling prophecy. When self-interest is defined more broadly, the adoption of cooperative attitudes and collaborative processes will follow.

There is increasing evidence, from international affairs to the advent of partnering to archaeology from the prehistoric period, that collaborative processes are more consistent with human nature than adversarial ones. Consider the steps that have been taken to loosen the stranglehold of identity-based conflicts that present themselves as ideological, ethnic, and religious wars (Rothman, 1997). From Northern Ireland, to the Middle East, to the Berlin Wall, huge progress has been made, even if the steps taken to keep the peace have been faltering at times. William Ury and Raine Eisler, in their separate books, point out that for tens of thousands of years, until roughly the last eight thousand, there was no evidence of the glorification of combat, conquest, wars and warriors (Eisler, 1991; Ury, 1999).

RESTORATION OF BALANCE

The engineer's comment about civilization being like a bird with one wing calls to mind what Joseph Campbell called the central myth of Western civilization. In the quest for the Holy Grail, brave knights battled dragons and all manner of evil, finding no rest in their search. But the Grail, a vessel filled with blood, is none other than the sacred feminine. (Appendix E elaborates on the qualities of the sacred feminine.) The Grail myth tells us that what we have been searching for throughout the history of Western civilization is *balance* of the feminine with the masculine. The feminine is part of all human beings, and when we fail to respect its qualities, such as its intuitive, relational, nurturing, indirect, and compassionate attributes, we deny part of ourselves, whatever our gender. Until we embrace this fundamental part of our nature, we are hopelessly and destructively out of balance.

The filters of the dominant culture distort both our lives and how we perceive what is real and important in the world. For several thousand years, we have accepted that a world deprived of the deep feminine and respect for gentleness is just a reflection of the way things are. Our parks are decorated with figures of warriors and conquerors. War metaphors define us in many arenas, from health care to conflict resolution to religion. These are old-mind ways of thinking that are beginning to yield to this sea change in paradigm that we are now experiencing.

There seems to be an inherent balance between self-interest and interest in the whole community, within the human psyche. How these intertwine in a mature and healthy psyche is shown in Spiral Dynamics,™ a model of human psychological evolution and personality states. Spiral Dynamics offers a whole new model of human nature to explain why we are as we are and what the development of the whole person is really about. Beck and Cowan demonstrate that:

1. Human nature has the built-in ability to change as the conditions of existence change, thus forming new systems;

2. When a new level is activated, we change our view of the world and our rules for living to adapt;
3. We live in a potentially open system of values with an infinite number of modes of living available to us; and
4. We can respond positively only to messages and other inputs that are appropriate to our current worldview [1996, p. 29].

The spiral ascends alternatively through me-views (survival, power, achievement, and flexibility) and we-views (kinship, purpose, consent, and globalism). It is not value driven: each level can be positive or negative; both the street gang leader and the great warrior draw heavily on the power level but in different ways. From the perspective of Spiral Dynamics, it appears that self-interest and societal interest was never an either-or proposition. The more highly evolved a person is—the more of these levels he or she has passed through—the richer and deeper the spiritual resources he or she has to draw on. The term *spiritual* is used here in a nonreligious sense to indicate the ability to function with a high level of refinement in thought, feeling, and intuition.

Spiral Dynamics offers research evidence to support those who would be hopeful about the ability of humans to make the best of changed circumstances—such as, the lessened interest in adversarial procedures and the movement toward taking greater responsibility for the resolution of conflict in which one is involved. It also provides a cautionary insight: people can respond positively *only* to messages and other inputs that are appropriate to their current worldview. Part of the purpose of this book is to support a broader worldview around conflict resolution and to woo those who still do not see the point.

This broader worldview is the *ubuntu,* holding that "a person is a person through other people." It appears in human affairs as the difference between cursing your neighbors because their children and their dogs make noise and taking them raspberries from your overloaded vines; as the difference between allowing time for a person being deposed—questioned by a lawyer under oath—to rest when fatigue sets in and insisting on boring ahead with the next fifty pages of questions. Generosity produces wealth: the neighbor gives you sacks of apples from his tree, and you have apple pies and apple crisps to share all up and down the street. A refreshed witness can better recall those things that might have been missed had questioning continued unabated. More reliable information is provided, and wasteful arguments are avoided later on. Wholeness expresses itself in the larger world as participation in life and community as you effortlessly walk your talk in your experience around conflict and in everyday life. When there is wholeness, there will not be a split between what you most value and what you do.

The old mind does not think. In words attributed to Peter Garrett,[7] "what mostly passes for thinking is thoughting—the replaying of old tapes involves no new thinking at all." It creates a powerful inertia that resists change tenaciously. It is embedded in institutions such as the formal justice system (Stuart, 1998) and in cultures, such as the lawyer culture, discussed in Chapter Six. And it is reflected in governmental and organizational persistence in following policies long recognized to be unneeded and even downright harmful to the objectives they allegedly support (Tuchman, 1992).

The new mind treasures wholeness and looks for ways of implementing it. This has not been lost on jurists, some of whom are among those engaged in the search, recognizing the limitations of justice as it has been pursued in the courts. Judge Barry D. Stuart of the Yukon Territorial Court writes this about criminal justice issues:

> Current bureaucratic dominance over community justice issues suggests a profound mistrust of local communities to be reasonable, prudent or knowledgeable about acting in their best interests. An anti-democratic, paternalistic attitude underlines most Justice policies, and denies the evolution of community-based partnerships that advance the collective best interests of the community, the justice agencies, the offenders and the victims [Stuart, 1998, p. 108].

Taking this open-minded perspective into the mediation field, New Zealand lawyer Roger Chapman wrote:

> It is not merely the outcome of the dispute which must meet the client's needs and interests; it is just as important that the process by which it is reached should be felt by the client to be appropriate and satisfying. However good the result may be when viewed in legal terms, the client will probably feel some dissatisfaction if it was arrived at by a process which the client did not understand; or if the client was unable to participate as fully as he or she wished;

or if the client did not have an adequate opportunity to explain
his or her perspective on the problem and know that it had been
heard; or if the cost was too high; or if the process endangered
important relationships [Chapman, 1996, pp. 186, 187].

Another example is the recent experience of Maryland, which
in the hallowed precincts of the chief judge's office, decided to consider how mediation and other collaborative processes might best
be implemented in that state. When all was said and done, public
discussions, which ultimately involved over seven hundred participants and every major institution—the courts, law enforcement,
juvenile and family service agencies, the educational system—came
up with one of the most far-reaching charters for the role of collaborative dispute resolution in the twenty-first century (see Chapter Sixteen).

In a very real sense, conflict resolution is everyone's business.
After hundreds of years of moving disputants further and further
apart from each other and making their exchanges increasingly
ritualized and formal, the tide has turned. In Native American cultures, when one is sick, the community comes together for healing
not just of the sick one but of the entire community. When the sick
one is healed, the community is healed. Conflict, by analogy, is not
something that happens just to one or another. The whole society
is affected, and it is affected by how that conflict is dealt with.

Mediation, restorative justice, peacemaking circles, partnering,
consensus building, and facilitation are all tools for allowing our
conflict resolution systems to get back into balance. There is an
intimacy and an accountability that allows human imperfections
to be self-correcting and problems to dissolve. This book is about
how these threads weave together to enable each one of us to participate in the design and development of dispute resolution systems worth having.

The Mediation Field Guide

Part One

Way Beyond Litigation

Speaking from the heart of Africa, Archbishop Desmond Tutu wrote:

> Harmony, friendliness, community are great goods. Social harmony is for us the summum bonum—the greatest good. Anything that subverts or undermines this sought-after good is to be avoided like the plague. Anger, resentment, lust for revenge, even success through aggressive competitiveness, are corrosive of this good. To forgive is not just to be altruistic. It is the best form of self-interest. What dehumanizes you, inexorably dehumanizes me. Forgiveness gives people resilience, enabling them to survive and emerge still human despite all efforts to dehumanize them [Tutu, 1999, p. 341].

Chapter One

The Big Shift

We dance round in a ring and suppose
But the Secret sits in the middle and knows.
ROBERT FROST

Let us look in on a group in Seattle that is just gathering. Let's pretend we're flies on the wall and have a fly's global awareness. It is a warm summer day. The lawyers are polite. It is obvious that there is only one person at the table who believes there is any hope the matter can settle. Lawyers for the plaintiff are there out of courtesy to the mediator, who has invited them to spend a day seeing what progress could be made. Defense counsel is going through the motions for his client, who initiated this mediation.

The dispute has been the subject of three lawsuits lasting more than four years. There have never been any negotiations. Each side has been committed to winning, but it was a long time before anyone asked what "winning" meant.

In the next eight hours, something important happens. The mediator listens, asks questions, caucuses with each side time and again. She shows the parties they need to know more about what the actual damages might turn out to be if the plaintiffs prevail. They discover that this information can be developed fairly readily, so they agree to recess and meet again in two weeks. There is cautious optimism; the parties see that they can at least agree on what is needed, who will get it, and when everyone will reconvene.

We come back for the second round and observe that by the end of the second day of mediation, the rough outlines of a settlement have been reached. We discover later that the details have been polished off in a third day, six weeks after the initial session. Hundreds of workers affected by this lawsuit get the benefits of the settlement. For everyone, the ordeal is over.

How long would this case have continued to be litigated without mediation? We can only say that this four-year-old dispute resolved in mediation, as do most matters mediated. We know the high success rate in mediation is independent of the dispute's maturity. Impending wrongful-termination disputes resolve in mediation before the termination. Intrafamily disputes resolve in mediation before the family relationship has died. Contract disputes between businesses resolve in mediation, allowing business relationships to be productively resumed.

The secret is now out: whatever your dispute, it's very likely to settle out of court. Ninety percent of disputes never reach the courts, and some 95 percent of those that do resolve without ever going to trial. These statistics suggest that people are passionately determined to resolve their own disputes—despite the biggest and most costly lawsuit industry in the world.

There is evidence of a major decline in civil litigation. During the last decade of the twentieth century, civil lawsuit filings remained steady across the board, despite a 12 percent national population increase. In California, long considered one of the most litigious states, civil lawsuit filings have decreased 17 percent while the state had a 15 percent population increase over the period from 1990 to 1999 (Judicial Council of California, 2001). What was at one time viewed as a litigation explosion has quietly gone away. At the same time, mediation has been increasing across the board.

Finding statistics is next to impossible due to lack of reporting and uneven reporting criteria. However, as an indicator, the National Association for Community Mediation estimates that in 1976, there were 10 mediation centers nationwide. By 1988 there were approximately 150 community mediation centers. Today it is estimated that there are more than 550. Some 100,000 disputes a year are referred to these centers, and about 45 percent of these are mediated. During the 1990s and before the consolidation of limited jurisdiction courts into courts of general jurisdiction, California reported a decline of 30 percent in the filing of small claims cases (California Judicial Council, 2000a).

What has happened? Have Americans lost their contentious-ness? Or is the futility of seeking our day in court finally sinking in?

WHAT IS LITIGATION?

Litigation is not trial. It is preparing for the trial that, 95 percent of the time, will not happen. Litigation is taking discovery, that is, formal inquiry into the matter by written questions, recorded inter-rogation, and requests for production of documents. Litigation involves interrogatories, questions posed in writing. Litigation involves devising answers that duck the questions.

Litigation is taking depositions—oral testimony under an oath of truthfulness—to get information or to pin down the witness to make it hard to say something different at the trial that will almost never take place. Deposition tran-scripts are prepared by long-suf-fering court reporters and transcribers. To make these long and boring depositions useful, lawyers or paralegals then spend more hours summarizing them.

Litigation is not trial. It is preparing for the trial that, 95 percent of the time, will not happen.

Parties in litigation often are required to produce all manner of business records, files, and other papers by the box and even in carload lots. These document productions, as they are called, tell both more and less than they should, but tell almost nothing about how the matter might prop-erly be resolved.

In litigation, lawyers appear in court to answer questions that make it easier for the court to manage its calendar.[1] They make or defend motions that sometimes complicate, rather than simplify, the situation, and they seek emergency orders (which are rarely granted) and seek to explain lapses and delays. New York lawyer and litigator John H. Wilkinson passes along the following story:

> Explaining how the law works to a group of high school students, a prominent New York lawyer put it this way, "You spend years and years in pretrial motion practice. I smother the other side with papers and they smother me with papers until we wear each other out and the judge knocks my head against his head and we

settle. It takes about three or four years [quoted in Wilkinson, 1990, p. vii].

Like war, in the words of Sir Winston Churchill, litigation is "mainly a catalogue of blunders."

One Los Angeles lawyer observed, "I have sinned. I cannot think of a case I have tried without stacks of depositions and boxes of organized and indexed but unnecessary documents. But that's the way I was trained and that's what the clients seem to want." You, as client, hold the reins. Will you use them?

HOW DO THE COURTS RESPOND?

Courts recognize the wastefulness of litigation activity. Judges believe that getting a reasonably early trial date will help force people to resolve their differences. Some adopt fast-track programs that require a lot of litigation activity right away, when no one knows if it will ever be necessary. This is expensive.

Not all courts, of course, take this approach. Some, such as Multnomah County, Oregon's largest urban court system, give a great deal of leeway for the first nine months or so after filing a case and then insist that trial occur within twelve months of the filing date, except for cases designated as complex, and even those typically are given only a few extra months. Because parties and counsel are aware of the early trial date, it gets factored in to how the case is managed. The leverage of delay has not disappeared, but its effects have been effectively curtailed in this court.

Recognizing that most cases settle, courts have begun to adopt mandatory mediation rules, which force people to sit down together and talk in the presence of a disinterested third party, usually a lawyer and sometimes a mediator. Some seventeen hundred courts now have alternative dispute resolution (ADR) programs to encourage ADR, though relatively few of them are mandatory. Mandating mediation has many implications—raising new issues like good-faith participation, too-rapid expansion of the demand for mediation, and impairment of the voluntary nature that makes mediation so effective.

Compulsory mediation seriously interferes with the qualities of voluntary mediation that tend toward finality. However, it is clear that when mediation is strictly voluntary, the programs still get relatively little use. The culture of the legal community, which has served as gatekeeper to dispute resolution processes since the establishment of courts of law, is still not predominantly invested in mediation. So it is a Hobson's choice. More and more, institutions are opting for a mandatory or opt-out model in order to give lawyers enough experience with the process that they become competent to discuss options with clients in an informed way. (See Chapter Eight.)

WHAT IS MEDIATION?

Mediation is a negotiation moderated by a neutral party to resolve conflict and address related concerns in ways that meet the parties' interests. The principals may participate fully. The mediation can rise to the level of diplomacy, but unlike litigation, it cannot fall to the level of a street brawl.

In civil mediation, the most common type offered for disputes affecting businesses and organizations, there is usually a joint session where all the parties come together to orally inform the mediator about the situation. It may run from a half-hour to several hours or even a full day. This is followed by caucuses: private meetings between the mediator and each side. In these caucuses, a party can give the mediator confidential information it did not want to disclose in the joint session, and the mediator will disclose what he sees as that side's hurdles, weaknesses, and problems. These private caucuses allow creativity and a certain anonymity as to the source of ideas about ways of resolving the matter.

Trust, often absent at the beginning, builds gradually as little agreements are reached, first by joint participation in the convening process, then by agreeing on ground rules, then on how the time will be organized, then through the read-back, that is, the mediator's artful acknowledgment of what has been said. People notice that their concerns are being addressed and begin to relax. The mediator works with both sides, and sometimes with the experts and counsel, inviting them into a constructive and productive dialogue. Animosities often soften, in part by the mediator's presence, in part by the mediator's modeling the values that the parties have sought in mediation.

In a typical civil mediation, the mediator may be briefed in advance of the mediation (see Chapter Ten). In convening the

mediation, the mediator describes the joint sessions and the caucuses and confirms understandings about how the time will be managed. Ground rules, such as common courtesy and one person
speaking at a time, may be agreed upon by participants. A written
confidentiality agreement may or may not be subscribed to by all
present, depending on available statutory protections. Then the
mediator listens to the presentations and reframes them in summary
form, highlighting what is important in all the talk by the attention
given to certain points. The mediator's skill in separating the constructive from the destructive, recognizing and articulating feelings
embedded in a presentation, and reframing contentions and statements, as well as teaching participants how frames work and what
they do to our perception, is a measure of the civil mediator's skill
and ability to generate trust. It begins the process of helping each
side to see the other's point of view. In caucuses, participants share
with the mediator what they will not share with the other side, discuss the hurdles their side faces, and develop options for resolution
as they come to a new perspective on their dispute.

WHO'S IN CONTROL?

In litigation, lawyers think they are in control, judges think they are
in control, and clients sometimes think they are in control. In fact,
no one is in control, nor is the litigation under control. Once begun,
litigation has a life of its own. It feeds on clients, lawyers, and judges,
all of whom become paler, but somehow usually keep walking and
talking. Many lawyers feel trapped by the profession they once loved.

Mediation is a different story. Generally in civil mediation, the
lawyer makes the presentation and response, although increasingly
lawyers are allowing their clients to speak directly, both because it
is effective to have them tell their own story and because it makes
the process more powerful for the clients. The lawyer advises the
client on the reasonableness of settlement options, for the client
makes the decision. The mediator is in charge of the process. The
clients or principals are in charge of all decisions. They need stay
only so long as the mediation is productive.

Any agreement is only as secure as the commitment behind it.
The security of a mediated agreement, like the security or enforceability of a judgment, is in practical reality directly proportional to

Figure 1.1. Security of Outcomes in Different Dispute Resolution Models.

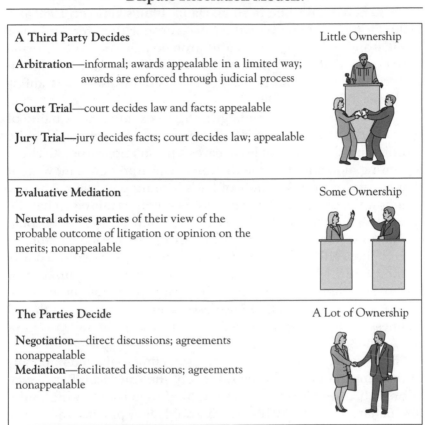

A Third Party Decides   Little Ownership

Arbitration—informal; awards appealable in a limited way;
        awards are enforced through judicial process

Court Trial—court decides law and facts; appealable

Jury Trial—jury decides facts; court decides law; appealable

Evaluative Mediation   Some Ownership

Neutral advises parties of their view of the
probable outcome of litigation or opinion on the
merits; nonappealable

The Parties Decide   A Lot of Ownership

Negotiation—direct discussions; agreements
nonappealable
Mediation—facilitated discussions; agreements
nonappealable

the degree of ownership the parties have in it. Adversarial processes like trial and arbitration have the highest rates of attack on outcomes, whether by appeal or by filing suit to attack or having to file suit to enforce an agreement (see Figure 1.1).

WHY ISN'T LITIGATION WORKING FOR US ANYMORE?

Our court system developed in England in a very different society and time to deal with problems very different from ours. In the United States today, it suffers from overdevelopment and has grown both form driven and rule driven as courts have struggled to keep up with what was perceived to be a tidal wave of litigation, which we already recognize has abated. California, for example, saw a 30 percent decline in small claims filings between 1989 and 1999. Filings of general civil cases—those with a demand over $25,000 and excluding family and probate matters—in California have declined about 22 percent in the same period. Jury trials in such cases are less than 1.5 percent of total dispositions (California Judicial Council, 2000a).

Finally some courts are beginning to examine the quality of their offerings. They are asking, for example, whether invoking the jurisdiction of the court at least leaves a person no worse off. There is growing momentum in the therapeutic jurisprudence movement that brings forward the study of law's healing potential.[2] The key is in how the courts see their purpose—whether merely to handle cases, which some courts still see as their only goal, or to become a dispute resolution center with many options, each capable of being tailored for the dispute, which has helped open the doors to mediation.[3] This spectrum in perspective is reminiscent of industrial history. Is a telephone company in the telephone business or the communication business? Is an oil company in the oil business or the energy business? Is a railroad in the railroad business or the transportation business?[4]

Many in legal and judicial circles still cling to the old-mind way of thinking about these things. Indeed, the American Bar Association (ABA) recently voted resoundingly against allowing multi-disciplinary practice (MDP), which would allow practice with other professionals, such as accountants and therapists. They thus left lawyers who practice with other professionals at risk for being adjudged unethical (Kelly, 2000a). In fact, MDP would open up job opportunities for lawyers with international accounting firms and make co-mediation of family matters by therapists and lawyers less risky, and it would give consumers a richer offering of professional services. The issue, for the ABA, was control—an old-mind issue if ever there was one. Plainly, it is just a matter of time until MDP is approved. Old-fashioned notions of control are as out of date as the horse and buggy.

The adversarial system has more than its share of old-mind control going. It has at times turned some lawyers into legal gladiators, poised to grab a large retainer and begin billing the hours for all the work that the war will require. Endless discovery and the full panoply of motions will be necessary. Nothing is to be conceded. Only the complete surrender of the enemy or the mandate of the court of last resort can end this dispute. Judge Thomas Reavley (1987, p. 789) of the Fifth Circuit Court describes this kind of lawyer as "the dinosaur of our times" and "a threat to every unfortunate client who enters the office." Few lawyers fit this description today, though the gun-for-hire mentality persists in many plush temples of the law.[5]

We have a contingent fee system in which counsel often advance costs to guarantee access to the legal system for many who could not otherwise have it. But with the increasing complexity of discovery and pretrial practices, this comes closer to requiring a banker than a lawyer. It is no accident that there are now venture capital firms offering to buy shares in lawsuits.[6] It is no better for defendants who may end up spending far more on legal fees and expenses than if they simply allowed judgment to be taken against them.

No small part of the burgeoning cost of litigation is due to the intricacy of claims and defenses and the few deterrents within the system to prevent delay for delay's sake. There are also ethical constraints that serve to hinder and delay the prosecution of cases: a lawyer's primary professional risk is to fail to assert a claim or defense. Thus, cases are tried on all possible theories in a climate where theories are proliferating, causing trials and arbitrations to take vastly more time and money than is necessary. In this way, the system rewards breadth rather than clarity of focus.

Few people know that when they retain counsel, it is likely to be two to five years before they see any results,[7] and the chances of going to trial are slim to minuscule. For plaintiffs in serious injury cases, this delay can mean lives of quiet desperation as they try to cope with their condition without the needed financial resources. It is common knowledge that injuries of all kinds—emotional, mental, and physical—are far slower to heal while the dispute remains unresolved.

When you spend years litigating only to settle the case by negotiation, you have done the equivalent of traveling from London to Berlin by way of Tokyo. True, you will reach your destination. But in the words of a famous World War II poster from which Uncle Sam glared over his pointing finger, "Is this trip really necessary?" (see Figure 1.2).

Figure 1.2. "Is This Trip Really Necessary?"

Lit-think—that is, our preoccupation with litigation—escalates disputes. When litigation is even just outside the picture, people often stop behaving constructively. Businesspeople stop trying to work things out and rush to the barricades, each side believing the other side is just trying to set them up (since they are trying to set up the other side). Frequently the motives we ascribe to others are our own motives, safely hidden from our conscious minds.

This destructive way of thinking about disputes—that we are engaged in war—in fact jeopardizes our interests. War requires that in order for us to win, the other side must lose. That is a formidable hurdle to achieving success in resolving the difficulties that brought us to seek counsel in the first place.

The damage to our quality of life from litigation filed without regard to its societal consequences is incalculable. A homeowner in an adult community with a minimum residence age of forty-five becomes pregnant. She sues and breaks the covenant limiting residents to adults. All over California, adult communities raise their minimum age to fifty-five, decreasing the age diversity of their groups and denying others like herself access at all. One may ask, was this trip necessary?

Consider another situation: does the family whose child was injured at a playground think about the possibility that their suit and others like it will likely close this and other playgrounds? Would they like to have had the opportunity to spread the risk of their actual loss (limited damages) without such consequences?

Peter Huber (1988) estimates that damages for accidents and personal injury cost individuals, businesses, municipalities, and other government agencies more than $80 billion a year. He asserts that the cost of liability insurance has skyrocketed, and as a result, many playgrounds, skating rinks, swimming pools, and slides have closed. He further suggests that certain prescription drugs, although legal, are not manufactured due to liability fears. He reports (though others have challenged him on these points) that 95 percent of the cost of childhood vaccines and 30 percent of the price of a stepladder represent the costs of liability insurance.

Justice and the justice system are not the same. It is more productive to think of litigation as a tool, one of several ways of securing results. The fact that it is commonplace has raised our threshold of outrage. We need to be resensitized. When an obstetrician's malpractice insurance runs more than $70,000 per year, when ice skating rinks and playgrounds are closing because of inability to secure insurance at all, isn't it time we noticed?

As Robert Ornstein and Paul Ehrlich (1989) point out in *New World, New Mind,* our old minds handle gradual change quite poorly. Once we are conditioned to a situation, whether nuclear explosions or acid rain or the decay of our infrastructure, it ceases to be important. It is, they point out, another example of the boiled frog syndrome. A frog sitting in a pan of water that is gradually heated will not recognize the risk and will die rather than jump out, even though a frog dropped into hot water will bound away instantly. We have much to learn from frogs about what it takes to survive in this world of ours.

HOW DOES LITIGATION SERVE?

Legislation is usually described as the way for the law to evolve. In the United States, it serves this purpose also, in part because our legislative process leaves a lot more to the discretion of courts than it does in the English system.[8] Many liabilities have evolved through litigation—the liability of doctors, hospitals, manufacturers, mechanics, lawyers. It has been the courts that established so many new responsibilities: skating rink owners for skaters, doctors and drug manufacturers for deformed babies. And many of the rights declared through legislation—such as the right to an environment free of discrimination based on age, race, sex, national origin, or disability—are given life by the courts. The increasing complexity of technical defenses may result in court decisions that encourage patterns of resistance rather than patterns of compliance—all in ways very costly to litigants and to the societal objectives the legislators seek to promote.

The law has evolved through decision after decision in case after case. Would people negotiating in good faith in mediation change rules of liability and the extent of damages without judicial precedent? It is unlikely. But even today, precedent is established by only a tiny percentage of cases. The need for precedent-setting cases is not served when cases settle or are otherwise disposed of, as well over 90 percent of civil cases did before the rise of mediation.

THE PROMISE OF MEDIATION

Mediation (like other collaborative processes, such as facilitation and consensus building and dialogue), unlike litigation, has the capacity to get to the underlying problems that otherwise will require legislation and move courts into new liability territory. Also, it frees up court time that would otherwise be spent processing cases that would settle without such ministrations. This allows more resources to be available for those cases that must be tried.

Mediation is infiltrating the institutional life of America in ways unforeseen just a few years ago. Mediation of child custody cases is widespread nationwide, and much of it is mandatory. As a result of the ADR Act of 1998, every federal court is required to have some kind of ADR program, and almost all of these involve mediation. Indeed, as early as 1997, eighty-seven of the ninety-four U.S. district courts already had established procedures for use of ADR (American Bar Association, 1997). The U.S. government has made a massive commitment to mediation, requiring it in department after department internally in several possible forms, including the workplace ombuds. The ombuds's sole responsibility is to help the employee get the problem resolved, something that more and more companies and other organizations are finding to be in their self-interest. Human resources can never cover this base fully because by definition these professionals have responsibility to management for the operation of the internal system. That conflict looms large in employee's eyes when the situation is perceived as particularly sensitive—such as when harassment or conflicts within management levels are involved.[9] Mediation programs are another form specified for federal departments' internal programs, and in many cases mediation for clients, contractors, and customers of the departments is also found. According to a listing of the Interagency ADR Working Group, fifty-four agencies of the U.S. government had ADR departments in 2000.

Mediation is infiltrating the institutional life of America in ways unforeseen just a few years ago.

One example is the Equal Employment Opportunity Commission (EEOC), long awash in adversarial processes that kept it mired in backlog. In 1991, in an effort to manage this backlog, the EEOC introduced a voluntary mediation program. This program has met with great success, and major settlements have resulted. Among them are the women's class action against Mitsubishi, resulting in a recovery of $34 million for sexual harassment. The growth of the program has been dramatic, as shown in Table 1.1.

Mediation has been used to deal with a number of high-profile cases, such as a class action that alleged systematic racially discriminatory practices by the U.S. Department of Agriculture.

Table 1.1. EEOC Mediation Program, 1997–2000.

Year	Amount Recovered in Dollars	People Involved	Percent Increase
1997	10.8 million	780	
1998	17.0 million	1,631	57
1999	58.5 million	5,260	244
2000	108.4 million	7,209	85

Source: Interview, EEOC Office of Research, Information and Planning, Jan. 25, 2001.

Under the settlement, black farmers who were discriminated against in their loan applications to the department between 1981 and 1997 will get $50,000 each and have their debts, many amounting to hundreds of thousands of dollars, erased. Those with more substantial claims may pursue them in addition.

Lon Fuller, one of the early visionaries in the field of mediation, described the fundamental promise of mediation. He saw the role of the mediator as significantly facilitating negotiations by allowing for increase in the speed and accuracy of the negotiations that would lead to a better overall agreement. To achieve this result, he advocated the practice of holding caucuses—separate meetings with the parties. The confidentiality of these caucuses invites greater candor and allows for venting of emotions without taking too great a toll on the other side or sides. Parties often feel a greater sense of safety in the caucus and are more willing to reexamine what is really most important to them (Fuller, 1971).

Mediation can be successful at almost any stage of the matter. For cases that will never be tried, this eliminates most of the transaction costs and delay. The cases that must be tried will be easier to identify and may be handled more effectively by courts and counsel, who will at last have the time to deal with them.

At the same time, mediation offers the potential to build teams and alliances among those currently or potentially at loggerheads. It offers the potential to revive business relationships soured by conflict. It offers the potential for participants to experience a positive, internal shift as a result of how this particular conflict was dealt with that can transform their way of handling other potential conflicts as well. And it encourages the development of creative options, considering new ways of doing things and the enhancement of lessons learned from the conflict experience.

Chapter Two

Mediation in Action

Be assured that if you knew all, you would pardon all.
THOMAS À KEMPIS

People are multidimensional beings, encompassing in their nature mental, physical, emotional, and spiritual aspects. Mediation can touch all of these, as the following four stories on the transformative power of mediation show.

A Case of Humility

Charlie Jacobson was in the prime of his career as a litigator—a partner in a large firm in a medium-sized city in the Midwest. He wasn't the first to defend this case: it had been pending for thirteen years in federal court. But he had devoted enough of his life to it that he devoutly wished it would be over. Nevertheless, good soldier that he was, he continued the meticulous defense work that was his hallmark, fighting every issue he could find with excellent research and long argument and with the approval, at least by default, of his corporate client.

The case was a court-certified class action based on racial and ethnic discrimination, brought by a group of sanitation workers against a waste disposal company. The case was being handled on a contingent fee basis, meaning the plaintiffs' lawyers would be paid only if and when they won. They were passionate in their advocacy and their sense of outrage at what had happened to their clients and what seemed to be continuing to happen. Excellent lawyers, they were appalled that there had never been settlement talks in the case. Yet like Charlie, they were fully convinced such talks would do no good.

A new management team from the company brought in a mediator, who persuaded the plaintiffs' counsel to participate in mediated negotiations. Charlie seemed hostile to the mediation. It was suggested that this was because settling was against his economic interests (he was being paid hourly) and that it was part of his way of life to punish the uppity plaintiffs for the impertinence of bringing the suit in the first place. If they only knew how tired he was of this case.

The plaintiffs were asking for more than $15 million. The employer's negotiators seemed to think $1 million would be more than enough. Yet the mediation took only three days—two days of negotiation spaced two weeks apart and a final day a few weeks later to complete the details of a complex settlement agreement that required the approval of the union, the court, and a large-class plaintiff.

After the initial joint session, the mediator focused tightly in the private caucuses on the specifics of the damage claims. Each party became involved in looking at possible ranges of recovery and some probabilities relating to them. During the first day, the mediator drew from the parties the best-case and worst-case scenarios, and encouraged the parties to devise noneconomic elements to be included in any settlement package.

As progress became apparent, the mood shifted from hopelessness and bare civility to cautious optimism. The managers felt hurt that the plaintiffs had not acknowledged the tremendous effort made to correct workforce inequities and discrimination, such as the old boy network, favoritism, and frequent racial and ethnic slurs. They therefore distrusted the plaintiffs' sincerity. On the other side, the plaintiffs' counsel continued to chafe at the apparent callousness of the defendant, as experienced through Charlie's defense.

At one point, the mediator had a brief moment with Charlie alone. Charlie had been going through the motions in the mediation, but it was plain his heart wasn't in it. Sensing an opportunity, the mediator asked, "Do you have a family?" It had been a long day, and both were tired and hungry. Before long, Charlie spoke softly of his little girl and how much he missed seeing her grow up. Gone was the brittle facade of the litigation lawyer. They talked about the difficulties of combining career with family life. The moment passed as the others returned, yet Charlie had changed. He was gentler in demeanor and much more creative in helping his client figure out how to structure a settlement that would work.

At another point a little later, the plaintiffs were ready to walk out. Had the plaintiffs' blind lawyer detected more commitment to settlement in the mediator than in himself? When mediation begins, the mediator is empowered by the parties' mutual commitment to resolving, if they can reach a satisfactory resolution. It is easy for mediators to forget the limits of that mandate in the heat of mediation. Remembering that it was the parties' case and not his, the mediator backed off. "If you decide you don't want to settle this case, that's okay," he told the plaintiffs' caucus. It is hard to come this close to resolving and walk out, particularly after thirteen years of litigation. After a long discussion among themselves, plaintiffs' counsel decided to see it through.

THE LESSON

Touching the heart reconnects us to reality—the reality that enfolds us, beyond the creation of our minds. Reminding Charlie of the human side of his life grounded him and enabled him through that lens to see the stereotype he had become. It also grounded the mediator, who had to let go of his growing desire to see the parties settle, so that the plaintiffs could squarely face the possibility of failure. Matters already in litigation are the inheritors of the encrusted roles and attitudes that the adversarial process engenders. So long as litigation dominates the mind, the minimal trust essential to movement remains elusive.

Both lawyers and mediators need enough humility to let the parties succeed or fail without foot dragging. The dispute belongs to the parties, something that lawyers and mediators sometimes forget. Lawyers can be transfixed by their advocacy, and mediators may be so focused on securing a settlement that they cannot allow people to fail. Many cases that might settle do not, and some that could settle so very well in fact settle badly.

> *Both lawyers and mediators need enough humility to let the parties succeed or fail without foot dragging.*

Another lesson is the risk of intentional misleading. Litigators know that much of what they say is intended to mislead the other side. There are serious consequences to this strategy. First, the other side believes it, and then the authors may come to believe it themselves.

The mistrust is self-perpetuating. When it reaches a certain point, talks become impossible because no one believes they will help. In this case, the exercise of focusing and clarifying the facts for the mediator led the parties quickly to their own satisfactory resolution. The settlement, in excess of $6 million, brought peace to hundreds of workers and a new day to the management of the company. The handshakes at the end were sincere.

Building Trust Through Sharing Control

Seventeen-year-old Kevin lived in a foster home with three other boys and Mary, his foster mother. It was two weeks until his trial for attempted murder. He had been snarling at the other boys and Mary, as well as not showing up for meals and generally breaking house agreements. The situation was tense, and Mary had been told that if the situation did not improve, Kevin would be moved to another home. She did not want him to go but couldn't talk with him. She asked for mediation to see if there might be an agreement to establish some guidelines for his staying, although she did not expect him even to agree to mediate. Surprisingly, he agreed. He said he had no particular issues to discuss and said almost nothing about his situation. His contribution was almost entirely limited to one-word replies to questions.

The mediation session took place in their home, with the other boys relegated to the basement to do homework. Kevin seemed a little uncomfortable with the fact that the mediator was a woman about the same age as his foster mother. Nevertheless, they proceeded.

The mediator began by asking Kevin again for his issues.

"I dunno," he replied.

She persisted: "How do you feel about being here?"

"Okay."

She gave him a chance to change his mind, then turned to Mary.

As Mary's many issues poured out, the mediator neutralized and clustered them so they did not appear as a litany of grievances: "Your concerns are about not calling when he isn't going to be home for dinner, not doing his home jobs on time, and being unavailable when you want to talk. These are communication issues, is that right?" Even so, the mediation seemed unbalanced.

Kevin agreed to the list, which also included behavior around the house and with friends, use of drugs and alcohol, angry outbursts, and his presence (or absence) at dinner.

They started with the least contentious issue: dinner time. Kevin rarely came home in time for dinner or called, yet he had been totally reliable about his 7 P.M. curfew. When the mediator inquired why, he replied, "I don't want to go to jail."

The mediator spent a lot of time asking him about his activities and intentions, as well as the effect the impending court proceeding was having on him. Each time he responded with a single word, a head shake, or a nod. The mediator gave him many opportunities to reply, pushing him so Mary could understand. Eventually she asked, "Am I pushing you too hard?" "No," he said softly.

The mediator acknowledged his responses through paraphrase and attempted to round out his expressions in order to put together his reasoning in a more coherent fashion. As she proceeded slowly, she would ask, "Am I putting words in your mouth?"

"No."

She worked to understand without appearing to cross-examine.

His interests were in spending as much time as possible with his friends, maximizing his independence given the very strict curfew, having a little fun, and releasing some stress. His demeanor was very subdued at this point. She took his information at face value, knowing that to assume manipulation would have denied him the opportunity to play this one straight. He was clearly terrified of his court date, feeling he would be incarcerated. All he could think of was that court date. Hanging out with his friends was the way he chose to handle it.

When the mediator turned to Mary to determine her concerns about dinner time, it became clear that her primary interest was respect. When asked why she needed an hour's notice that Kevin would not be there for dinner, she couldn't explain. Then Mary shifted. Influenced by Kevin's responses, she was willing to relinquish all of her demands, including adequate notification, having the family together for dinner, and being able to provide good food for the boys.

She began to see Kevin's behavior in different terms—not so much disrespectful as self-comforting. Even his explosions made perfect sense. She had been through this sort of thing before with the other boys but had been deeply hurt by Kevin's apparent total disregard for her and the others. She knew he was in a bad spot; his case was likely to be bumped up to adult court and result in a long sentence if he were convicted. A dedicated and loving parent, Mary had been trying very hard to be supportive.

Mary's shift was the turning point in the session. Her compassion for him overtook all other needs, and she told Kevin she would back off. Taking the pressure off him also took it off herself. The tension in the room evaporated. Mary recognized this was not the time for negotiation, but simply a time to show her love.

As the mediator and Mary talked casually to close off the session, Mary mentioned that Kevin had not provided his lawyer with the list of friends who could testify on his behalf. By now the mediator had established a good rapport with Kevin and could quiz him safely. She asked him the state of the list. Kevin told her it wasn't finished, that he needed more addresses and more telephone numbers. The mediator told him to bring the list.

Kevin returned from the basement with a scrap of paper containing first names, some addresses, and a lot of blanks. He allowed the mediator to go over the items one by one, extracting as much information as he could provide, rewriting the list, and making another list of those he needed to call for more information. He placed calls as they all sat there but needed to catch some people at a different time.

Kevin needed more information about four key people. He said he would do this the next day around dinner time. He was starting a part-time job for the Christmas holidays the next day and wouldn't have time to provide the information to the lawyer. But the lawyer urgently needed the information to get the defense together, so Mary said, "I'll call for you, Kevin." Kevin hesitated for a moment and then handed her the list. The mediator sensed the drama, but did not understand it until Mary explained later in private: "Kevin has never before told me the names of his friends or anything about them. They were involved together in drug deals. What he gave me was his list of contacts."

THE LESSON

The trust built in the mediation allowed Kevin to let down the guard that separated him from everyone else, even his loving and dedicated foster mother, when he badly needed help. The mediator built rapport with Kevin by giving him control of her understanding. It would have been easy but destructive to pump him for information. Fleshing out his replies as she checked with him to see if her understanding was correct allowed him to control what she knew and to remain silent. Slowly the mediator drew out his underlying interests. Her simultaneous sensitivity to Mary's underlying interests allowed Mary to shift to common cause with Kevin. The bottom line was that a young man who had gone far toward destroying his life was offered, and accepted, the chance to win the support of his foster mother while playing it straight. Life lessons like this are pure gold.

Transformation Is Where You Find It

Several years ago in a southwestern city, two families, good friends and close neighbors, enjoyed a particularly warm relationship. Both attended church, though of differing denominations. Both were considered kind, generous people with a high sense of community responsibility. Both were highly regarded by neighbors and colleagues, both before and after the events that ensued. Although one couple's children were grown and the other's were aged two, four, and six, they had much in common and enjoyed good times together. The beautiful little two-year-old girl, Mary, was especially beloved by the older woman, who doted on her. Let's call the older couple Edwina and George Ruggles and the younger parents Laura and Rob Clemons.

Then one day, all of this changed. The women had met at the park for a picnic. The children were playing, and at one point Edwina called Mary over to a bushy area to show her something. No one was concerned, as Edwina loved the child dearly. Laura will never forget what happened next. Screams came from the bushes. As Laura was rushing toward the sound, Edwina emerged covered with blood, saying, "I've just killed your daughter."

If a nuclear bomb had fallen on these families, and this neighborhood and this community, it could not have had greater impact. It turned out that Edwina had suffered a psychotic break. She had been troubled with psychosis for several years. When she started having thoughts about killing one of her own children, she recognized that she was getting out of control and sought treatment. The terrifying thoughts finally subsided, and she was fine as long as she was on medication. She continued in therapy and on medication.

Edwina and George had moved into this community several years earlier from the East Coast. Some months before the attack, her local therapist here had given her hope that at long last she might be cured. Edwina was a particularly generous person by nature and deeply involved in volunteer community services. And so gradually, to the delight of Edwina and George, her medication was reduced, and eventually it was stopped. As this was taking place, the therapist never spoke to either Edwina or George about possible danger signs or situations that would put Edwina at risk for a recurrence.

Laura rushed over and grabbed her daughter, stanching the blood flow from her daughter's neck, willing life and vitality back into her daughter's body.

Somehow she got Mary and her other two children to the hospital, and Mary was successfully treated for what turned out to be minor injuries despite several stab wounds around her neck.

Four years later, Mary was a beautiful, completely normal six-year-old with only one scar on her neck. Four years later, her mother could hardly allow her children to play at a friend's house without dissolving in terror and guilt, despite several years of therapy and tremendous progress in putting her mind and heart back together.

As the criminal proceeding against Edwina dragged on, Laura had gone public with her outrage time and again. She had tried in every way she knew how to see that Edwina was put behind bars and kept there, despite the unanimity of the therapeutic community that Edwina was completely incapable of controlling her actions in the grip of the psychotic break, and that with medication, she was in no way a danger to society. Both families had moved out of the neighborhood. Edwina had been given probation (the state does not recognize insanity as a defense) of ten years, but several months before the mediation, she had been placed in custody to serve out her term due to a minor infraction of the rules of probation. And so at the mediation, there were only George, with his lawyer, and Laura and Rob Clemons and their lawyer.

The mediation was to resolve the civil damage action that Laura and Rob had brought against the Ruggleses. The mediation was begun and continued in private caucus with each side separately. This can happen in situations of deep trauma, where one party is extremely fragile or trust is exceedingly low. In such situations, the mediator nevertheless will often work toward some kind of joint meeting in order for the healing process to begin. This may be done, for example, in medical malpractice cases in which mediation has laid the groundwork for an opportunity; the doctor may make a heart-felt apology to the former patient (when the doctor so desires).

Laura and Rob were a loving, gentle couple whose marriage was deeply faith based. Rob, having more distance from the events, supported Laura every step of the way, recognizing the space that had to be traversed before healing could occur for her, yet never moving so far ahead that she could not keep up. They brought photos of their three children and placed them on the table in their caucus room. With their lawyer, a compassionate man who was a friend of both families (as both sides knew), they set the focus on getting the best result possible for their children.

Through what must have been a tremendous effort, Laura had finally let go of the focus on the need for vengeance. The children's photos symbolized that commitment. Little Mary's eyes sparkled out of her picture, next to her two bright, attractive siblings. As the mediator asked about Mary, her story unfolded. "She treats it as just another thing that happened," said Laura. "Her brother came home one day from school, making a deal out of a painful scrape on his arm. Mary said, 'Yeah? So I got stabbed.'"

In all conflict, letting go is perhaps the hardest part (see Appendix D). In this one, the self-blame that hid behind the accusation was especially difficult. Yet as the mediator spoke confidentially with Laura's therapist, who had been on telephone standby during the mediation, it became clear how important resolution was to Laura's continued progress. The pendency of the litigation was hampering her recovery, and so the mediator proceeded.

Initially the mediator spent time with each side, drawing out what each most wanted from this mediation. As each one's hope of reaching a final resolution that would allow the past to pass away into history strengthened, so would their chances of reaching it. The mediator's own optimism and confidence in the parties' ability to do this added yeast to the mix. Wherever the line had been drawn, it was no longer sacrosanct if crossing it would achieve that resolution. Separating how satisfaction might be achieved from the goal of achieving satisfaction is an important step in breaking impasse, whether in a commercial dispute or an interpersonal one.

The mediator hypothesized that the best result for the parties would occur if there could be personal contact between George Ruggles and the Clemonses so that some of the demonization could abate, as different information and understanding came to the light. Laura's healing ultimately would depend on her gaining perspective on Edwina and George's side of the tragedy. But to set this as a goal would have almost done violence to Laura, whose own timing needed to be respected. And so the mediator sought to model the values the parties held in common (though not necessarily regarding this matter) in order to encourage them to live those values in the situation at hand.

As opportunities permitted, the mediator worked to introduce into the Clemons's caucus the idea of a possible meeting with George Ruggles. This became uncomfortable for Laura, who could see where the mediator was going. During a pause, she told her lawyer she didn't want to do that. He told the mediator, who at the next opportunity in the Clemons's caucus simply said, "You know, if you don't want to meet with George Ruggles, you don't have to.

You have complete control over how that might play out. If you decide that there are some questions you want answers to or perceptions that you want to test, you may have the opportunity to do so. If you decide that's too much, you certainly don't have to." By letting go of any desire to see the parties reconcile, the mediator allowed Laura to know that she had control.

In the defense caucus, the mediator had informed George that there might be a possibility for a meeting before the day was over. He said he would like that very much. Yet the mediator had doubts about whether it would be helpful. George was a gentle, sophisticated, and good-hearted person struggling to take care of his wife of forty-five years and provide for her care in the future. Still, he could have played the lead in *The Godfather.* His rugged face was impassive, and he tended to rock back in his chair, legs crossed, steepling his hands, looking aloof. "It's a family characteristic," he told the mediator. The mediator offered to George and his lawyers a reflection of what he saw and began demonstrating some techniques from neurolinguistic programming, a powerful and widely accepted theory of human communication that uses nonverbal communication strategies. Gradually as the day wore on, he noticed George sitting forward more and with a bit more expression on his face.

It became increasingly obvious to the mediator that talking about money in Laura and Rob's caucus could be painful and would bring up residual passion for vengeance. One's aspirations in a conflict often far exceed what is realistically possible. Despite careful groundwork by the Clemons's lawyer, Laura in particular still had very high expectations concerning the value of the claim, particularly in light of the situation the Ruggles were in. To do conventional reality testing—focusing on damages, for example—would reopen wounds just barely covered over. So the mediator began working with the defense. There was already a court order for restitution of more than $30,000 that George was prepared to pay as part of the mediation. Most of George and Edwina's assets were in a retirement plan exempt from execution (collection through the enforcement of a judgment). The expenses of Edwina's four years of probation had been enormous: multiple therapy sessions, legal fees, and a twenty-four-hour-a-day guardian. How much more would the defense allow the mediator to test for? (Mediators of necessity test various hypotheses of what is available readily and how much might become available for resolution. This affords some distance on what parties actually *say* in mediation—something mediators normally take with a grain of salt.) Although no dollar figure was offered or indicated, from the discussion the mediator got a pretty good idea where they hoped to land and, beyond that, of what might be possible, having in mind the protected form in which assets were held and the immense demands on the Ruggles's resources, now and in the future.

In the Clemons's caucus, the mediator discussed how different sums of money could be used for their children's college education. Using a structured settlements consultant (a professional in deferred payment, special annuity contracts that are often used to facilitate personal injury settlements) whom the mediator had on telephone standby, they talked about the possibilities for the children, staying in the examples in the ranges of possible settlement. At one point, the lawyer's fee loomed large, and the lawyer figured out how to reduce it while still receiving fair payment for his efforts. As elements began to fall into place, possible ranges were tested by "what ifs"—*what if* the other side were to do this much . . .

As discussions of possibilities flowed back and forth, the mediator learned more about what life was like for George and Edwina—how it was to get through the blaring accusations from friends and on radio and television and in the press, getting through the criminal proceedings, and the effort to make the arrangements so that absolute compliance with the terms of probation could be accomplished; then, after so much success, having your wife whisked away and then spending weeks just trying to jump through the hoops that would let you see your wife in prison for the first time.

In their caucus with the mediator, the Clemons's questions flowed: "How could they . . ." and "Why didn't they . . ." and "What about . . . ." The mediator followed the flow, not disclosing what George may have told him in confidence, but nevertheless raising questions about what George's version of events might be—for example, "I wonder what George would say about that. Maybe there is a reason that simply hasn't come out, because the forum didn't lend itself to real communication."

With the use of a structure (a form of annuity contract and a partly deferred payment), the parties reached an agreement that evening. The lawyers throughout the day had been quiet and sensitive supporters of both their clients and of resolution. Now they turned to crafting a simple but adequate memorandum of agreement.

As the memorandum of agreement was being circulated, Laura asked if George could come in and sign it in front of her. She didn't think she could talk to him, but when he came in and tenderly apologized, she began asking him some questions, thus beginning to clear away the underbrush of assumption and projection. The tension in the room subsided visibly, and no one present was left untouched.

THE LESSON

The mediator here modeled the values the litigants and their lawyers shared, bringing these into the process where they were accessible to everyone. The lawyers' sensitivity was drawn in, and the parties, nestled in the safe environment, did what needed to be done. Some of the values modeled in this mediation are set out in the following list.

Values	*As Modeled by the Mediator*
Respect	Respect of the parties' own process and timing; respectful and intense listening to the parties and their lawyers
Honesty	Vulnerability—the openness to be wrong and to be corrected without guilt or blame
Humility	Holding lightly to his beliefs about how things might go
Trust	Trust in the parties' ability to do the best thing for themselves and for the situation
Courage	Courage to say what is needed to be said in the moment, even if it makes him unpopular or distrusted for a time
Forgiveness	Without judgment or criticism of anyone on account of anything
Resourcefulness	Being prepared with the appropriate tools, including communication technology, personal presence, and a standby expert

As this story demonstrates, transformation is an interior process, personal to the parties, the mediator, and the lawyers. Each can be open or closed to being touched by something numinous—something the Canadian-born teacher John de Ruiter (2000) calls "nectar"—that sort of tender sweetness that draws awareness to the heart level. It is never found in the mind. If we would have this fruit, we have to go up in the tree. We cannot go up in the tree and stand on the ground of our opinions and judgments at the same time. In this case, the parties brought their own vulnerability, a critical resource for authentic communication that can transform almost by itself.

Vulnerability Works

This case involved nearly two hundred tract home owners of roughly half that many parcels—the vast majority of properties in a new coastal development— who had battled for two years to recover against various defendants for land-slide problems and massive construction defects. The situation and the litigation had riven the community, dividing those who sued from those who did not and dividing litigants one from another, depending on whose property was most at risk. The development was situated overlooking the picturesque Maine coast. Several homes had been condemned. Very expensive homes had received very expensive fixes along the way for defects, but these had failed to solve the problems created by building in such punishing conditions. The market for everyone's property had collapsed. Lenders refused to lend on the properties, regardless of whether they were at risk. Just about everything that could have gone wrong did go wrong.

Finally, in judicial settlement conferencing, the case settled. A committee of home owner litigants worked for months to come up with a formula for distri-bution of the settlement funds. Meanwhile, the details of winding up the settle-ment and tying up loose ends had repeatedly delayed the expected receipt of settlement funds. The judge stayed with the case, taking on one crisis after another. The way he dealt with these triggered what seemed at times like tidal waves of rage and frustration to wash over the community. To top it all off, when the committee came up with its distribution formula, a substantial por-tion of plaintiff home owners split off, hired a lawyer, and prepared to do battle over the proposed division of settlement funds.

The remedy available to the plaintiff home owners under an earlier agreement was arbitration. If any plaintiff home owner filed for arbitration against an otherwise agreed-on plan, everyone affected would be held up yet again. The community would again be divided between those seeking arbitration and those defending the plan, an almost unthinkable situation, yet it was widely believed to be completely and utterly unavoidable. How could it happen that one plaintiff home owner in this fractured community would not pursue that remedy? How could arbitration not happen?

Faced with this prospect and being unable to assist because of potential con-flicts of interest (lawyers cannot represent some clients against other clients), the law firms representing the plaintiffs sought a mediator.

After two days of briefing on the situation, including a site inspection, the mediator developed a design for getting the mediation together. There were three proposals on the table: the committee's proposal, the opposition proposal, and a global proposal that said in essence: "Let no one get any specific monies. Fix the situation. Restore value to the properties." Reasonable proponents for each of these were identified and agreed to offer themselves as representatives for those who could not or did not care to attend the mediation. Great care was taken to keep that representative status loose, so that people understood they were giving their representatives discretion to do what they thought was best at the mediation, not simply vote their position going into it.

In a series of communications, all plaintiffs were informed of the decision to use mediation and of the mediator's background, qualifications, and experience. Notice of the mediation was given, which included a review of the proposals and identification of the proponents. People were given the opportunity to go along with whatever happened in the mediation, select a representative, or attend the mediation. They were urged to attend if they felt they needed to have a voice in the final determination. Most of the home owners responded. Many selected representatives, a few indicated they would go along with whatever came out of the mediation, and many chose to attend.

Those planning to attend received a third mailing describing in very general terms the process that the mediator was designing. ("It couldn't be described," she later explained, "because it had to be largely invented on the spot. Too detailed an advance description would provide fuel for process objections if it turned out changes would need to be made at the actual mediation.") Both the notice of mediation and the preparatory materials sought to lower expectations—emphasizing that there would *seem* to be no progress, that participants would get frustrated, and that this was all necessary to securing a result everyone could live with.

The home owners who attended the mediation were basically opinion leaders, those who had been involved in leadership of one of the groups in some way and the most vocal and determined objectors. Prior to the mediation, the mediator received more than 650 e-mails and handled numerous telephone calls and responded to more faxes and letters. Crisis after crisis emerged during this period, some among constituencies, some among opinion leaders and those with representative status. Many were serious enough to keep the mediation from happening at all. Frustration was at an all-time high. It was not a hopeful scene.

The day before the mediation, thirty-six chairs were arranged in a large semicircle facing the mediator and a projection screen was installed. All key documents had been committed to film so there would be no need for tables and papers.

People arrived early and began talking in their groups. When they sat down, all thirty-six of them, they sat in their own groups. Many had not spoken for years to others who were present. The tension crackled. As the mediator was setting up the newsprint pads, argument started to break out. The mediator intervened: "I am here solely to help you get what you want." She wrote "Contract" on the pad on the easel and wrote under it, "The mediator is here to help you." "But I need something from you to do that," she continued. "I need you to tell me what you think I need to know. Would you agree to do that?" First there was silence. Then a slight nodding of assent. "You will tell her what you think she needs to know," she wrote on the easel. The contract was made.

On another sheet, she wrote "Ground Rules." "I need one ground rule here in order to be of any use to you at all," she continued. And on the easel she wrote, "It's okay to make mistakes." "You know a lot more than I will ever know about your situation," she said. "I *will* make mistakes. And I need for that to be okay. Can you agree to that?" The assent was quicker this time.

"If the conversation goes the way it has started," she continued, "I can't be of any help to you. I don't know how to help you with that kind of conversation. Would you let me do a little training—nothing new; it's what you already know. But it's just good to have it in mind as we proceed here. Can you go along with it?" Profound silence followed. Then someone said, "It's okay by me," and most others joined in.

The training consisted of reinforcing the preparatory materials—showing through the Kantor four-player model[1] that each one had a role and that the important thing was for participants not to get stuck in a single role but move around from role to role. The basics of inquiry were discussed, and destructive argument distinguished. "Rather than looking for what's wrong with what someone else is saying," said the mediator, "look for what is most useful in it. Inquire into the thinking behind it, and offer your own thinking for examination. Think `curiosity' rather than `critique.'" The fatal attraction of wallowing in the past was already clear. At the conclusion, the mediator asked, "I wonder if it might be helpful to practice this?" The groan was audible. "Was that an 'Oh God, no!'" the mediator asked. Everyone agreed. And that was the end of it.

A few more ground rules were collected from the group, including one that turned out to be key: "Celebrate every agreement." There were many impasses faced and transcended as the morning wore on. Despite the tremendous effort that had been put into the committee's formula and the fairly offhand way some of the other proposals were developed, each was given equal treatment.

Each proponent had a chance to make his or her argument. When discussion time came, what looked like an easy issue to agree on turned out to be impossible to resolve so soon, and another issue had to be taken up amid much discouragement.

As the discussion continued without visible progress, people kept asking to take a vote. So the mediator called for the vote. It was split. She said, "Now what are you going to do?" There was silence. "Be a little more patient, so you'll have the chance to see how consensus works." They were and it happened finally, the first agreement of substance. There was no one who couldn't live with it. It went up on the easel under the heading "Agreements," with everyone understanding that all agreements were tentative until the end. The mediator did a little dance and whooped like a cheerleader around the room. Interim paperwork was wadded up noisily, and the group turned to the next subject.

A couple of times someone called the mediator on a misstep. She acknowledged it each time. These were blame-free and guilt-free exchanges.

Once every half-day, the mediator did a check-in, asking each participant in turn, "How do you feel, and what do you think?" "This proved invaluable," she explained later, "because I would otherwise never have had a reading of what was really going on. There were a few remarks about 'touchy-feely' but all in good humor."

The toughest issue for one subgroup ended up being last and was dealt with by use of the check-in, with people's creativity growing as the right to speak went around the circle. By midafternoon on the second day, there was a one-page agreement everyone subscribed to with great enthusiasm. Papers were torn up and crushed noisily, and many people cheered. People stood in line to subscribe to this agreement that all agreed they could live with.

There was never a problem with any of the people who attended. The biggest objectors became some of the most constructive players. There was a gradual relaxing of positions and viewpoints, and in the latter stages, members of the group began collecting the consensus. In the most intractable issue, at one point it was down to one person who felt he couldn't live with the formulation. He held his ground, and others soon joined him. But as the discussion deepened, each of them, including him, eventually decided that the majority way really was the best way. Several said they had been persuaded by the discussion. In breaks, people were talking across groups, and the suspicion and cynicism and critical approach gradually evaporated.

THE LESSON

What changed this group was in large part the mediator's vulnerability. She claimed no power for herself but instead gave the group complete control over her and how she worked. Her process was completely transparent. She made it safe to make mistakes. She invited criticism and accepted it as part of the process. The four-player model legitimized everyone. No one needed to fight for their position or their view. Everyone held a veto, and no one needed to use it. It was a clear, clean use of shared power.

Every step of the way posed risk of falling into the chasm that yawned close by. But in the end, what had been a warring, bickering, suspicious, resistant group of powerful individuals coalesced into a remarkably effective working group. At no time was there anything less than respectful listening, which became increasingly characterized by real interest, curiosity, and a desire to be constructive.

Shared power *grows* power. Control is its antithesis. Worse, control is an illusion. What we think we are controlling we are rarely, if ever, actually controlling. We are coming into a time when sharing of power is the way power will be exercised. Those who share power grow in power, since there are so many others adding their power, and no power is being wasted on futile attempts to control what is in reality a completely dynamic process. In this way, everyone can rise to the top.

Instead of being the group from hell, this group became a group of *exceptional litigants*. Every group of litigants has that potential. But by using power to try to control, manipulate, or influence the direction of the process, a neutral party, whether mediator or a settlement judge, has the ability to blow it away. It takes commitment to be small and weak in the face of such a situation. But in this way, the mediator gave sharp-shooters nothing to shoot at. It wasn't fun anymore—perhaps better to play the game and see where it leads. As it turned out, instead of two days in hell, people enjoyed themselves and were rightly proud of what they accomplished.

> *Shared power grows power. Control is its antithesis. Worse, control is an illusion.*

These stories demonstrate the transformative power of mediation. People coming to mediation are often stuck. Previous discussions, if any, have proved fruitless. Each side is mired in its one-sided view of the matter and continues to see it in the same old way. Participants are often emotionally stuck as well and need a new perspective for the situation to change. When mediation is an art form, it is never laid on the parties by the mediator nor are the parties bent, spindled, stapled, and folded in order to be made to accept that new perspective.

In the hands of artists, such as these mediators, mediation allows the interplay of timing and sensitivity to bring out the best in people, allaying their fears. With Charlie, it enabled him to become more himself and be more sensitive to his client's needs and how to satisfy them. With Mary, it allowed her to see that by helping Kevin meet his needs, hers too would be met. With the Ruggleses and the Clemonses, it allowed each family to end the destructive gridlock with dignity and a lightened heart. And with the larger group of exceptional litigants, it created momentum that had the effect of drawing all of the other more than two hundred home owners into agreement.

Chapter Three

Strategies for War and Peace

Better to be quarreling than lonesome.
IRISH PROVERB

Have you seen one of those bumper stickers that says, "Hit me, I need the money"? They are a reflection of *lit-think*. Lit-think is a knee-jerk reaction to perceived injury or affront that throws people into fight mode and propels them toward litigation. It is an attitude that both individually and societally dominated American consciousness toward the end of the twentieth century. It drove us to lawyers for advice on everyday business affairs. Far more than we thought, it arose from our emotional response to what we read and heard.

THE BASIS OF LIT-THINK

Lit-think is based on fear. We fear that we will not get our share, that we will be taken advantage of, that we will lose something of great value to us. Businesses and all kinds of organizations act on the same principles.

Fear is pervasive in our society, exposed as it is to violence. If we did not fear that someone would sue us, we would not increase our liability insurance and curtail our operations down to what the carriers consider safe. Insurance, intended to make us feel safe, seems at times to confirm the reality of our fears.

The insurance companies are not the enemy. Carriers work on calculated margins and long-term contracts to manage the risk they assume. Initially insurance was inexpensive, with sales promoted by telling people all the horrible things that could (but had not) happened. Now, what was only a fanciful parade of "horribles" forty or fifty years ago has happened through the maw of litigation. Insurance today protects us from litigation while by its very nature encouraging litigation through the presence of readily available cash. Fifty years or so ago, a prospective plaintiff had to contemplate first winning a lawsuit, then forcing a defendant to pay, by perhaps losing his business and his house and causing such internal stresses that he might lose his family or even his life. At that time, community values did not encourage litigation.

In the United States today, the insurance industry feels besieged by ever broader liability and larger judgments. Yet its commitment to using mediation is still weak, although mediation spells major relief from litigation costs. By embracing collaborative problem solving, carriers could do much to discourage the flight to the courts of more and more disputes with wider and wider sweeps of liability. Examples are the increasing volume of huge lawsuits over consumer issues and multistate environmental issues.

The habit of blaming and the pervasiveness of fear are hard to shake. If we did not fear that we might not get our share, we might not sue a doctor over a relative's death or sue our architect or engineer because we did not get a perfect house. We do not expect someone we meet on the street to be perfect, and we do not sue unless we are willing to live with the consequences for many years. Litigation places a barrier between the parties to a dispute that impedes the humanizing of the dispute. Lit-think keeps us stuck in our own view of the situation, oblivious to the necessity for considering what reasonableness there might be on the other side. The following case illustrates how lit-think kept the parties from resolving a very costly dispute in the early stages.

Getting Past Lit-Think

The corporate owner of a solid waste landfill in Colorado wanted to build a gas-cleaning plant in order to recover fuel from the decomposing waste and help lower the cost of operating the landfill. The divisional manager found a reputable engineering firm, a deal was struck, and the plant was built, but it didn't function.

As the dispute escalated, the divisional manager and the plant's advocate quit. His successor and the rest of management scrambled for cover, pointing fingers at the contractor to explain why this multimillion dollar investment wasn't working. None of the corporation's executives had a personal stake in the plant's success.

When representatives from both sides met, the accusations flew. Then there was another meeting. By this time, the corporate owner sought legal advice on how to avoid paying for the plant construction. The corporate owner came to the meeting seeking not the benefit of the contract but the cheapest way out. It wanted the contractor to absorb the cost of the plant, which it considered a total loss.

The contractor's management thought the plant was well designed and constructed. Its investigation showed that the problem was actually a change in the type of waste being dumped at the landfill—something for which the building had not been engineered. They believed the plant could be made to work and wanted to talk about how to do that work, not about how much they should pay for what they saw as the client's problems. Not surprisingly, the discussions went nowhere.

A couple of years into the litigation, the owner decided to invite the contractor to mediated discussions. In just two days, the two parties negotiated a settlement that would save each side hundreds of thousands of dollars. Mediation at the beginning might have enabled both sides to deal creatively with the situation, saving a fortune in fees and expenses.

The owner in this situation had acted in a way that was adverse to the deal, justifying it on the grounds that the other side was preparing for litigation. This is an example of lit-think. Since the contractor was always trying to make the system work, this justification was in fact only the owner's projection.

THE LESSON

Action taken to protect ourselves, coming as it does from fear and projection, is often adverse to the deal or the relationship and makes resolution of the problem highly unlikely. Rarely do we question our assumptions about the base motives of the other side. It's comforting for a while to rationalize that our destructive actions are okay because the other side is doing the same. But the pleasure doesn't last. We need either to verify those assumptions or abandon them. Even if the other side is behaving offensively, we still need to evaluate the consequences of proceeding ahead with full adversarial action, because we're very likely to settle eventually anyway. Much of our effort and resources will have been wasted before getting to that point.

PRACTICAL PEACEMAKING STRATEGIES

A peaceful system is one that moves toward stability while allowing for change. It is dynamic, not static, and so it requires constant attention. To paraphrase the words of John F. Kennedy, peace, like democracy, is never a final achievement. Part of practical peace-making is recognizing our part in how things came to be the way they are. Bernd Huppauf (1993, p. E17), professor of German at New York University, notes, "The dividing line between ourselves and those whom we fear is an illusion: violence is as much a part of each of us as it is of our society." Tipping the balance toward peace and away from violence, war, and other adversarial activities that can be life threatening requires "concrete and localized acts of peace."

There are two fundamental strategies for making peace on a day-to-day basis: listening and speaking from the heart. Following them will help align values, goals, and the means for achieving them—within organizations and within individuals.

Listening

Intensive listening is a profound communication of respect. And respect is the cornerstone of peacemaking. To show respect, we find ways of trying to put ourselves in the other's position. This is not the same as being "nice." It is far deeper and far richer. We do not jump on others for not being able to express what they mean perfectly, seizing on their words, disinterested in any subtleties of meaning. Instead, we look behind the words to the feelings and beyond the feelings to the deeper meaning. We are open, receptive, interested, and attentive; we are tough on the problem but gentle on the people.

Intensive listening is a profound communication of respect. And respect is the cornerstone of peacemaking.

You may be familiar with the teaching of the pointing finger, which I first learned about from the Northwest Indian elder and teacher Johnny Moses. It graphically demonstrates that whatever you accuse another of is three times more true of you. Look at the other three fingers of your hand as you point, and you'll see where this wisdom may come from. Blaming is still in fashion, but it evaporates into a new understanding of personal responsibility under this teaching. I have seen a group of workshop participants suddenly deprived of words by it, as the members strove to dance around their old tapes concerning how their lives were distorted by their parents' failings.

Our keenness for another's faults or weaknesses derives from our own unconscious self-judgment, for we most resent in others the things we disown in ourselves. The charge "You're just being manipulative" often comes from a manipulator. It is only by loving and respecting our imperfect selves that we can ever respect others (Edelman and Crain, 1993).

There is a way of checking whether you are projecting on and judging another: the test for your level of *warm okayness*.[1] Here's an exercise to try:

> *Exercise in Nonjudgment.* Take a minute now to think of something you are "OK" about—but that bothered you at the time. Bring that situation to mind. Notice any tightness in your body—around the jaw, the belly. Notice your breathing. Now see if you can become warmly okay with it. Check it out in your jaw, your breathing, your belly. Notice the difference.

Everyone who has done this exercise in one of my classes seems to find that what they thought was okay-ness was in fact a cold okay, masking continued judgment. Real okay-ness is being warmly okay. That's the qualitative difference.

Once you are warmly okay and that emotional hard edge is gone from your relationship to opposing parties and to the situation, you can trust yourself to speak. Whether or not you understand the other side of the situation, keep the dialogue going. Listen deeply, and be willing to talk around the point if necessary rather than always to the point. As a teacher of mine liked to say, there is more to talking than flapping your gums. Even in the biggest shouting match, some of the words going across the table carry useful information.

William Isaacs in his book *Dialogue and the Art of Thinking Together* (1999) speaks of listening to the spaces between the words. We cannot listen effectively without coming from a place of stillness inside.

We all have such a place; it's part of the human operating system. In far earlier times—in the savanna and the arboreal forest—it allowed early humans' senses to fuse with the world around them so they could participate directly in that world. By calling on these powerful inner resources, we can do so again at some level.

In the heat of the fray, stop! Listen carefully to what you are saying and what the other side is saying and not saying. Look for the assumptions underlying their view *and* your view. Isn't there something there on which to build a discussion? The willingness to listen and to keep discussion going is effective even if it comes from only one side. It is entirely in your hands. Patience is the touchstone.

Patience Works

The parties in the mediation, the board of directors of a charitable organization versus two design firms, were at loggerheads. The organization was in the process of remodeling an old hotel in a midwestern city to create a retirement facility, and its board was demanding damages from the design firms for delays. The architects, for their part, were demanding their fees. The negotiation consisted of the board's repeatedly forwarding its demand for delay damages. Each time, the architects explained how the contract and the situation at the job site showed that the problem was the absence of a competent contractor. In response each time, the board would lay out its demand. In the course of the four-hour confrontation, the architects had kept talking not just about why the delay damages claim made no sense, but about a variety of issues, throwing in such information as the situation permitted. The tension was enormous.

Eventually the board caucused to reexamine its priorities. The board's real concern, on reflection, was to get the facility built within the loan commitment. As this became the focus of discussions, differences began to narrow. After fourteen hours, an agreement was struck that made a great deal of sense to each side: both fee claim and damage claim were dropped. The local architect agreed to stay on the project to help the board get someone competent on the job site.

THE LESSON

This successful resolution could have been lost if the architects had been impatient with the apparent stalemate earlier in the mediation. It might never have been found if the board had not paused to examine its priorities. When you think of settlement strategies, it may help you to think of preparing to listen. Most people prepare what they are going to say. They do nothing to prepare to listen. The exercise in nonjudgment on page 39 may prove useful in that regard.

Speaking from the Heart

Speaking from the heart means speaking honestly. It does not require compulsive truth telling. It means going beyond what you think people want to hear to what is really true for you. It means refraining from expressing something different from what you feel, whether the expression is verbal or nonverbal (a shrug, a smile, or a frown, for example).

Children's remarkable ability to ask penetrating questions no one else seems able to ask derives from the fact that their words, thoughts, and feelings are aligned. If they do not understand, they haven't yet learned to say they do. They never heard of a stupid question and do not put up a front. Many people believe it is sophisticated to say what they think people want to hear. It is true you cannot be a good negotiator if your feelings are on your sleeve. But really good negotiators are authentic, honest, and fully congruous in feelings and words or actions. This congruity gives them an authenticity that engenders trust. It does not make them an open book, but it does make them trustworthy. Expert negotiators act in ways consistent with credibility.

Consider an employee who has just been told to do something he does not believe is right. A response of "Oh sure, no problem" deprives his boss of the opportunity to check the proposed action herself to see if it really is what she wants done. It deprives both of the chance to see if there might be a better way to do what is needed, and it creates an untruth between them, which is likely to cause trouble later. The honest expression of the employee's reservations will not occur unless trust between the two is sufficiently high.

When we are committed to speaking congruently, we respond better after the fact when some excess we have committed is brought to our attention. We recognize and acknowledge the overkill and let it go, and perhaps we even apologize. The knee-jerk defense or explanation, auto-speak (that is, talk generated out of reach of the heart), is much more common, but it has no place in an environment of authenticity. "The human heart is an 'analogue' device: continuous, fluid, wavelike. It cannot be broken down into information packets and beamed somewhere only to be reconstituted exactly as it was before" (Isaacs, 1999, p. 389).

When you are coming from your heart, you have immense capacity to handle what others might judge to be outrageous words and actions. You can look at disruption as an opening to another's heart—that rare and valuable honest communication—that invites true connection. Examples of the effectiveness of applying this principle can be found in abundance in the peacemaking circles initiated in First Nation Communities in the Yukon Territory. The circles draw together affected family members (the perpetrator's family as well as the victim's family), community members (merchants, for example, in the cases of theft or vandalism), and the prosecutor, defense counsel, judge, and perhaps the arresting officer. In speaking of peacemaking circles, Judge Barry D. Stuart of the Yukon Territorial Court writes:

> Until it is experienced, it is difficult to appreciate the ability of people in the Circle despite their pain and anger to search for higher ground. The overwhelming energy of a Circle is positive. The value of expressing anger, frustration, hate or fear cannot be discounted. These emotions reveal to offenders the deeply felt responses of a community or a victim to their crime. These feelings force offenders to deal with the human dynamics of their actions [Stuart, 1998, p. 95].

When we sit in a circle with those who hurt us and those we have hurt, our hearts may more easily be touched. Violence and cruelty are products of the hardening of the heart, for unless the heart is hardened we would suffer from our own misdeeds more than those we have hurt. The circle allows the perpetrator a window on the pain he or she has caused, and the dawning of awareness of that pain is life changing. All of a sudden, life becomes more real. What we live in most of the time is illusion—and illusion created by our own minds.

As Peter Senge writes on this same theme:

> Thought *presents* itself (stands in front of us) and pretends that it does not *represent*. We are like actors who forget they are playing a role. We become trapped in the theater of our thoughts. This is

when thought starts, in [David] Bohm's words, to become "incoherent." "Reality may change but the theater continues." We operate in the theater, defining problems, taking actions, "solving problems," losing touch with the larger reality from which the theater is generated [1994, p. 241].

Speaking from the heart may take a little practice. We may have to sift through a pile of little lies that candy-coat and weaken the experience of daily life until we find what's real inside. It gets easier with practice.

THE GROUNDWORK OF MEDIATION

The cornerstone of mediation is the awareness that in all likelihood the matter in question *will* settle. To resolve early, through negotiation, is the most rational decision, unless for some reason you do not want to resolve, even on terms that are satisfactory to you. (See the section "When Is It Unwise to Mediate?" in Chapter Eight.)

If the matter is not yet in litigation, focus on drawing together what is needed to have a reasoned discussion about resolving: girding yourself with only the essential information and loosening the hold of any destructive attitudes.

Do a preliminary investigation, looking possibly toward a joint investigation. Information gathered jointly will have much more acceptability to both sides. You might want to gather important documents and check the financial impact of what has happened or threatens to happen.

Because attitude is important, assess your emotional involvement as well, recognizing that anger and fear narrow perspective and get in the way of effective discussions. Recall the story of the Clemons and the Ruggles families in Chapter Two. By the time of the mediation, much of the young mother's thirst for vengeance had been transcended. This allowed a huge breakthrough in the healing process for those involved in this tragedy, and it allowed that chapter in their lives to begin to close once and for all.

When you begin to recognize your own emotional contributions to your perspective and position, take steps to address these emotions so that you can be more effective in your efforts to resolve your disputes. The perspective exercise described in Appendix A is a useful technique for recognizing and detaching from the emotional freight that comes with most disputes, allowing one to regain a balanced perspective. The more that you do to loosen your hold on your beliefs about how things were and need to be, the greater are your chances of getting real satisfaction. Keep in mind the "rule of one": it takes only one side to change the entire nature of a discussion. By the simple act of looking at the assumptions on which rest your own perspective and position, you create an openness to something new entering in—new understanding, new insight, new information, and new possibilities for achieving satisfaction.

MAKING MEDIATION THE CONTAINER

The legal system has become the envelope or container for most disputes that are filed as lawsuits. It need not be so. Because some 95 percent of filed cases settle, it makes more sense to use a container designed to produce the following results:

- Separate those matters that really need to be tried from those that will settle
- Reveal the negotiated resolution that awaits the vast majority of matters
- Maximize the development of insight, awareness, compassion, and common ground that is the natural by-product of a wholesome resolution of the conflict

Mediation can be such a container. By using a negotiation focus right from the beginning, you have already taken the first step in this direction. This does not prevent you from using litigation artifice, such as setting depositions and document productions, as a means of displaying your commitment to taking the hard road if necessary. Such steps sometimes create trade-offs, such as postponement, which can be used to win agreement to the early use of mediation. You may consult with a lawyer about what information will be needed to secure a satisfactory negotiated resolution. You and your lawyer may consult with a mediator about the steps to take to resolve through mediation (see Figure 3.1). These are critical planning steps.

Figure 3.1. Steps in Resolving Disputes.

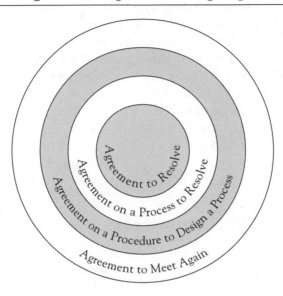

Agreement to Resolve

Agreement on a Process to Resolve

Agreement on a Procedure to Design a Process

Agreement to Meet Again

Source: Interaction Associates.

If the matter is in litigation, case management planning is already taking place. Periodically lawyers and clients meet to discuss the case, sometimes for a half-hour, sometimes for a day or two. These meetings usually focus only on litigation strategy. They will be far more productive when, instead, the primary focus is on laying the groundwork for effective negotiation.

Here are a few techniques for bringing an unruly lawsuit to negotiated resolution in a timely and cost-effective way.

Manage the Case Strategically

Focusing on securing a negotiated resolution defines the environment in which all activity takes place. The strategy will fail, however, if you shelve it when litigation activity grows intense.

Organizations are composed of shifting power groups. When you oppose an organization, be aware of the need to cultivate those groups that favor a resolution you would find acceptable. Your goal is to enlarge their voice within the decision-making structure of the opposing party organization. This helps secure satisfactory results by keeping you from making a devil out of your opponent and keeps alive the possibility of serious settlement talks.

Most people are familiar with the good guy–bad guy style of managing contacts with the opposing party. Tactics for handling that gambit are discussed in Fisher and Ury's *Getting to Yes* (1981) under the heading of "dirty tricks." Such games generally serve merely to block meaningful communications. A good counterstrategy is to name the game, bringing it out in the open—for example, "You seem to be using good guy–bad guy tactics here. I don't believe that's helpful." Such games are a symptom of dysfunctional communication: no one is really listening; each is taking a role, wearing a mask.

Do the Most Critical Discovery First

Discovery, you will recall, is the name given to formal information-gathering tools used in litigation: depositions, interrogatories, and requests for production of documents. Analyze proposed discovery activities by asking yourself a number of questions:

Exactly how does this help you and the other side evaluate settlement options?

What do you need from this witness for this purpose?

Can you get an agreement to come back for more questions later if need be?

How strong is that expert's opinion, and how will he or she stand up to cross-examination?

Is this an expert who could help draw the other side's expert into more reasonable territory?

The tendency in litigation has been to take important depositions last. The reason is what is known as the "one bite rule": you get only one crack at a nonparty witness without an agreement to the contrary. Therefore, you do not want to depose a key witness until you know all the questions you want to ask. You can get around this by negotiating for agreements with opposing counsel and the witnesses themselves, if need be. If I were the deponent, I might be happy to agree to a short deposition now at the price of a possibly a longer one later. The willingness to cooperate should come as no surprise, yet it is rarely sought.

Dance with the Courts

Wherever the court has taken an interest in helping parties to move cases along, your best interest may lie in seeking the court's support for your efforts to resolve through mediation (see "Winning the Judge's Support," the case example in Chapter Ten). Judges increasingly are throwing their support behind voluntary mediation. Unless they detect a purpose to subvert the rules, they will do all they can to help you. Agree to pinpointed discovery, if any at all, and try to postpone the rest while you try to negotiate a resolution.

An early but reasonable trial date is in your interest, whichever side you are on. The practice in some courts of requiring immediate and substantial discovery, however, is not helpful. This approach actually hinders resolution by hardening positions and keeping counsel and parties busy. It is diametrically opposed to what a negotiation focus would dictate.

San Diego, California, pioneered the Fast Track system, designed to move cases to trial earlier than the three to five years that was all too common. Still, like so many rule-driven reforms, this system proved itself the litigator's full-employment act. In tracked cases, parties were plunged into vigorous discovery to meet court timetables, long before they knew whether or not it was necessary. This benefited defense lawyers, who are usually paid by the hour, but hurt plaintiffs' lawyers, whose own funds often finance litigation costs for clients. There was an explosive growth in area law firms to meet the vastly increased demand for foot soldiers in the discovery wars. Overnight, many major Los Angeles firms that until that time had bypassed San Diego set up or merged with local offices. According to Julie Haig, executive director of the San Diego Bar Association, a voluntary organization, the Association saw an increase in the *rate of growth* in memberships of about 18 percent in the period between 1988 and 1989 and a decline of about 75 percent again in the rate between 1990 and 1991. A judge, writing of the reforms when they were first implemented, related that "[t]he institution of Fast Track has meant full employment for court reporters" (Huff, 1989, pp. 227).

Fast Track has now been taken statewide. According to lawyer Kenneth M. Sigelman, a member of the board of governors of the Consumer Attorneys of California, in 1983—before Fast Track—it took five years to get to trial. It was common to have sixty cases trailing (waiting to be assigned for trial) in Los Angeles County— that's sixty sets of attorneys and sixty sets of litigants, lawyers, witnesses, and experts. With Fast Track, it is far better. One can expect a trial date eleven or twelve months from filing the complaint.

In San Diego, the court sets deadlines for exchange of expert reports earlier than those required by statute, so there might be a little more opportunity for mediation before the trial. This step has proved helpful to lawyers and to litigants.

San Diego still has no overall mandatory mediation program, which is perhaps a blessing in disguise. For according to attorney Sigelman, virtually every serious personal injury case is mediated on a voluntary basis. The most common time for doing so is after depositions of percipient witnesses but before the much more expensive depositions of experts. These voluntary mediations have replaced the mandatory, court settlement conferences—the latter now no longer take place at all.

A few departments in San Diego have been experimenting with early court-ordered mediation. In these cases, mediation takes place before much, if any, discovery is taken. This approach may work well in certain types of cases in which the basic information is known on both sides of the table. It is premature, reports Sigelman, to report a positive result in cases in which, for example, not enough is yet known about how the injury occurred.

Another experiment involves San Mateo County's Multi-Option ADR Project (MAP), which has been in operation since 1996. This voluntary program, co-sponsored by bench, bar, and community, makes referrals to trained and experienced attorney and non-attorney neutrals as well as private judges. MAP reports around 90 percent of participants, both attorneys and litigants, are satisfied to very satisfied with the program (San Mateo Superior Court, 2000).

Programs such as this one give choices to lawyers and litigants— an approach that raises levels of satisfaction with the legal process. They are a far cry from the aggressiveness of early Fast Track in San Diego, which forced so much unnecessary discovery at litigants' expense. Now it is apparent that lawyers are becoming accustomed to using mediation, in particular, and they work it into the management of the case with cost-effectiveness in mind. This is a significant improvement achieved through the court.

Use Mediation to Gather Reliable Information

Negotiate during the setting up of the mediation or once mediation has begun for the information you need. Instead of written interrogatories, convene a mediated discussion between principals and experts. Such discussions can greatly narrow the range of issues and broaden the areas of agreement. When technical issues are complex and overarching, this type of mediation may be co-mediated. For example, a facilitative mediator, charged with keeping the process on track, may work with a technical co-mediator, charged with putting the resulting questions, agreements, and output of the process into terms that make sense from a technical point of view.

For safety and simplicity, it is helpful not to give a single mediator two roles. When the mediator is also the technical expert, trust can fall as the differences between parties become more intense. A mediator who takes a position opposing one or another party may lose critical effectiveness as a neutral.

Although mediated discovery may not yield an overall settlement, it will have saved significant time and money. Trustworthiness of information need not be an issue. You can satisfy yourself as to completeness and authenticity by gaining agreement that the information will be provided under a declaration under penalty of perjury, the way authenticity is often ensured in discovery. In litigation, authenticity in answers to interrogatories and productions of documents used to be ensured by a notarized statement that the information was true and correct or complete. Over the past decade, many jurisdictions have changed to the declaration under penalty of perjury, which does essentially the same thing but without a notary public.

Avoid a Battle of the Experts

Another important step in preparing a matter for negotiated resolution is to control the use of experts, one of the biggest cost sinkholes in disputing. Mediated negotiations may secure neutral expert opinion from the beginning.

To secure an agreement for use of a neutral expert, there are many points to negotiate. It is difficult to hold this complex a negotiation together outside the protection of mediation, for it is all too easy to get suspicious of the other side's motives. Nevertheless, it can be done and produce great savings of expense and time. The parties share the expert's cost. Moreover, a neutral expert is more likely to persuade than an opposing party's expert.

Table 3.1 covers most issues both sides might want to consider in negotiating for a neutral expert.

It is a bit unsettling to send a neutral expert out to investigate something when you have no idea how it will turn out. What if the expert comes out against you? Well, that's life. What better time to know your problems than early on? What you risk, if the expert is wrong and against you, is that the other side gets a bit too cocky. That's nothing new, and you have tools for dealing with that. What you gain is an opportunity to increase acceptability of your view or another constructive view of the situation through an expert who has the ear of opposing counsel and the

Table 3.1. Neutral Expert Checklist.

- What qualifications are needed in the expert?
- By what method will you select the expert?
- Who specifically will have contact with the expert?
- Are the other parties entitled to know what each has communicated to the expert?
- Shall the expert be able to investigate outside his contact with the parties?
- With whom may the expert talk?
- Just what will the expert be told about the underlying dispute? By whom? And how will this be communicated?
- What provision will be made to check on the expert's progress to be sure the work is on track?
- What kind of report does the expert need to produce?
- What can be done with the expert's opinion?
- Can the expert be used by any party in the event adjudication is required?

opposing party, whom you must persuade in order to succeed through negotiation.

STRATEGIES FOR MANDATED MEDIATION SITUATIONS

Some states are mandating mediation in some, most, or virtually all civil lawsuits, and more are expected to do so. In Florida, a leading example of mandated mediation, Sharon Press, the director of the Florida Dispute Resolution Center, reported that in 1999 over 122,000 court-connected mediations took place. There are in addition a substantial number of mediations in which courts are not involved.

The U.S. District Court for the Northern District of California has now taken court-wide its Multi-Option Program, which presumes that mediation or some other form of ADR will be used but leaves the choice of process to the parties. This relatively less coercive approach resulted in higher ratings for litigant satisfaction in a study done by the Federal Judicial Center, which reported that attorneys who had selected their process were more likely to report that it lowered litigation costs, that it reduced the amount of discovery and the number of motions, that it was a fair process, and that the benefits of the process outweighed its costs (Federal Judicial Center, 1997). In the several counties comprising the San Francisco Bay Area, lawyers are routinely required to use mediation, arbitration, or early neutral evaluation. Early neutral evaluation (ENE) is a process in which the opinion of a neutral lawyer with subject area expertise is expressly sought. The motivational implications of providing litigants and their lawyers with choice are enormous but often lost in old-mind thinking.

When we find ourselves in mediation not of our own choosing but through a mandatory court program, we often shoot ourselves in the foot by not taking the initiative. Thus, we suffer through a short or long, going-through-the-motions procedure, neither investing in it nor being capable of drawing the gold from the conflict. Here are some tips for dealing with the mandatory mediation:

1. Take the initiative. *You* decide the best time for mediation. Many court programs still offer mediation as an end-game strategy. That's an old-mind strategy. You cannot use mediation as

the container for the dispute unless you bring mediation and a commitment to mediation on board early.

2. Find a suitable mediator. An evaluative mediator whose job it is to give advice on the probable outcome at trial or to weigh the merits of the case (see Chapter Nine) is of little value to you early in the disputing. There usually is not enough information yet for this person's opinion to be meaningful. Consider finding someone who is resourceful, creative, and free of a heavy need to know—indeed, someone who is perhaps expert in what he or she *doesn't* need to know. There are special situations where you might want to use a neutral evaluator—not necessarily a mediator—in order to get a sense of the lay of the land in the particular type of dispute you are involved in. However, if you have used mediation as the envelope, you can bring in this neutral as part of that process. In this way, your generalist mediator may be more effective on your behalf. Moreover, your timing is likely to be a lot better. Except in run-of-the-mill cases, neutral evaluators operate best not early but late, after the story has been clarified and the key points needing attention in a negotiation setting have been identified.

> *Consider finding someone who is resourceful, creative, and free of a heavy need to know—indeed, someone who is perhaps expert in what he or she* doesn't *need to know.*

3. Use the court. Courts may have some flexibility in their approach to your use of mediation. Even with a mandatory program proposing mediation late in the litigation, sometimes the court can nudge a reluctant party to be more cooperative simply by showing interest in the process. Sometimes when mediation is underway, conflicting court requirements can be placed on hold without threatening the integrity of the case processing system. If you don't ask for court assistance when you need it, you'll never know.

4. Follow through. Even if you end up unable to reach complete resolution through mediation, use the process to shape and manage the litigation or arbitration that will follow. Clarify and segregate issues that will require trial. Negotiate for stipulations

of fact that will allow you and your opposing parties to pinpoint and even prioritize the key conflicts, thus containing transaction costs and improving on the chances that the ultimate decision will be useful.

Be Persistent in Pursuing Negotiated Resolution

Remember your goal: to settle does not mean to compromise. To settle is to resolve, and it may also include an internal letting go of the conflict. It's how you settle that determines whether you gave up something of value.

If the opposing party stonewalls, bide your time. There will be opportunities to penetrate the facade through court status conferences and informally at depositions. Repetition alone may win the day. Strategic discussions occurring in the fleeting moments when you can relate to an opposing party or counsel primarily as a human being can win agreement to your approach, for it will be heard with new ears.

Managing a case for early negotiated resolution requires finesse. Everything that happens or that fails to happen presents an opportunity to plant the seed of an idea, to assess the situation and strategize anew. In this work, mediation, not litigation, is the better tool.

Chapter Four

Transformation in Mediation

*Non-linearity means that the act of playing the game has a
way of changing the rules.*
JAMES GLEICK, *CHAOS: LIFE IS NON-LINEAR*

If you have been involved in serious conflict, you may agree with
me that it is a fertile ground for transformation, not unlike grave
illness and near-death experiences. Lives can be and are transformed by how conflict is transcended, in relationships, communities, businesses, government, global affairs, and all kinds of
lawsuits. In the hands of a mediator who has the capacity to create
an environment where transformation is a possibility, mediation
can provide a container for such occurrences.

The way conflict is handled in our culture creates major distortions in people's lives. Everything—work lives and personal lives—is
affected. As soon as there is an inner tightness, a personal insistence
that something be *my way,* there is conflict, and the push that
comes from this creates resistance. It causes a sort of darkness in a
person's life that few recognize but everyone knows is there. In the
classes I teach, a person who truly lets go of his holding against
another person becomes visibly younger, more beautiful, and
brighter. Everyone in the class can see it. There is a softness and
gentleness in the person that is so sweet, and the person can hardly
believe how long it took to let go.

In the absence of forgiveness, when that holding spot is
touched, there is reaction, and it is often strong and often unpleasant. The old tapes about how a person or organization has been

wronged emerge to play themselves once again. In conflict, every side has a story about what happened in which he or she is the victim (Cloke and Goldsmith, 2000). There is a strong sense that *we're right* and *they're wrong*, which sets up a whole series of adverse consequences. Our insistence on our version places filters on our perception. Someone who is in conflict mode often cannot appreciate what is going on now, so heavy are the filters imposed by remembered past experiences. Past hurt held onto often prevents awareness of opportunities for healing, reconciliation, and renewal.

Lawyers are caught up in these stories. Many lawyers say that when they first hear about a dispute, they are at their most objective. They have not yet taken up the cause, and their perspective is relatively unclouded. But after they have begun serving as advocate, their objectivity is covered over by the fallout of the pursuit of winning. Lawyers can maintain a certain degree of detachment, but they find that they often have to work at it. The greater the inner development and resources of the lawyer, the easier it is to compartmentalize the advocacy role. But as we will see in the next chapter, this is not something the legal profession has much valued historically. Nevertheless, there is a trend away from the past toward a more holistic way of being a lawyer.

THE BUSH-FOLGER MODEL: TRANSFORMATIVE MEDIATION

Since the publication in 1994 of *The Promise of Mediation,* by Robert A. Baruch Bush and Joseph P. Folger, a movement has swept the field, aggressively challenging those who seek "merely" to problem-solve and to find resolution to difficulties presented by the parties. The term *transformative mediation* has become synonymous with an approach that advocates that a mediator subordinate these simpler goals—settlement of the dispute—in favor of a goal of "engendering moral growth toward both strength and compassion" in those who present their disputes for resolution, through a variety of techniques aimed at generating recognition and empowerment (Bush and Folger, 1994, p. 28).

Bush and Folger deserve great credit for legitimizing the concept of transformative mediation. Thanks to their pioneering work, transformation in mediation is no longer something one might talk about only quietly, among friends. While I do not believe the model, as taught, goes very far in tapping the potential for trans-formative mediation, I honor their contribution to opening the door to exploring that territory.

It speaks volumes about the barrenness of formalistic, evaluative processes that Bush and Folger should evoke an opposing model such as this—one that so profoundly engages the mediator's *mind* in efforts to enhance opportunities within mediation for empowerment of the participants and for greater recognition of each other. In my experience, empowerment and recognition are natural by-products of flow in the mediation process, requiring no great effort on the mediator's part. Indeed, the more effort there is from the mediator, the less likely there is to be flow. But the Bush-Folger model must be understood in relation to what it was created to oppose: the widespread model of mediation that is itself aggressively effortful, that is, the problem-solving model in the hands of those not yet graced with *mediator mind. Mediator mind* respects the parties' wisdom, experience, and understanding, and it allows the mediator to make himself or herself available to help remove obstacles to the parties' ability to use these resources effectively. Mediator mind is not anxious to *do something* or *tell someone something.* Mediator mind is in touch with the heart and is the expression of the heart without any loss of the skills and abilities of a highly trained mind or the benefit of prior experience.

So great has been the impact of this movement on the thinking of many in the field that any discussion of transformation as it might happen in mediation is likely to be judged by how it conforms to this model. Largely because it is a mental model rather than a heart-based one, there has come to be a certain orthodoxy in the way many Bush-Folger-trained mediators look at their work and how they do it. It is looked at as either-or: either you're a transformative practitioner according to the model or you're *merely* problem solving. This has tended to isolate practitioners and weaken the ability of the vision to leaven the field.

The Problem with the Bush-Folger Model

The Bush-Folger model focuses the mediator on "helping to transform the individuals involved, in both dimensions of moral growth. . . . It means encouraging and helping the parties to use the conflict to realize and actualize their inherent capacities both for strength of self and for relating to others" (Bush and Folger, 1994, p. 82). Bush and Folger believe that "if this is done, then the response to conflict itself helps transform individuals from fearful, defensive, or self-centered beings into confident, responsive and caring ones, ultimately transforming society as well" (pp. 82, 83).

Improved listening, recognition, and empowerment in mediation participants are natural by-products of good mediation. These help participants to function better in the mediation. But for the mediator to bring an agenda to the mediation that is not the parties' agenda is a risky proposition for the participants. A mediator pushing her own agenda to heal me might very well miss opportunities to understand me and my needs more deeply. Her slate is not clean; it has writing on it. As Thoreau wrote, "When I see people who want to help me, I run in the opposite direction." He recognized that those who seek to help are often motivated by their own need to be seen as a helping person. A person with such a mind-set can turn aggressive when his or her helpfulness is unappreciated (Palmer, 1991).

Bush and Folger criticize mediators who focus on problem solving as being too likely to miss relational issues and opportunities. Their model is responsive to this perceived need. It focuses not on agreement but on relational issues and opportunities. The lawyer-minded mediator is looking for a fix, a settlement. That is his agenda.

The Bush-Folger transformative mediator is looking for improved relational capacities and has specific steps to take to secure them. Although this is laudable, it is still an agenda. The two perspectives share commitment to an agenda that is not needed.

The agenda reveals that the mediator is coming from a place of "not okayness" focused on "what's not right." That attitude deters transformation and deeper healing. A mind focused on its agenda is not open, relaxed, or available to the participants in the situation. It blocks flow.

There is an honesty that is communicated when, however bad the situation, the situation is accepted just as it is, and the people involved in it are accepted just as they are. From that place of acceptance of things as they are, far greater creativity, healing, and empowerment can emerge than could ever come from service to an agenda. Flow can happen.

The dramatic and favorable results of the USPS REDRESS program show how much can result from touching even the tip of the transformational potential inherent in mediation. Transformation will have moved deeper when the statistics start to show greater creativity and fellow-feeling and more cost-saving ideas and pleasure percolating. It can come from the way an organization is run. Or it can come through the way an organization manages conflict and conflict resolution.

Bush-Folger model mediators have been criticized because their mediations are lengthy. This criticism is to some degree unfair, given what they set out to do. If it takes three or four hours rather than two (as it does in the USPS REDRESS program), then let it. Perhaps "McMediation" (as the two-hour version has been called) is not appropriate in cases in which there is a continuing relationship, such as that of neighbors or fellow employees. Programs now limited to two-hour mediations might offer a two-stage process, with some cases quickly disposed of by the presence of a mediator for two hours while others are referred to a mediator with more time and perhaps more aptitude for addressing the relational situation.[1]

Bush and Folger contend you cannot mix, let alone marry, problem solving with transformative mediation (Bush and Folger, 1994, pp. 108–112). But theirs is a mental model. Mental models are two-dimensional in a multi-dimensional world. It is the heritage of the *argument culture*. There is still a felt need to hang on to the "rigor" of academic debate, even in discussions about processes such as mediation.

What is missing is a culture of wholeness—with the body in service to the mind, the mind in service to the heart, and the heart in service to life itself. Until such a culture begins to permeate the field, many will be stuck in such dichotomies—*either* problem-solving *or* transformation—when reality is in its nature so very much greater than these. Test your own wholeness with the exercise on non-judgment in Chapter Three.

In truth, the best mediation is both problem solving and transformative. And it is neither. There is no agenda to be either problem solving or transformative. There are no mandates, other than established ethical considerations that are honored automatically in the pristine process I'm describing. The mediator need not think, "Do this," "Do that." There is room for participants to do what they came there to do and what their openness—happening in the mediation process itself—allows. With reflective mediation, there is an opening for many approaches simultaneously.

REFLECTIVE MEDIATION: REAL TRANSFORMATIVE MEDIATION

The term *reflective mediation* is used by Lang and Taylor in their book, *The Making of a Mediator: Developing Artistry in Practice,* to describe one who mediates with artistry. I have given the concept greater depth by taking it out of the reach of the purely mental and basing it in the heart. As we explore this new foundation for reflective mediation and flow, the differences in the two approaches become more apparent. A heart-based approach is not so much a model as it is a way of being in the mediation process. Rather than the language of holding—as in holding on to flow—there is the language of letting go—as in letting go of the illusion of control. Instead of words like *making,* there are words that propose *allowing.*

Mediator mind defines one's role as more catalytic than active in nature.

The term *reflective* has at least two levels of meaning as used here. In one sense, the reflective mediator brings a relatively clear mirror to the participants so they can see the wisdom, compassion, and understanding they bring to the process. In another sense, reflective refers to the mediator's self-awareness—the consciousness of internal states as well as external words, timing, and actions.

Reflective mediation is mediation from the inside out. It is something a mediator grows into. A reflective mediator sees his or her role as catalytic in nature rather than proactive, for this is essential to operating in *being* mode rather than *doing* mode. In doing mode, one is acting in support of one's own agenda, not the parties' agenda. In being mode, one still acts, but with a power, precision, and effortlessness unapproachable in doing mode.

The reflective mediator is highly present in awareness and also is highly skilled and open to helping the parties find within themselves the resources for creatively addressing their surface (problem-solving) and deeper (transformational) desires. In this way the reflective mediator creates a safe space or container in which all can work to remove the barriers to the participants' achieving whatever they are able to achieve. Such a mediator has no reservations about providing information as needed by the parties but is more likely to turn questions around rather than to answer them directly, because doing so throws people back to their own resources, where most of the time the answer is to be found.

A reflective mediator is self-aware, but not self-focused. Such a mediator will notice when he has an agenda and let it go. He will notice when he is judging someone or someone's behavior and let it go. As he notices his assumptions, he will test them with the parties involved, perhaps by bringing them forward and inviting comment. He will notice when he is being controlling and relinquish control back to the parties. Such a mediator will invite correction, showing that it is okay to make mistakes and that he will share power. He will embrace surprise. He will recognize himself as a player among equals, rather than imagining himself apart from or above others.

With such a mediator, flow is invited. Such a mediator will relax into the flow and not attempt to hold onto it, because doing that cuts off flow. This relaxation increases flow and invites the parties to likewise relax into it, which vastly increases the effectiveness of the process and the healing that can take place within participants. Reflective mediation is both effortless and fearless. The reflective mediator is not concerned about looking good or playing it safe.

There is no "how to," no series of moves, no particular practices that distinguish heart-centered reflective mediation. The distinguishing characteristics are the openness, vulnerability, lack of agenda, and quality of attention that the mediator brings to the table. Over time, as a mediator grows in reflective practice, there is a sense of doing less and less and reaching better and better outcomes for the participants.[2]

Reflective mediation is the most powerful approach to the mediation process I have ever experienced. In this approach, the mediator is *in* her power but does not *use* that power—for using power is an automatic disconnect from the source of all life. Using assumes separation—a doer and doee, an actor and one who is acted upon. The user of power has needs that inhibit flow: the need to look good, the need to be right, the need to vindicate a personal agenda, and the need for recognition. When the mediator is in his power, that power is available to everyone for the mutual benefit of all concerned. It is not important where the power comes from nor where the ideas come from nor anything else that would merely provide a feel-good experience. Being in your power is very hard to describe, but it is real.

Transformational potential is the capacity to see people, events and situations in a new and even profound way. It is the ability to let go of blame, guilt, and judgment and to go forward in life to seek restoration of business and personal relationships that have been fractured by conflict and misunderstanding. It is a reflective mediator without any agenda as to the outcome who creates far and away the greatest opportunities for such transformation. Such a mediator is free to see you, not just your problems. When you are truly seen, your heart is touched and, depending on your response, there is no limit to the good that can come to you.

Wisdom is not for sale. No degree and no amount of experience ensures it. You can detect wisdom in prospective mediators perhaps more through what *is not* said than through what *is* said. If you are tuned in to it, you will recognize it. In this way, you can ensure that the door to transformation will remain open in your mediation. And no one will have an agenda to push you or anyone else through it. Sometimes, we think of the other side, "If *only* they would see. If only *they* would understand." To go fishing for understanding is the surest way to prevent it from happening. Understanding comes of its own accord. Otherwise, it is not real and it does not come from the inside but from the outside, which sets up resistance and a negative spiral.

If transformation of a relationship is something of interest to you, seek a mediator with no agenda either to solve your problem or transform you. Such a mediator will have no self-conscious application of techniques and tools to change you. Such a mediator will create, and invite participants to share in maintaining, a container to hold the conflict while such sorting, soul searching, and exchanges as present themselves may take place in relative safety. Transformation is not something you can make happen. It is only something you can allow to happen. By the wholeness the mediator brings to the conflict, by modeling constructive behaviors, and by the respect shown through deep listening and acknowledgment, participants are drawn into deeper levels of awareness and functioning. Fears subside, and people's capacity flowers. Transformative mediation allows this gold to come forward.

Such a mediator will not place a finger on the scale of outcomes. Rather, respectful of the parties' wisdom and inherent good judgment (once the layers of conflict-based complexity and its fruits are peeled aside), this mediator will work with perceived reality, with problems as the parties see them, toward developing more than one acceptable option for resolution, being firm on the agreed-on process in order to achieve goals the participants brought with them. While doing this, the mediator will be gently inviting participants to a broader view of the conflict, themselves in relationship to it, and the possibilities.

Transformation is not something you can make happen. It is only something you can allow to happen.

With such a mediator, the participants retain control. At any time, any of them can put a stop to a mediator initiative by simply saying, "No. I won't go there now." With such a mediator, that will be completely acceptable because this response will have been invited honestly. The door will remain open, but there is no urgency, no necessity for someone to walk through it. No push-resistance is created. Anything else is disrespectful.

Transformative mediation requires a quality of excellence, and there are those who are seeking to define what it is that makes for excellence in a mediator. Michael D. Lang and Alison Taylor's book, *The Making of a Mediator: Developing Artistry in Practice,* is helpful in this effort. Both authors have been leaders in the field of mediator education. Among the characteristics they cite as indicators of those for whom mediation is an art form are the following (my comments in italics):

1. They engage in a continual process of self-reflection.
   I would include in this being in touch with their own inner and outer states and loosening the hold of their own beliefs and assumptions as they are able to do so.

2. They rely on models and theories to guide and inform their practice—theories of interventions, of justice, of power, of dispute formation and resolution, of interpersonal interaction and behavior.
   I would say they are aware of their models and theories and they hold these lightly.
3. They use the process of experimentation to test their observations, perceptions, and formulations of the experiences, beliefs, and needs of their clients.
4. They are willing to see perspectives other than their own, to experience surprise.
   I would say they invite and are open to other perspectives because they are interested and they welcome surprises.
5. They are open to new information about their practices; life-long learners, they are open to new strategies and techniques.
   And beyond these, to wisdom.
6. They do not see themselves as experts, but they acknowledge that both they and their clients have expertise to bring to bear on the conflict situation.
   I would add that they do not see themselves as sole managers of the process, but they seek to involve their clients' own expertise and contribution to the work of building and maintaining the mediation container, which will allow the most powerful results for the parties. They are comfortable sharing power.

What Lang and Taylor are looking for in a mediator is the ability to create flow. They define *flow* as "that sense of deep concentration, absorption, joy, and accomplishment that are some of the best benefits of being human" (Lang and Taylor, 2000, p. 213). They identify measurable benefits of flow: increased productivity, heightened self-esteem, and enhanced creativity. It seems there are levels to flow, for something approaching flow can be experienced in the mind and perhaps even in the emotions. Yet what I am calling true flow is deeper than that.

To me, flow doesn't produce a sense of accomplishment, any more than would being present at a birth or a death or watching your team's quarterback throw that long pass in the third down to make a touchdown. Rather there is a sense of being present at a miracle, in which one is merely an instrument along with other instruments that are being played in a way that could never have been devised. True flow involves a deep interconnectedness among those participating in it. Each heart is touched. It is not clear where the energy and the power are coming from. We feel awe in its presence, and it could be coming from one or both or all who are present. Effort falls away and the impossible and inconceivable and numinous happen. True flow is an affair of the heart, not an outcome-oriented experience in the mind. And there is dignity to it.

A mediator who can open transformational opportunities has personally experienced transformation. In the same sense that you cannot give what you do not have, you can only *be* in the world in the way that you truly *are* on the inside. You cannot by thought or deed make yourself into a transformed person. The extent to which you let go of your belief systems and agendas speaks to the extent of your transformation. Such a mediator will recognize and bring the parties into flow if possible. In flow, things that seemed difficult become almost ridiculously easy to do or become obviously of no consequence. The second through fourth stories included in Chapter Two are good illustrations of the influence of flow. The following story shows the effect of even the tiniest touch of flow.

How Flow May Happen

This was a mediation between government officials responsible for management of a historical facility and leaders from the surrounding community who wanted more voice in how things were done at the site. In advance of the mediation, the mediator met privately with each of the eight participants. On the day of the mediation, there were grumbles as most participants communed with their apprehensions about "spending a day with those people." But within an hour and a half, it was as if both sides could not do enough for the other side. One participant observed, "I've lost track of the 'us' and the 'them.' What they are saying is just what we were saying." "Same here," said someone from the "other" side. What happened?

There was a shift in perspective. Going into the mediation, each was prepared to jockey for position on an advisory council that was to be created. This wrangling continued until tempers began to flare. The community leaders reiterated their sense of having been ignored. The agency managers retreated to their position: "We're charged by law with the management of this facility. We can't delegate that." As the conflict grew louder, the mediator then asked two strategic questions. To each side, she asked: "Do you need these folks here in order to do what you want to do?" Each side rather grudgingly agreed.

Everyone of course already knew this. The historical site was created and sited near the community largely due to the hard work of the local community leaders. Such prosperity as the community then enjoyed was in large part driven by the presence of this historical site. By the same token, the agency managing the site depended heavily on its devoted core of volunteer workers, whose efforts at the site brought in close to $1 million in revenues annually, which were then used to enhance the site. Yet because of the conflict, this interdependence had become a source of frustration rather than a source of enjoyment.

The mediator then looked at each member of the group and asked the second question: "When's the last time you took a vote in your family?" First there was silence—then laughter as everyone recognized the implications of the question and their response.

In the subsequent discussion of the concept of consensus, each side recognized that it actually had a veto on anything the advisory council came up with. Everyone was in exactly the same boat, only this time, they recognized it for what it was. People quickly began proposing to give more seats to the other side. Each side worked diligently trying to come up with the very best advisory council, not those who could hold turf for one or another side. The conflict evaporated.

This was the last advisory council to make it through the department involved, for the department had decided to abandon that model (one wonders, were they too contentious?). The application for this one was approved in record time and continues to this day, to the great satisfaction of all involved.

THE LESSON

Any mediator who was trained in the process and understood it might have suggested consensus. But a mediator who was microfocused on empowering this person or recognizing that person could easily have missed the timing that strategic intervention requires. Nor would a mediator focused on bargaining have been able to see the bigger picture so easily. Here, people were energized and committed because the flow happened with the strategic intervention. A less artful introduction of the consensus model would not have done that. That's a small example of flow. The mediator in this story did not plan the intervention. There was simply an openness to the participants' and to the mediator's own inner resources.

Lang and Taylor point out that the lack of flow leads to disappointment, a sense of lost opportunities and failed interventions. Because mediators have so much potential influence on the parties and the outcome of the mediation process, it is important that they have good feedback loops going, that they be self-reflective during the process, and that they share with the participants, to the extent possible, the management of the interaction. Such steps guard against the pernicious use of the mediator's power—intentional or unintentional (Lang and Taylor, 2000, p. 216). A high level of practice skills is assumed for artistry in mediation to occur.

What flow feels like from the participant's perspective is, at first, chaos and frustration as expectations collapse, then a slight willingness to pitch into the effort to do what you came there to do. This gradually picks up steam until you and the others are doing more than you ever thought possible. And at some point, with your hardly becoming aware of it, you may find yourself in flow. It can all come clear, why you are there, why the conflict is in your life in the first place, what there is to do, perhaps what there is to let go of (or that it has been let go of), and even where the best path now lies.

With a mediator open to bringing conflicting parties into flow, there is powerful support for negotiators to be effective. Negotiators are encouraged to "consider a wider range of outcomes and options, concentrate on looking for areas of common ground and focus more on long-term considerations, to be more flexible in setting limits and in letting sequence and issue planning flow freely" (Fukushima, 1999, p. 2).

Even average negotiators can look good in the safety of a good mediation setting, using fewer "irritators" (words or phrases that have a negative value in persuading the other side and actually cause irritation) and being able to tap into a better sense of timing instead of making premature counterproposals or getting into defend-attack spirals. They may become able to label behaviors strategically, drawing attention to what is helping to move the process forward and avoiding labeling disagreements. They may become comfortable asking more questions and more likely to share their internal state, for the expression of feelings is directly linked to establishing trust (Fukushima, 1999).

Some have asked, "Why would a company or agency be interested in reflective mediation and in flow?" It is simple mathematics. They've invested in a conflict, whether as a carrier, a disputant, or a counsel. Why not get the full payoff? There is a great deal that all participants—counsel, companies, executives, negotiators—can learn and much they can receive from the transformation of conflicts they are involved in that will greatly promote their future success. Why define their interest so narrowly—for example, "Just get rid of this dispute!"—that they never get the lesson? Those who ignore lessons from conflict are doomed to repeat the mistakes that led to the conflict. They only hurt themselves and they lose their opportunity to make a contribution to a more civil world.

THE QUALITY OF TRANSCENDENCE

Mediation can be offered in forms that range from the simple shuffling of people and problems to an almost magical transcendence of people and events. Problems resolve or they do not resolve as participants determine. The difference is, as Table 4.1 shows, in how committed people are to the outcomes. In the wider ranges of mediation potential, there are internal changes in participants, often including the mediator, that can be described only as grace. To participate in such an experience with an open heart is much like attending the birth of a baby. The physician or midwife does not "make" the baby or even in most cases "deliver" it but is privileged to be present at this extraordinary event. So can it be in mediation.

Imagine what it means to an injured person to give up the fight for redress from injuries and come to terms with the fact that money can never compensate for physical, relational, and emotional losses. Or what it means for an employee or former employee to be heard, understood, and acknowledged when things at work have gone off the rails. Or what it means to a manager to take fully in, without defense and excuse, how things she did or failed to do contributed to the conflict, so that she is empowered to see that it does not need to happen again, so that difficulties can be picked up earlier, when they are smaller, reducing both pain and suffering and also increasing the effectiveness of her organization. Or what it means to a doctor whose imperfection injured someone he was committed to caring for, to be able to apologize

Table 4.1. Spectrum of Mediation: Flow Toward Resolution.

Shuffling People and Problems	Potential for Transformation	Grace
Leads by pulling or pushing.	Leads by modeling.	Makes leading irrelevant.
Mediator sees the situation or the parties as needing fixing. Fails to address fear, anger, blame, projection, narrow view of self-interest, insistence on being right, stuckness.	Reflective mediation invites inquiry, curiosity about other perspectives, compassion, digging deeper into how one's values might best be served, in enlightened self-interest.	All find the best outcome effortlessly, allowing initiation of release of fear, anger, blame, and projection, appreciation of broader self-interest, and compassion for another.
Works only with symptoms.	Uncovers insight into root causes. Shows way to healing.	Allows healing. Motivates addressing of root causes.
Parties are done unto.	Parties are invited to lead.	Parties lead.

for the unintended injury that occurred. Or what it means to two chief executive officers, bickering and fighting about some perceived past wrong, to recognize that there was basically a misunderstanding at bottom and that they are now free of these misconceptions and all of their progeny to do business together again, productively and creatively.

There are ways of approaching a conflict that produce significant insights, new perspectives, even new paradigms—much larger expanses of new ways of being true to one's values. And there are ways of sidestepping all of that potential. There were varying degrees of flow in the four case studies in Chapter Two. There was a touch of it in "A Case of Humility," considerably more in "Building Trust Through Sharing Control," and still more in "Transformation Is Where You Find It." There was even more than that in "Vulnerability Works," because in that story, the mediator was personally the most out of the way, which made the process almost completely transparent to the parties. In the first instance, the mediator's move was largely self-conscious—an effort to get a reluctant player to play. There was a bit of that in the second instance, although the mediator was willing to go a lot further out of her comfort zone. In the third instance, the mediator devised and followed a game plan but was open to changes in it from the parties. In the fourth instance, the whole process evolved on the spot. Although the mediator had some idea of how it might go, there was little momentum or personal insistence in her ideas, to borrow from Canadian-born teacher John de Ruiter. In the fourth example, the lack of momentum of the mediator's ideas made it safe to criticize and even to reject them; it dispensed with guilt and blame and allowed the mediator to model the behaviors everyone at some level was able to put into practice in the meetings.

It is not yet acceptable in legal circles to talk about the heart and its pivotal role in conflict resolution. It will be a while, it seems, before emotional intelligence is much valued in academic discussions around mediation. But it is happening elsewhere. In speaking of his experience with what emotional intelligence can bring, through peacemaking circles (described in Chapter Three), to the sentencing and rehabilitation of convicted persons, Judge Barry Stuart writes:

> My experience is consistent with many others, especially with police officers, courtworkers, and probation officers who become directly involved with community justice. Getting involved with the community creates if not for the first time, certainly the most significant belief that crime can be successfully addressed, that the process can beneficially impact upon victims, offenders, families and communities—and that the original motivation to take up a career in justice—to help others, to help the community *can* be realized [Stuart, 1998, p. 107].

There are significant benefits to a more community-based approach to criminal justice. Peacemaking and sentencing circles restore the treatment of criminal offenders to the community. This community-based approach represents a sharing of power by the authorities. But the end result is far lower recidivism rates so that the system itself is less overwhelmed. Significantly, people who participate become motivated to get more involved in their communities.

Great change is happening around the edges of the box that contains mainstream thinking. Another example is what is happening in the business world.

LESSONS FROM THE LITERATURE OF BUSINESS

Today's business literature is filled with models of transformative practice. Peter Senge's seminal work, *The Fifth Discipline,* shows how individually and organizationally we can move out of our mentally created reality into a way of being that is more creative and more deeply satisfying; we can move away from shallow fixes that do not move toward a holistic way of being and seeing. Senge's strong medicine is based on the thinking of David Bohm, whose *Thought as a System* and *Wholeness and the Implicate Order* have influenced a generation of thinkers and teachers. It exposes the personal and cultural illusions we have inherited from the mechanistic world-view of Descartes and linear Newtonian thinking. By using analogies from the mechanical world, such as leverage, Senge uses a familiar framework to open people to the tremendous distortions in perception that come from mental models of how it is. These are buried so deep that we do not even know that they exist, let alone that they color the way we experience ourselves and the world around us. It is life-changing work to begin to accept responsibility for the way things are. Senge writes:

> There is no blame. We tend to blame outside circumstances for our problems. "Someone else"—the competitors, the press, the changing mood of the marketplace, the government—did it to us. Systems thinking shows us that there is no outside; that you and the cause of your problems are part of a single system. The cure lies in your relationship with your "enemy" [1994, p. 67].

Can the paradigm of systems and wholeness have an impact on the universe of conflict resolution? It can and it will. It is just a matter of time until the whole fabric of society is permeated with what now seems like a radical new way of thinking. Senge provides a personal observation on the effect of abandoning blame: "So long as I saw the problem in terms of events, I was convinced that my problems were externally caused—'they let me down.' Once I saw the problem as structurally caused, I began to look at what I could do, rather than as what 'they had done'" (1994, p. 160).

William Isaacs's book, *Dialogue and the Art of Thinking Together,* along with several others on the subject, describes how people in business, community, and organizational settings are learning to engage in thinking together. Isaacs describes dialogue as a conversation with a center but no sides. It exposes the fallacy in the notion that for things to work, we need to fix something or change someone. It assumes there is an underlying wholeness that we can access when we listen deeply to all of the views that people may express. Dialogue brings us together in association to allow us to create a quality of listening and attention that includes but is larger than anyone's individual view.

Isaacs (1999) tackles the problem of the closed heart head-on. "Through dialogue," he writes, "we learn how to engage our hearts. This does not mean wallowing in sentimentality. It refers, instead, to cultivating a mature range of perception and sensibility that is largely discounted or simply missing from most professional contexts" (p. 47).

The term *dialogue* comes from the Greek: *dia,* meaning "through," and *logos,* meaning "word" or "meaning"—"meaning flowing through" (Isaacs, 1999, p. 19). I agree with Isaacs that flow—the free flow of substance from one level of being to the next—is present all the time, but that in our awareness, we are often out of it. What maturation and wholeness of the person means is recovery of a feeling for this sense of intimate participation in one's own life.

The steps to true dialogue mirror those inherent in a problem-solving/transformative negotiation or mediation. It begins with the sacred act of listening and all it takes to do that. Krishnamurti, the Indian philosopher, wrote: "If we try to listen we find it extraordinarily difficult, because we are always projecting our opinions and ideas, our prejudices, our background, our inclinations, our impulses; when they dominate, we hardly listen at all" (1968).

As a visually dominant society, our sense of hearing (the purpose of listening) is significantly underdeveloped—reserved, if available at all, for music, perhaps because it completely bypasses the rational left brain. Yet authentic communication requires the same kind of listening—open, nonjudgmental, cleansed of our all-too-ready reactivity, opening the way to true response. True listening has a sense of curiosity in it. If judgment and criticism are there, they are part of the armoring we impose on ourselves through memory of past experiences, including cultural, family, and personal conditioning. When we listen intensively, we connect with the speaker in a way that allows us to walk in his moccasins; we derail reaction in favor of reflection that can lead to creative and healing response.

Another cornerstone of dialogue and of problem-solving/ transformative mediation is respect. By showing respect, we send the message to the other person, "I see you" (it is the greeting used in Zulu). So much violence derives from a sense of being invisible— of being a person of no account, no value. Each of us is nourished by respect, by an "I see you." Its impact on people is profound. Listen to what an offender says of one of his old comrades in crime:

> I see what he's got now—I know what he used to have because we hung out together—did it all together. Now he has a good life—got the respect of many people—heard many people say he should run for Council—now that's a long way from what they were saying about him before [Friend of a past offender in the circle—Kwanlin Dun, 1992; quoted in Stuart, 1998, p. 106].

Is there any reason in conflict situations to deny another person this most basic acknowledgment? Indeed, there are myriad reasons to give it: the other person is put on notice that this is not to be a charade—you are willing to engage personally in the search for a mutually acceptable outcome; you are present to whatever may happen.

Thomas à Kempis's observation at the beginning of Chapter Two of this book, "Be assured that if you knew all, you would pardon all," speaks of respect. By what arrogance do we approach another, thinking we know what is important about that person— thinking we know what her motivations are, thinking we know how and what she thinks? Respect is a value, one that is self-implementing when we allow it to be. Bringing respect to a negotiation, to a mediation, draws everyone to a higher plane of functioning. Simple respect is life-giving.

Suspension is another fundamental of dialogue. It asks that we put on hold our tendency to fix or correct another, that we release our hold on certainty. Instead we ask questions to learn what this is about. How does it work? What value is in it? Curiosity replaces reactivity. There is no invitation to the dialogue dance in mediation as a rule, but there could be. Parties and counsel can learn the art of suspension and also learn inquiry rather than argument.

Suspension of certainty and judgment, respect and deep listening, cultivating the art of inquiry, and reducing reliance on destructive advocacy: these are all tools that can be used to good effect in any negotiation and mediation. This by itself would immensely enhance the transformative potential of the process. Imagine inquiring into one's own motivations, looking beneath what is being asked, taking in the midst of the most bitter of conflicts a fresh and nonjudgmental look at the architecture underlying what is being said and questioning the flow of meaning. Imagine routinely challenging your own certainty that something is so by looking for what is missing and stepping back from the argument long enough to allow its workings to be revealed. These are some of the techniques of transformative mediation you can practice any time.

In the same sense that all healing is self-healing, all transformation is self-transformation. If you want to get your money's worth out of conflict, be prepared to go deep—deep within yourself, deep within the conflict, deep within each and every person involved and within what each is saying and not saying. By starting with yourself, you clear the decks for action. Park your opinions and judgments at the door. Return to the innocence you once knew—to being vulnerable. You will lose none of your functionality. The heart knows better than you do how to use your experience, your mind, your emotions, your will. The power of a heart that is opened and softened is a power aligned with the power of life itself. It is a power that includes everyone but treats no one as special, that calls forth the best that is in people and that evokes great creativity. It is the power of love (de Ruiter, 2000).

Part Two

Obstacles to Resolution

To quote from Pogo, "We have found the enemy and it is us." How many times have we come to the end of a blind alley, realizing that it was not the opposition but our own blindness and mistakes that did us in? How can we learn to see these as they are developing?

Chapter Five

Self-Made Stumbling Blocks

*Finally, you understand that the real motorcycle
you're working on is yourself.*
ROBERT M. PIRSIG,
ZEN AND THE ART OF MOTORCYCLE MAINTENANCE

In our less rational moments, we might willingly hurt ourselves in order to hurt another. Not infrequently, litigation is pursued with such self-destructive motives. Not until the end do we discover how much the exercise really cost us.

A story is told in Russia of a farmer who was plowing one day when he accidentally captured a genie. He was given one wish. "But whatever you get," the genie said, "your neighbor will receive double." The farmer thought for a long time. "Blind me in one eye," he said (Sidney Lezak, personal communication, October 1981).

A major difficulty in securing cost-effective legal representation is our societal approach to the lawyer-client relationship. Problems arise because often clients are not clear about what they want to accomplish. They hold on to fantasies: cost-free vengeance or the belief that something will be done now (a near impossibility in the tangled world of the legal system). When they finally get focused on what can be accomplished, they become more reasonable and therefore get better results. In a sense, the litigation waltz is usually no more than an elaborate ritual to get litigants to tap into that part of themselves that knows what their long-term interests are and what it takes to serve them. In *New World, New Mind* (1989), Paul Ehrlich and Robert Ornstein show how the mind that served primitive humans so well over the millennia utterly fails to help us cope with today's world. People filter information so as to make it manageable and reduce it to caricatures—a sort of mental short-hand. They respond quickly to sudden change but hardly at all to gradual change.

One of the reasons that Americans have put up with an excess of litigation so long is that we have become habituated to it, and we no longer question the delay, expense, and inconvenience. Today, it is the old mind that holds mediation at bay, insisting that prolonged but customary litigation activity take place first.

KEEPING MEDIATION AT BAY

There are certain things some of us just cannot accept. Chief among them is change. As Lewis Carroll put it in *Through the Looking Glass,*

> "I can't believe that," said Alice. "Can't you," the Queen said in a pitying tone. "Try again: draw a long breath and shut your eyes." Alice laughed. "There's no use trying," she said. "One can't believe impossible things." "I dare say you haven't had much practice," said the Queen. "When I was younger, I always did it for half an hour a day. Why sometimes, I've believed as many as six impossible things before breakfast."

Many of the following rationalizations used to put off or avoid mediation ignore the reality that mediation excels at dealing with just such concerns:[1]

• *This matter won't settle. The other side is too unreasonable and there is too much hostility.* Mediation is a process in which both sides are encouraged to be more reasonable and less hostile. In mediation, the parties may be able to discover why previous efforts at settlement failed, and then devise solutions.

• *I've settled many matters before without a mediator.* It is true that in the long run, almost all disputes settle. The question is when, how well, and at what cost.

• *We don't need to settle this case. If I wanted to settle, I would just call the other side.* It is always possible to lose in court or end up with less than you deserve. In mediation, you can at least find out what your choices are. You may still decide not to resolve, but this decision will be an informed one.

- *Why mediate? We have a mandatory settlement conference with a judge coming up soon.* Mandatory settlement conferences with a judge are often too brief to help. In many, there is pressure to settle. Mediators, in contrast, have been trained in communication and process skills most judges are unfamiliar with.

- *This dispute is too complex for mediation.* Mediation works extremely well in complex cases because each item can be negotiated separately or as part of a package. Also, it is much easier to untangle complex situations in civil discussions. And if the matter cannot be settled, it has at least been simplified and made less costly.

- *We don't trust the other party. They have not acted in good faith.* Mediation is a process in which remedies can be created that do not depend on trust. For example, one side's performance can be contingent on completion of an act by the other side; authenticity and completeness can be sworn to under penalty of perjury. Trust, which is destroyed by the adversarial nature of litigation, is often restored in mediation by the nature of the process.

- *We've completed discovery and have a trial date. Why should we mediate?* In mediation, when both sides agree, both have won, and they have laid the groundwork for a peaceable future relationship, however distant it may be. At trial we may still lose, for despite discovery, there may be some surprises.

- *Mediation will only provide the other side with an opportunity for free discovery.* Each side has control over how much information it discloses in mediation. Both sides will learn more about each other's case in mediation, but the truth will come out at trial anyway. Surprises do not necessarily help or produce fair results. Since this is a nonbinding process, there is nothing to keep the parties from changing their minds. When mediation results in agreement, a document is prepared that makes the settlement final and binding. It sticks because the parties are invested in it. Before agreement, the parties have a right to change their minds, try out an option, or make sure the final result feels balanced and fair.

- *The only way to teach the other side a lesson is to get a court judgment.* That may be right. But it is often we who end up being taught the lesson, because of what it costs us to get that result. Only later may we realize that we could have done as well or better in a negotiation and have conserved the resources squandered on litigation in the bargain.

PERSPECTIVES: OURS AND OTHERS

We often lose perspective when it is our ox that has been gored. People whom we have dealt with for years take on a sinister look; we project our own anger on them and then are frightened by what we see. We take their angry words literally and convince ourselves that they speak softly for devious purposes. We attribute to them serious destructive capabilities, in part to justify our own adversarial buildup.

When I was in college, a rosy-cheeked, robust, good-looking accounting graduate student was convicted of the brutal rape-murder of another student. On the eve of his execution, the newspaper portrait of him showed a man with thin lips, dark shadows under his eyes, and a sickly look. It later emerged that the photograph had been retouched to make the attractive young man look evil—perhaps to make the public happier with the execution.

In disputes, we do much the same thing with our minds. We no longer see the enemy as we did before the dispute arose. The mere thought of the other makes us tense or angry. The other side sees us in much the same way, hears us in much the same way, projects on us in much the same way, and ignores what we're really saying in much the same way.

RESTORING BALANCE TO PERSPECTIVE

Distorted perception adds immeasurably to the burdens of the situation. Nevertheless, there is a certain satisfaction we derive from feeling right. To regain balance, we need to be willing to let that go. That does not mean letting go of our claim or defense or weakening our will in any way. It instead means letting go of the victim stance, of the pleasure of feeling wronged.

Regaining balance may require only a few quiet minutes of work. Most of us find it hard to dispel the emotional side effects of disputing. We become so stressed that it affects our day-to-day lives. Perspective always distorts, and the distortion reaches epic proportions in conflict situations. By taking just five to ten minutes to do the perspective exercise in Appendix A, you can unload a conflict sufficiently to open up a host of options you never imagined were possible in an emotionally laden situation.

One of the problems with business disputes is the number of people who think that their emotions get parked at the door of their place of employment. It is not acceptable in many cultures—including to a large degree the culture surrounding courts and lawyers—to talk about emotions. Yet the emotional mind is a major part of our makeup and a major determinant of our decisions and our actions. Daniel Goleman (1995) observes:

> A view of human nature that ignores the power of emotions is sadly shortsighted. The very name *Homo sapiens,* the thinking species, is misleading in light of the new appreciation and vision of the place of emotions in our lives that science now offers. As we all know from experience, when it comes to shaping our decisions and our actions, feeling counts every bit as much—and often more—than thought. We have gone too far in emphasizing the value and import of the purely rational—of what IQ measures—in human life. For better or worse, intelligence can come to nothing when the emotions hold sway [p. 4].

If you find yourself in a situation where it's not okay to talk about emotion, here's a secret: talk about perspective. Use the perspective exercise in Appendix A, and share it with others. Because perspective is highly colored by emotions as well as other thoughts and beliefs, loosening the hold of perspective gets you to the same place as dealing with emotions. There is no need to sort, analyze, classify, or prioritize your inner states. With the proper tools, any "garbage" can easily be made to fit within a standard trash can.

Such clearing is sometimes called forgiveness work. It does not mean condoning or making okay something that was definitely not okay. It means separating what others have done in the past from what we are doing to ourselves now by holding on to destructive emotions about what they did. We give up the sour satisfaction of holding another responsible in order to secure the far greater pleasure of reclaiming power to get results in the situation.

For example, when I hold my mother responsible for not providing me with a good maternal model, I inhibit my own ability to be the best mother I can be. I blind myself to the qualities and habits in myself that I disliked in her, making it impossible for me to become the kind of person I want to be. When you hold anger toward a former partner over a financial debacle in the partnership, you blind yourself to your own contribution to the situation, making it more likely you will repeat the pattern.

You may ask, What good is it to regain a balanced perspective when others may remain distorted in their perceptions? The answer is that clarity is catching, just as confusion and fear are catching. Once you are clear, you become far more creative and far more effective in moving the situation toward a resolution that serves you. This helps to clear the other side's perceptions too.

Until we clear our perception, our perspective, we are likely to hurt ourselves more than others could. With even a modest emotional burden, we are likely to stir up unnecessary legal work for which we pay one way or another. We may snarl and sulk around, or play Camille, the eternal victim, for the next few years. There are endless variations. In either state of mind, mediation seems pretty unappealing, and so we add to our problems rather than resolving them.

Rage appears empowering, but in fact it holds us hostage. We may be powerful in blocking another's path, but we are usually powerless to get a result that works for us. A balanced perspective allows us to lighten up and regain personal power and effectiveness. And it allows us to see the advantages of mediating.

HOW WE LOSE EFFECTIVENESS

A variety of inappropriate tools, attitudes, and perceived needs deprive us of effectiveness in negotiations—and in fact, in all of life. By knowing them for what they are, we can make the choice to let go of them. They are simply patterns of reaction that have long outlived their usefulness.

Tools That Bite

The heavier the emotional charge is on a dispute, the more likely we are to use high-risk negotiating strategies when we finally do decide to negotiate or mediate. These tend to defeat negotiations and make a mockery of mediation.

Secrecy and Deception

People conceal or misrepresent their preferences and priorities when they believe that if the other side knew their true desires, they would never get satisfaction. It is a marketplace strategy expected to lead the merchant to offer a lower price. However, this technique may prevent the other side from offering the very thing we most want. Discussions become more a performance than a negotiation (Susskind and Cruikshank, 1987).

Intransigence

Refusing to move is a strategy often based on fear,[2] for example, the belief that moving off a fixed position shows too much interest in resolving. It is a refusal to negotiate that passes up the opportunity to resolve now. It invites retaliation, which means an end to the discussions. The effect of intransigence is to keep you from finding out what is the best that can be accomplished short of an adjudication. If you leave with no acceptable agreement, wouldn't you like to know that it was impossible to reach agreement and necessary to seek adjudication? Or would you rather wait until the courthouse steps to find out that, in fact, there was an acceptable agreement that was waiting for you before you spent all that extra money and committed all those additional resources to the fight?

Blaming

Some people come to mediation bristling with accusation of everyone and everything in sight. Sooner or later the mediator gets into this person's sights, causing such severe erosion of trust that any chance for a positive outcome is lost. If the other side does not like your offer or demand, it's the mediator's fault. If you find the other side's offer repugnant, it's the mediator's fault. Blaming is a control strategy that gets you nowhere. If nowhere is where you want to go, this approach serves your purposes. Mostly it defeats the very goals you think you are serving.

When blaming crops up, reach inside yourself and flip the little switch to partnering mode. Think of the mediator as your partner in seeking resolution. Ask questions. What am I missing? Why is this so difficult? Help me to understand why we are stuck.

Attitudes That Impede Resolution

Certain attitudes reduce our ability to satisfy our interests through negotiation and mediation. They usually function undetected just below our awareness.

Asking for More Than Satisfaction

Sometimes we reject options that meet our interests because we think the other side is gaining more or losing less than it should. If something satisfies our interests, it is sufficient, whether or not the other side got its just desserts. To hold otherwise is to subordinate our self-interest to our desire to hurt the other.

Loss Aversion

Sometimes we focus so intently on not losing anything that we undervalue our gains. Arms negotiations provide an example. American arms negotiators often felt that what the Russians offered to give up was not worth nearly as much as what they asked us to give up. Since we always had substantial superiority over the Russians, this attitude was self-defeating. It took years to reach an agreement that could have been reached readily in the absence of loss aversion.

Believing Our Own Puff

When we are out of balance, the mere fact that we are offering to give something up may cause us to become much more attached to that item. The old cat-clawed sofa that wouldn't bring fifty dollars at a yard sale becomes a valuable "antique" after we have offered to let our nearly ex-spouse have it. The other side sees this valuation as dishonest, and it heightens distrust. It is particularly destructive when both sides are doing it.

Knee-Jerk Reactivity

Often we dismiss proposals that might in fact serve our interests quite well, just because the other side made them. Studies confirm this. In one sidewalk survey, pedestrians were asked to evaluate a hypothetical nuclear disarmament proposal. They were told one of three explanations: that the United States proposed it, that the Russians proposed it, or that a neutral third party proposed it. Reactions were highly favorable when it was attributed to the United

States, unfavorable when it was attributed to the Russians, and in between when it was attributed to a neutral third party (Stillinger, Epelbaum, Keltner, and Ross, 1988; Stillinger and Ross, 1991).

Asking yourself, "What's this based on?" helps unveil such reactivity masquerading as thought. It is useful to keep in mind that much of what passes as thinking is in reality "thoughting"—replaying old stuff we thought before.

Needs That Do Not Serve

We confuse desires based on fear with real needs.[3] We then convince ourselves that nothing will suffice unless these false needs are met. Do any of the following needs sound familiar?

Need to Control

Controlling people usually feel they must make the final proposal. They must put forth proposals for the other side to consider, not vice versa. This need to control alienates the other side, pushing it to wrestle for control also. The antidote is to force ourselves to work from the other side's proposals if no mediator is present. We may also use mediation to mask the originator of proposals, so they may more readily be considered on their merits.

Need to Be Right

It can be difficult to accept now what we rejected a while ago, even when it makes sense. It is a mark of statesmanship to do it gracefully: "You know, you were right about that. I see what you're driving at." This approach, when sincere, engenders trust and makes it easier to reach overall agreement.

In the forgiveness workshops I teach, we explore the physiological and emotional impact of disputing. In one exercise, participants are asked to observe the physical effects of the rage engendered by a situation. They are then asked to imagine that the other side has taken out a full-page advertisement in the *New York Times* or their local newspaper, saying, in effect, "I was wrong. You were right. I'm terribly sorry." To date, not one participant has felt any lessening of the rage in contemplating such an action. This illustrates an important truth: nothing another person does can relieve us of what we choose to cling to. The need to be right reflects an immature way of thinking that stubbornly insists that others accept our views *now*. Life does not work that way. There is only honor in letting it go.

Need to Keep Fighting

Even when we get 110 percent of what we want in a settlement, we often feel as if we are giving something up. We're giving up the dispute, with all that entails. There are payoffs for being a victim; we attract sympathy or maybe even something more tangible. We give these up for a greater good only when we are ready. Recognizing when we are in this loop is a good way to stop this mental train that is going nowhere.

Need for Vindication

The rosy view that our day in court will mean that the judge says "You're right" is largely illusory. There is only a small chance a case will be tried, and then there is no guarantee of a clear decision on the merits. The few well-publicized court victories hide legions of the disappointed.

Need to Be Nice

Niceness is camouflage for far more dangerous feelings and reads that way to the other side. People feel dishonored when they are not trusted with the truth. This is a key cause for so many wrongful-termination actions: people intuitively know when they are being lied to. Neither side is willing to risk disturbing the atmosphere in order to see if progress can be made on deeper issues.

People feel dishonored when they are not trusted with the truth.

Cordiality masks the real problems. We may start out being cordial and quickly slide into a real fight when anger springs up unexpectedly. There is no point in taking that risk, we reason. Mediation allows tough subjects to be tackled with dignity and without offense. With or without mediation, antagonism is not a necessary part of a dispute.

Accepting responsibility for being part of the problem is the first step in securing resolution, even if we have actually done nothing.

It may help to think of this as claiming responsibility rather than blaming another or ourselves. By taking that step, we recognize that it is within our power to end our suffering. While pain is in the heart and cannot be erased, suffering is in the mind. When we loosen our grip on our own conclusions and our insistence, new possibilities that were covered over by our judgments and opinions swim into view. It's like a breath of fresh air.

The only difference between a stepping-stone and a stumbling block is in how you use it.

The only difference between a stepping-stone and a stumbling block is in how you use it.

Chapter Six

The Lawyer Culture

He who sues my client is my friend.
LAWYER PROVERB

If you are involved in any kind of general, civil lawsuit, any mediation you have will likely involve the participation of lawyers. (This is not true of domestic relations cases, where lawyers are often not present, by agreement or by court requirement.) Increasingly, civil litigation mediations are initiated by lawyers. These lawyers are often extremely helpful in moving a matter from impasse to negotiated resolution. However, the way lawyers are trained to think can and often does impede early entry into the mediation process, with consequent loss of many of its benefits. In addition, adversarial training and many years of adversarial litigation experience can and do influence lawyers toward more of an evaluative, bargaining model of mediator (more like the settlement judge) than a more subtle, wide-ranging facilitative-transformative mediator. This background also takes its toll on a lawyer's perspective. For these reasons, it is important to consider the effect of the lawyer culture on the mediation of civil disputes.

To understand lawyers and their impact on the way mediation is becoming available generally, to say nothing of the way you may be influenced to think about it, it is important to understand something of what is happening inside the legal profession.

THE LEGAL PROFESSION IN CRISIS

A Newtonian vision has dominated the practice of law and the training of lawyers for more than a hundred years. According to this view, law is a system of principles and rules that may be applied almost mechanically to people and situations in order to reduce the ever-threatening chaos in human affairs. The training of lawyers and judges has, since the nineteenth century, been focused on the development of intellectual acuity and the skills of argument and critique. More than any other field, the legal field is permeated by what Deborah Tannen (1998) calls the argument culture. And in this system, even the argument is to be pristine, devoid of values, moral concerns, emotion, and, inevitably, human concerns. Facts are important only tangentially, in that they serve to shift focus from this line of decisions to that one. Clients are merely a distraction, albeit an essential one.

Moreover, more than at any other time before, the legal profession has lost sight of what it means to be a lawyer. There is no longer agreement that it means, for example, dedication to principles of fairness and the public good over economic gain. Steven Keeva, senior editor of the *ABA Journal,* writes:

> Beginning in law school and continuing into the practice, the message comes across loud and clear: What really matters is winning. . . . From this primary message flows a number of secondary directives: never admit ignorance; never let your weakness show (better yet, to be sure that doesn't happen, don't even acknowledge it to yourself); develop a mask that suggests certainty, aggressiveness, strength (which, more than likely you will come to confuse with your real face); kill or be killed [Keeva, 1999, p. 10].

In such a culture, there is little attention to the true art of persuasion in the classical sense—the kind that implies interactivity between speaker and those addressed, between lawyer and client. Aristotle, in his discourses on rhetoric in *The Art of Persuasion,* gives a lot of attention to the emotions, such as anger, fear, shame, pity, indignation, and envy, and to resources, such as emulation and calmness, pointing out how they set the stage for how a speaker and his or her message will be received. Considerable emphasis is placed on the fine art of listening, something almost completely absent from the education of lawyers—these classical rhetoricians of the modern age. Why has the training of lawyers ignored the study of human character and emotions? Perhaps it is the personality characteristics of those who are drawn to the law.

Susan Daicoff identifies the following characteristics, which are often intensified during law school, that distinguish lawyers from the general population:

1. Lower interest in people, emotional concerns, and interpersonal matters
2. Less humanitarianism
3. More likely to be cold and quarrelsome, and less warm and agreeable
4. More into masculine traits (including argumentativeness, competitiveness, aggression, and dominance)
5. Having a high need for achievement based on an external or internal standard of excellence (includes competitiveness) [Daicoff, 1997, p. 1410].

The toll the personality structures have taken on lawyers is a heavy one. Studies by the ABA and others agree that about one-fifth to one-quarter of lawyers are very or somewhat dissatisfied with their jobs, and the rate of depression and alcoholism among lawyers is about twice the rate in the general population (Daicoff, 2000). The effect of anger, frustration, and anxiety on the immune and cardiovascular system is well documented. The lack of a "trusting heart" has been described as a key risk factor by Duke University's Dr. Redford Williams, who has researched the relationship between hostility and dying young. Among his findings from a sample of physicians were these:

- Those with the highest scores on a test of hostility during medical school were seven times as likely to have died by the age of fifty as were those with low hostility scores [and] that

- Proneness to anger was a stronger predictor of dying young than were smoking, high blood pressure and high cholesterol [Goleman, 1995, pp. 170–172].

Moreover, Williams found that a network of friends and family relationships has proved to be a strong indicator of health and longevity (Goleman, 1995). The requirements lawyers often place on themselves leaves precious little time for nurturing these life-giving resources.

Many lawyers find themselves trapped in work they abhor, drained of personal meaning and meaning-ful contact with others.

Law has been practiced in the most dehumanized way imagin-able over the past two decades. It is small wonder that all is not well.

In large part, these "best and brightest" practitioners of the law have relegated themselves to the elegant playing of mind games with one another. Not surprisingly, as human consciousness in our culture emerges from the straitjacket of early industrial era think-ing, many lawyers find themselves trapped in work they abhor, drained of personal meaning and meaningful contact with others.

THE BREAKING POINT

In the increasingly demanding practice of law—with more and more billable hours being required—lawyers are suffering. In 1990, the Young Lawyers Division of the ABA conducted a survey on career satisfaction, *The State of the Legal Profession,* and found that between 1984 and 1990, there was a 20 percent decrease in those reporting satisfaction with the practice of law as a career. In a report the next year, the ABA stated that of lawyers admitted to the bar since 1967, approximately one-third reported dissatisfaction with the practice of law (ABA, 1991a). And in a response to a 1994 survey by *California Lawyer Magazine,* over 70 percent of California lawyers said they would not go into law again if they could begin their careers anew (Greenberg, 1996).

In a 1995 follow-up survey, less than 15 percent of lawyers in private practice firms of three or more lawyers reported they defi-nitely would not consider a career change (ABA, 1995). Reports of negative experiences increased in all categories, with the highest incidence found in lack of time for self and family. In the 1991 ABA report, *Breaking Point,* this problem was described as *time famine,* in which 50 percent of all lawyers in private practice reported working 2,400 hours a year or more and 45 percent reported billing 1,920 hours a year or more. What is lost in all this work is the opportunity for development of the whole person through nonlegal education and association with others in various contexts. The *State of the Legal Profession* report estimated that about one-third of childless lawyers stated that their decision not to have children was based on career demands.

Human wholeness encompasses emotional intelligence, a key part of our physiobiological tool kit (Goleman, 1995). Imagine a fish that has just flipped itself out of the water. It is lying on the bank and the water is right there, so close. Emotional intelligence (assuming the fish had it) would energize its body, and it would be able to splash back in the water. But this fish is different. It can think. And it thinks, "Should I or shouldn't I?"[1] Emotional response is many times faster than intellectual response, according to Goleman. Like the fish, a person who self-defines only in terms of intellect lacks that ability to respond quickly. What is missing is attention to growth of the whole person, essential to the full development of any professional.

What the absence of wholeness leaves available to the client is often an overworked, overwrought technician seeking to apply deep but very narrow knowledge to a stubborn problem that refuses to fit within the mold. Lawyers recognize that it is strange that patients are seen by medical professionals as their disease or condition. Yet it is not uncommon for them to see clients as cases in the revenue stream that feeds the unending demands of one's status or partners, rather than as individuals with problems that require more humane consideration than simply the application of the Band-aid of legal opinion.

The ABA's *Breaking Point* report showed that lawyers' increased levels of mental and physical stress have an impact on service to clients. In another survey of a random sample of 10 percent of the practicing lawyers within Washington State, one-third reported suffering from psychological, behavioral, and physical symptoms indicating the presence of depression or alcohol or cocaine abuse. Similar data have been collected in other jurisdictions (Andrew and others, 1992). More than 70 percent of those surveyed reported observing lack of courtesy and incompetent representation at times. According to the 1991 *State of the Legal Profession* report, nearly one-fourth reported encountering lack of courtesy often, which cannot fail to interfere with effective representation of clients.

OLD-MIND THINKING

As popular author Deborah Tannen (1998) points out, we have in this country a culture of critique that impels us to approach the world and the people in it in an adversarial frame of mind. The effects of this are nowhere more strongly felt than within the legal profession and the legal system. Argument has been, and still is for many, its lifeblood. David Wexler, a leading exponent of therapeutic jurisprudence, points out that "intellectual inquiry in a culture of critique focuses on criticism rather than on integrating ideas from disparate fields" (Wexler, 1999, p. 263). This makes it difficult for us to welcome new ideas and insights, to take what is useful from a situation, and to learn from what is not working and be creative with it.

The spirit of inquiry is essential to collaborative conflict resolution. The culture of critique, the worship of argument, and the glorification of conflict all discourage and denigrate this. Argument and criticism are important and valid intellectual techniques, but they have been much overemphasized and misused as a result of the argument culture in which the legal profession has so long reveled. This facet of the landscape within the legal profession is important for us to know.

NEW-MIND THINKING

Yet the seeds of transformation are at work, within the legal profession as elsewhere in the world. The therapeutic jurisprudence movement seeks to identify and pursue opportunities to integrate the learning from other fields into how law and the legal system serve. For example, rather than using destructive approaches such as longer incarceration for getting convicted addicts to stay with their rehabilitation programs, there is a new willingness to look at what the mental health field has learned about how to increase adherence to treatment. Although recidivism following incarceration is usually common, in the peacemaking circles I wrote about in Chapter Three, the incidence of recidivism has been almost trivial—less than 10 percent (Barry Stuart, interview, Oct. 25, 2000). These changes represent a highly important move toward power sharing, a concept totally unfamiliar to the legal community as a whole but beginning to infiltrate it in part through the ADR community, through therapeutic jurisprudence, and through restorative justice. These are only a few examples of what I believe is likely to become the new look of the law and the legal system.

Daicoff (2000) refers to this type of development as the *comprehensive law movement.* It encompasses preventive law and problem-solving/transformative mediation. It includes therapeutic jurisprudence, restorative justice, holistic law, collaborative law, creative problem solving, and specialized courts. It has the potential to draw any conflict away from the more formalistic rights- and power-based approaches, with their tendency to exacerbate the harm that comes from the underlying causes, so that the parties have readier access to collaborative processes with the potential to heal.

This is a significant concern to clients: whether the lawyer who serves them in a conflict resolution situation is *all there* or only an actor playing a role and whether the tools the lawyer is skilled in using include collaborative processes with that healing potential.

With this background, let us consider some of the ways lawyers package their services.

LAWYERS IN NEGOTIATION

Mediation is a facilitated negotiation, so it is useful to think of negotiation skills when building a mediation team. The genus lawyer has come in roughly two species for the past one hundred years: the transactional lawyer and the advocate.

The transactional lawyer helps structure deals, negotiates and writes contracts, and plans estates. When these lawyers function at the deal-making level, they can develop excellent negotiation skills. However, those who specialize in contract drafting can be as wedded to words as anyone else. As one lawyer put it, "Even three or four words could be the exact focus of later litigation. I'm going to do everything I can to see that my client isn't hurt in that fight, even if the deal suffers." No wonder these lawyers are sometimes called "deal breakers." Their focus is not on the deal but on its representation in written contract form, so that *if* litigation over it ensues, their client will be in a favored position.

The advocate speaks for us in adversarial forums, such as arbitration or the courts. Once litigation begins, however, we usually have an advocate, even if we had a transactional lawyer involved earlier. Advocates can be so steeped in adversarial strategies and behaviors that they find it difficult, if not impossible, to engage in constructive advocacy and effective negotiation. Some recognize this and stay as far away from mediation as they can. Still, lawyers in growing numbers are becoming more creative and compassionate and find themselves right at home in mediation, regardless of the nature of their day-to-day practice. With the increasing spread of facilitative, traditional mediation, even lawyers little transformed from old-mind thinking are challenged to drop their adversarial stance and learn how to disagree without being disagreeable. Lawyers find this form of practice a type of work that draws on their breadth and depth as well as their legal expertise.

Whoever represents us influences how others involved in the dispute or its processing see us. If our lawyer or other negotiator is arrogant or disinterested, boorish or angry, we are viewed in that way. If our lawyer is dignified, intelligent, responsive, and wise, we are presumed to have these qualities too. Adversarial advocates often equate themselves to soldiers and litigation to war. In fact, however, litigation is more like a ritual dance that leads most of the time to a negotiated resolution.

Like tribal dancers, lawyers put on giant masks and costumes and ritually fight each other.

Like tribal dancers, lawyers put on giant masks and costumes and ritually fight each other, using not sticks and magic hoops but acres of trees neatly pressed into paper on which tiny symbols line up in rows. They fight with words, as if only their adversary's death itself would amount to victory. Yet they settle before the final act. Litigation is much more like theater than like war.

The kind of lawyer we use has a lot to do with the quality of our experience in resolving disputes. Soldier-lawyers are often aggressive and may tend to take on themselves authority they should not have. At times, they wage the battle for their own glory or economic gain instead of those of the client. And they invite problems of professional behavior and ethics as well as major problems with perspective. This is a very expensive way to make use of a lawyer.

THE NEW PARADIGM IN LAWYER-CLIENT RELATIONSHIPS

New mind does not condone playing games in this important relationship. There's no room for manipulation, passive-aggressive behavior, or trying to duck our share of responsibility. When the client shoulders a fair share of responsibility, the lawyer can be most effective.

Client Control: An Evolving Concept

A phrase commonly used by lawyers, particularly in the past, is *client control*. Not so long ago, a lawyer who did not have client control was looked down on by other lawyers. When applied to procedural agreements, client control affirmed that the lawyer was properly vested with authority.

The concept of client control has also been used in settlement negotiations. It has been used to mean that when the lawyer speaks, he has authority. The client is not going to come back and want to renegotiate the deal. In fact, sometimes lawyers have agreed to resolve a matter without talking with the client, at times before the client even knew discussions might take place. Often these discussions are very, very brief. And if the client was not a party to these discussions, the lawyer might use verbal threats, a form of force, to win the client's acceptance—for example, "If you can't accept this, I will probably have to withdraw from representing you."

This is not to say that whenever a lawyer feels she must withdraw from the case that there is expressed or implied force. Sometimes a lawyer needs to withdraw because she has lost effectiveness. But whatever lawyers do, they are required to act consistently with the client's interest. Thus, in the context of a settlement negotiation conducted without prior discussion and clear understandings between lawyer and client, it is problematic. And as you might expect, clients have been able to nullify settlement agreements that were reached without their approval.

The idea that the case is the client's and not the lawyer's has not always been accepted, but it is clear that clients are entitled to be consulted about the settlement of their case. And it is they who determine how a case is pursued, how and when negotiated resolution is pursued, and what outcomes are acceptable.

Increasingly, client control is coming to mean that the client is in control. This new relationship requires that the client take more responsibility for what happens in the course of the representation.

Mediation puts clients back into a position of control, participating actively or passively in joint and confidential discussions. In this model, there is plenty of opportunity to assess options, and agreement is reached only if it is acceptable to the clients. As a result of the mediation, we have a better understanding of the range of realistic settlements.

Mediation fits with today's greater recognition of ethical standards concerning the limits of legal representation. The Model Rules of Professional Conduct were adopted by the ABA in 1983 as an ethical standard for lawyer representation suggested for consideration and adoption by the various states. Rule 1.2 states, "A lawyer shall abide by a client's decisions concerning the objectives of representation . . . and shall consult with the client as to the means by which they are to be pursued. A lawyer shall abide by a client's decision whether to settle a matter" (American Bar Association, 2001).

Although these rules are not binding until adopted by the supreme court of the state in which the lawyer practices, they provide a shorthand way of talking about long-established requirements. Rule 1.2 has been adopted, more or less, in approximately forty-five jurisdictions. Mediation satisfies the lawyer's ethical responsibility to inform us sufficiently so that we may make wise decisions. By contrast, when only lawyers participate in the negotiations, settlement possibilities can be presented with what seem to be strings attached.

To decide what kind of outcomes meet our true interests, we need a serious talk with our lawyer. Trying to talk to a soldier about long-term interests is often futile. For such discussions, we need a counselor-at-law, worthy of the name.

Lawyers as Counselors-at-Law

A counselor helps us clarify our objectives, decide what resources to commit to pursuing them, and assess how much delay can be tolerated. A good counselor-at-law will find what our real interests are—beyond our stated goals, which are often very short term—and devise realistic options to serve our best interests. Like a skilled coach, this lawyer helps us regain our balance and effectiveness.

The personal injury plaintiff's lawyer has even greater need to be such a counselor. The client's suffering may be so severe, the disruption of his or her life so traumatic, and the consequences of losing so terrible that decisions about handling the matter and about seeking and evaluating settlement options are major life decisions for the client. Keeping the client well informed in a considerate way and respecting the client's need to make the key decisions are all part of the work of lawyer-counselors.

Business lawyers also need to be counselors. Organizational clients often have political problems. This is as true for labor unions and churches as it is for corporations. As counselor, the lawyer may be called on to help keep the group functional while seeking direction for the handling of legal matters. For example, some clients are reluctant to suggest mediation because they believe the other side would reject their overtures. The lawyer might work to secure an offer to mediate from the other side, so that the clients would be able to consider the option from a fresh viewpoint.

Lawyers as Storytellers

Good negotiators are storytellers. The lawyer as storyteller first listens very carefully to her client. When put together by the storyteller, the story is not likely to accuse others of wrongdoing so much as to raise questions.

Storytelling seeks to incorporate not only the client's view of truth and reasonableness but the other side's as well. If we do not recognize something of ourselves in the story, it cannot persuade us. The fact that we may well be accusatorial at trial does not mean it is appropriate to be that way in day-to-day contacts. It just makes people hard to deal with.

The lawyer as storyteller sees the steps leading up to a trial as a series of opportunities to enlarge acceptance of her client's story by the court, the opposing party, and opposing counsel. Little by little, the story will be refined to include as much of the other side's story as it can, narrowing the areas of disagreement.

At each step of the way in mediation, counsel decides what, if anything, to disclose and how to disclose it. This moment-by-moment decision making is the forte of the lawyer as storyteller, for in storytelling, timing is everything. It is the storyteller who can redirect the energy from oppositional channels into problem-solving channels.[2]

HOW MEDIATION AFFECTS LAWYERS

The legal profession has approached mediation cautiously, finding it inconsistent with their training, experience, and the way things have always been done. But these supports are crumbling with clinical legal education, negotiation, and ADR training in law school and also through mandatory and quasi-mandatory mediation programs as well as market changes. One example of the market changes is how lawyers are paid.

The widespread practice of hourly billing has led lawyers and law firms to focus on hourly billings rather than on results, pitting their interests *against* clients' interests in many cases. Standard case-handling procedures often require sufficient legal work to make this prediction come true, except for firms working primarily on a contingent fee basis, when economy of effort is key.

Hourly billing is coming to be seen as a poor measure of value. Lawyers are recognizing that modern electronic research capabilities, document assembly software, and the pervasiveness of desktop computers enable them to generate work product in far less time than ever before. Clients are finding that they prefer paying for partners' expertise rather than associates' education, and so the whole money-making system of having numerous associates working long hours on client matters is threatened (American Bar Association, 1996). Steven Brill (1993) states that "demand for the product that most big law firms now sell, which is hours rather than solutions—is going to drop by as much as a third" (p. 65). Brill celebrates a Houston law firm for its value-

based billing and staffing policies. The firm's policy is "to make money on our work, not on our hours. Our rates ($300) per hour for a lawyer of 13 years' experience) are high, but . . . our bills are low," observed one partner in the firm." The firm's flexible pricing schedule includes a kicker, or bonus, when results are especially good. This suggests that clients need a clear understanding of the kicker arrangements in advance.

Research shows that alternatives now becoming more common include flat fees, incentive fees, contingent fees, and bonuses (Ricker, 1994). One-third of law firms surveyed for the ABA Section of Litigation by Price Waterhouse and by Altman Weil Pensa between 1993 and 1995 indicated that alternative pricing strategies were critical to their success. So can it be critical to yours.

Whereas law firms in the past looked to the client for the motivation to resolve (LaMothe, 1993), now alternative fee arrangements are pushing at least a significant proportion of law firms toward earlier resolution. Some 80 percent of corporate clients interviewed in 1995 preferred using flat-fee arrangements. Lawyers are beginning to realize that effective and efficient legal services and satisfied clients will produce more business with the potential for higher per unit compensation for lawyers as productivity rises. To the extent this touches more and more types of disputes, fewer disputes will continue to fester unresolved, as they did in the past, until the courthouse steps come clearly into view.

Value—what it costs to resolve the dispute—is a major focus among heavy consumers of legal services, such as insurance companies and corporations (Reed, 1989). *Value-added* is becoming a watchword among lawyer watchers, as the profession moves to alter the decades-old pattern of basing fees on time spent rather than results achieved. A firm in Portland, Oregon—Cosgrave, Vergeer and Kester, LLP—seeking to establish a better basis for a long-term relationship worked out an arrangement for a stepped-down fee with a client, CGU/North Pacific Insurance. It provides for a substantial rate reduction in cases not resolved within the first seven months of representation. "This aligns the interests of the firm with the interests of the client in expeditious resolution," said attorney Eugene H. Buckle, "and our case load from this client has significantly increased" (personal communication, Oct. 18, 2000). Until lawyers change their minds about how disputes may most effectively touched by the legal profession and legal institutions.

Unfortunately, many court reforms spring from the belief that the courts can take better care of litigants than lawyers can. Even court-mandated mediation may give rise to special problems that slow the acceptance of mediation in the legal community. For example, in one jurisdiction, construction cases were routinely referred to a single special master for discovery management and settlement mediation. This gave him a virtual monopoly, and counsel reported that it also materially increased the cost of handling these cases, where settlement was not readily achieved. After the parties had given settlement their best shot, they still had to drag through settlement exercises, often requiring a lot of expert time and expense. Situations such as this have meant that mediation could be seen by everyone as a problem rather than as a solution to problems.

The California Judicial Council, pursuant to recommendations from a task force, has recommended changes in rules and sought changes in legislation to eliminate abuses of ADR references such as this. Moreover, the county involved, San Mateo, has put together an interesting collaboration of the courts, community organizations, members of the bar, and the ADR community—the multioption ADR referral program described on page 48.

INERTIAL DRAG FROM THE CULTURE OF THE LEGAL PROFESSION

Leonard L. Riskin wrote in 1982 about the relationship of lawyers to mediation. He states that the lawyer's philosophical map rests primarily on "two assumptions about matters that lawyers handle: (1) disputants are adversaries—i.e. if one wins, the other must lose, and (2) disputes may be resolved through application, by a third party, of some general rule of law" (pp. 42–43).

Litigation fits this mental map like a glove. The lawyer whose main tool is litigation is like the jeweler who made jewelry with a pipe wrench. "Oh yes," the jeweler said when queried, "It looks awkward, but I use it very, very well."

In the 1980s, these two assumptions, along with the demands of the adversary system and the expectations of many clients,

tended to exclude mediation from most lawyers' repertoires. Today, court-instigated mediation favors the selection of evaluative, advisory lawyer-mediators. As more and more jurisdictions mandate mediation for matters in civil litigation, as law practice experience continues to be made a prerequisite for membership on court panels, as more and more lawyers become mediators, and as more and more lawyers select the mediator and mediation model, there is a tilt toward a model of mediation that is closer to court settlement conferencing than to traditional, facilitative mediation. The former chair of the ABA's ADR Section, Kimberlee Kovach, and Professor Lela Love have observed, "Two factors have driven the mutation of mediation: rapid expansion of court-connected and lawyer-dominated programs and the failure of courts to distinguish among ADR process options" (Kovach and Love, 1998, p. 71). Previously they wrote, "Many practicing mediators have an evaluative orientation. Yet most trainers, teachers and professors don't teach evaluation as a permissible component of mediation. The courts and the legal community are largely responsible for this paradox" (Kovach and Love, 1996, p. 31).

"Lawyers," Riskin (1982) argues, "are trained to put people and events into categories that are legally meaningful, to think in terms of rights and duties established by rules, to focus on acts more than persons. This view requires a strong development of cognitive capabilities, which is often attended by the under-cultivation of emotional faculties. This combination of capacities joins with the practice of either reducing most nonmaterial values to amounts of money or sweeping them under the carpet, to restrict many lawyers' abilities to recognize the value of mediation or to serve as mediators" (p. 45). Both Riskin and Daicoff are quite clear about what the legal profession as a whole brings to collaborative processes. Daicoff further suggests that those who would be lawyers are attracted to the profession because they have personal characteristics that are skewed toward the cognitive and away from anything having to do with feelings. This causes some to downplay the personal realities in favor of the litigation gamesmanship. A newspaper article illustrated how legal advice causes people to overcome their best instincts, with predictable regret.[3] The mother of a bully failed, on the advice of counsel, to ask after the condition of the much younger child whom her child had harmed. The mother described the poignancy of her later chance meeting of that child's father on the suburban train. Consider also this comment from a client after losing his case for a reduction in his support obligation:

> My lawyer told me in deposition, only to answer the questions and not to elaborate. This left a lot of unexplained statements which my former spouse's lawyer used to discredit my claim of vastly reduced income. I lost my good job a year and a half before we separated. We had used up all our savings when my spouse filed for divorce. But when I tried to fill in the gaps in court, the judge told me to be quiet. My lawyer never told my story and I lost. So I kept on paying when I didn't have the money until I was forced into bankruptcy [Rodney Gietz, interview, Oct. 17, 2000].

That kind of rigid litigation-oriented thinking and the traps it causes people to fall into are well known within the profession.

Another example is that it is still common for lawyers to advise their clients not to talk with the other side, when that is the only way there is any short-term hope for the situation to sort itself out. Good lawyers, by contrast, have long coached clients in order to help make the communications safer and more constructive. For old-mind lawyers, it is as if that vain hope for the day in court (which has about a 5 percent chance of happening, even when the case is filed) is as much a trap for them as it is for their clients.

One might think that with all of the changes going on in the profession and in the way disputes are being managed, by clients and by the courts, lawyers would now be thinking differently about mediation and other collaborative processes. It can only be old mind that causes lawyers to continue to treat mediation as an end-game strategy and look to it primarily for evaluative mediators. Nevertheless, the disincentives for change built in to the lawyer-client relationship during most of the twentieth century are weakening. There is also a strong cross-current to this: the lawyer's innate desire to be helpful, which is now finding more ways of expressing itself through the holistic lawyering movement (discussed in Chapter Seven), facilitative mediation, the emergence of therapeutic jurisprudence, and the comprehensive law movement.

So when you are looking for a lawyer, consider evaluating whether new mind is at work or old mind. The lawyers of new

mind—and some of them have been practicing law for decades—
are a different breed. They are excited about the new frontiers in
the law: about the concept of law as a healing profession, how institutions can be bent to be more responsive to peoples' needs, and
new opportunities to enhance their skills and more effectively use
whatever resources are available to help clients.

The McGill Center for Creative Problem Solving at California
Western School of Law is an international center for this perspective, which also is fully represented in the law school undergraduate
curriculum, according to Executive Director James Cooper. Cooper
reports that since the Center was founded in 1997, hundreds of
lawyers, prosecutors, judges, law enforcement officers, and justice
department officials in fifteen Latin-American countries—in addition to many more from the United States—have been through the
Center's training program. In the Center's model, the lawyer is
seen as fighter, designer of preventive strategies, and creative problem solver (James Cooper, interview, Jan. 24, 2001).

The International Alliance of Holistic Lawyers (IAHL), founded
in 1991, now has over 900 members from twenty countries, and it
is the only membership organization in the new movement to make
law a healing profession. Most of the other organizations, such as
the Therapeutic Jurisprudence Network, the Collaborative Law
Institute, the Preventive Law Movement, and the Restorative Justice
Movement, are academically based and do not have membership
organizations, although their influence touches many.

Though those who are pioneering a more humane approach
to law are few in number, their influence is increasing and will continue to do so, given the larger societal trends from which they
grow. Margaret Mead once said, "Never doubt that a small group
of committed people can change the world. It's the only thing that
ever has."

THE IMPACT OF LAWYERS ON MEDIATION

All counsel pertaining to a particular dispute are usually involved
in mediation if one counsel is. This is because lawyers are under
ethical constraints about talking directly to other parties who have
lawyers. These can be waived by the nonattending lawyer but must
otherwise be respected. Blanket waivers are made under certain

circumstances, such as when a party's negotiator is a lawyer. In many insurance mediations, the claims professional does not have counsel present, although the plaintiff or claimant usually does. Also, where one counsel is especially trusted by opposing counsel, her participation will not necessarily draw in all the others. One of the things that can happen in mediation is that the most knowledgeable lawyer can become literally the expert for the situation— trusted by all parties and counsel. Sometimes this trust is dispersed among the lawyers present, as each one contributes his or her special knowledge or expertise. Such is the magic of mediation.

Even counsel who are not present can inform client and mediator about desirable formulations for any settlement agreement. Not infrequently, counsel who have been on the sidelines during a mediation will step forward at the conclusion to write up the agreement until the formal documents are prepared.

Once the dispute reaches the problem-solving stage, counsel serve by seeing that reasonable agreements are reached and that they are secure, safe from disruption caused by subsequent counsel review or some facet that was overlooked. Here is where the legal mind and training are of greatest service.

Generally lawyers are present during the mediation of matters in litigation. If they are not working effectively together, part of the mediator's work is to make that relationship more functional. Lawyers who are committed to the process are an excellent resource. When they do not participate, the culture of argument or critique may take over, and they may undermine what the parties do in mediation. By overprotection bred from a lack of understanding of the trade-offs, they spare us a moment's headache so we can enjoy a long-term disability.

A new kind of lawyer, lawyers for the negotiation, is emerging. These lawyers are committed to wholeness within themselves and for the client. As you will see in Chapter Seven, holistic lawyering is becoming a reality, and with its emergence comes a new set of lawyer and negotiator skills.

There is a whole skill set that may come into play that most traditional advocacy would not recognize. Constructive advocacy is an art form. It involves offering not only ideas and positions but the thinking and assumptions underlying them, inviting others to share their thinking and examine their assumptions. Ideally, it combines constructive advocacy with inquiry—inviting others to come and reason together. Traditional advocacy seeks to persuade others to one's own point of view. Constructive advocacy means looking into what you do not yet know and to how others see things and understand them. It means having a sense of curiosity and interest even in the face of your own opinions or assumptions. There is a certain restraint in constructive advocacy, as if you were suspending judgment, position, and opinion.

Agreements reached when such constructive approaches are used are not only secure. They embody and implement trust in a way old-mind win-lose advocacy would not recognize and might not even credit. And they reflect mutuality.

Refusing to mediate until most pretrial legal work is done robs clients of many of the benefits of mediation. This makes no sense from the client's point of view, except when there is so little information available that it is impossible even to lay the groundwork for exploring settlement options.

Lawyers nevertheless have persisted in this old kind of thinking in part because clients were not paying attention. No more. The future belongs to those who will solve problems and help clients become free to creatively move on with their business and their lives.

Chapter Seven

Selecting and Using a Lawyer for Your Mediation

The devil is an angel, too.
MIGUEL DE UNAMUNO, *TWO MOTHERS*

A lawyer acquaintance with some twenty-five years of experience still shakes his head, remembering that he used to think his job was to wield the tools of the legal system to win outcomes that would satisfy clients. He changed his mind the day he saw that legal remedies were too limited and the system was too costly and slow to make this kind of outcome possible. "I'm a problem-solver," he said. "At the beginning, I check my gut feeling for whether or not the matter will ultimately be negotiated. If the overwhelming odds are that it will settle, I make my strategic decisions from then on in that context."

Some lawyers are not prepared to wean themselves away from heavy reliance on the legal system. For some, the consideration is economic. Another lawyer asked this man, "How has this affected your practice?" "I'm busier than ever, and I'm getting better results for my clients with a lot less effort," he replied.

A growing number of lawyers offer outstanding competency in the fine art of moving disputes from impasse to resolution, through the deft use of litigation, mediation, and other tools. The trick is to find them. Here are some suggestions on how to do that.

KNOW WHAT TO LOOK FOR

The difficulty in selecting a lawyer is knowing what to look for and being clear about what you and the lawyer each is responsible for. Many clients look for a father figure and then proceed to hand the lawyer the power to make decisions that only they should make in the exercise of their own good judgment. This is unwise and unfair. It is you who must be satisfied. It is not enough for the lawyer to tell you that you should be satisfied. If your expectations are unreasonable, the lawyer's job is to bring this to your attention early and often, giving you the opportunity to make the best use of his or her services.

At times in the initial interview, you may get an exaggerated sense of the value of your case. Perhaps the lawyer has emphasized the positive side to show sympathy or to get your business, or perhaps you have not been completely candid in what you have disclosed. When problems with the case become evident, even good lawyers who did not encourage unrealistic expectations may be slow to explain to clients that their expectations are too high. There is a saying, "You can't cheat an honest person." This reflects a truth: our gullibility springs from a desire to believe things we know inside are not true, that are too good to be true. However it happens, for many cases the moment of truth is the courthouse steps. It is still true that delay in the trial date spells delay in securing a settlement.

In states where a range of mediation models is familiar to a number of lawyers, such as Washington and California, more and more the plaintiffs' lawyers are seeking to have cases mediated. An article in the *Recorder*, a San Francisco newspaper for the legal community, carried this headline in February 1994: "ADR Forum of Choice for Harassment Claims." This has been a recurring theme in reports since then. The trend for using mediation in harassment and all other types of discrimination claims has continued upward. From the point of view of a lawyer working on a contingent fee basis, the economics are compelling. Where a satisfactory result is readily achieved, some plaintiffs' lawyers will voluntarily reduce their fees below the agreed contingent fee percentage because their time was so productive.

Responsible lawyers give a balanced evaluation at the beginning, including the risks. They will not play to the prospective client's sometimes frayed emotions. They outline the steps needed to move from where things are to final resolution and the timetable for these steps. They are largely expected to be familiar with mediation and to be able to advise a client on options for its use, as well as concerning other dispute resolution processes, such as neutral evaluation. A good lawyer will welcome questions, be willing to discuss the possibilities of mediating early, and will not mind if you take notes during the interview. Allow the lawyer to review the notes at the conclusion to ensure they are accurate, and then leave a copy. Some lawyers will also give you copies of their notes, particularly if they are fairly complete.

A lawyer-client relationship isn't like a marriage, where in the old view the two become one. It's more like a joint venture.

A lawyer-client relationship isn't like a marriage, where in the old view the two become one. It's more like a joint venture. The lawyer's interest is close to the client's but not identical. It is good to be alert to potential conflicts without letting them become a preoccupation.

CHECK REPUTATION

Reputation is a good place to start in evaluating a lawyer. Generally you can check a lawyer's reputation with other lawyers. If you do not know a lawyer well enough to do this, get a friend who does to inquire for you. You may want to use some of the questions set out in this chapter to be sure you get the information you want.

If you have a lawyer in mind but are not certain of his or her skill in the mediation arena, talk with a mediator or client the lawyer has experienced mediation with. The public often has a superficial view of what a lawyer is, does, and should be. But because mediation is more accessible than the legal system to the layperson, a client who has been through mediation with a lawyer may have some useful insights. Skill in mediation is quite different from skill in litigation.

Success in mediation depends in large part on a party's negotiation skills. The mediator usually cannot negotiate for one party without losing the trust of the other party. The mediator will protect the integrity of the process and ensure that to the extent possible, each side understands the deal it is making or the options it is rejecting. This is why it is important, when lawyers are needed, to have one who is sophisticated in the use of mediation and equipped with good negotiation skills.

INTERVIEW PROSPECTIVE LAWYERS

In interviewing prospective lawyers, do not be put off if a lawyer whose strength is in negotiating—that is, a lawyer for the negotiation, as we discussed at the end of Chapter Six—may recommend associating trial counsel even before proceeding with mediation. The trial lawyer's reputation, even when she does not participate in the mediation, is a useful bargaining chip. Lawyers with a good trial record will inspire more favorable settlements at the negotiating table. The negotiation lawyer may conduct the mediation. Negotiation is rarely the forte of the trial lawyer.

It is good practice to interview two or three prospects. Here are some questions to ask yourself about a potential lawyer and then some questions to ask prospective lawyers:

• *When you've told your story, do you sense the lawyer's concern for you as a person?* A compassionate lawyer can often best convey your concerns to the other side. I am speaking here of a person who transcends the hubbub, not one who merely hates loud noises. Compassion requires comfort with oneself. In a lawyer, as with all other professionals, it must merge with a high level of competence. In any representation, you will be well advised to keep the focus on gaining satisfaction of reasonable goals, recognizing that overzealousness is no asset. Sometimes lawyers view clients as merely a vehicle carrying the problem to which they will address themselves, never seeing them or anyone else involved in the matter as first and foremost human beings. This fragmented approach to you and your situation does not bode well for quality representation, particularly if early and satisfactory resolution is your goal.

• *How well does this lawyer listen?* One of the handicaps of being the information resource that lawyers are is that what you know about the subject can clutter the mind and reduce attention. Some lawyers listen simply to determine what cubbyhole your situation fits into. Increasingly, though, they are learning to listen more deeply and avoid jumping to judgment too quickly, in order to develop more appropriate, creative, and responsive approaches. If the lawyer really listens, this is a good sign.

• *Does the lawyer seem resourceful?* Does she offer several different approaches and strategies to secure a prompt, negotiated resolution? If so, she will be able to retrieve the situation when things get polarized, as they frequently do. Litigation often bogs down. The lawyer who can think in extrajudicial terms is going to be more useful than one who thinks primarily about litigation activity.

• *What does the lawyer have to say about other matters like yours?* Listen for personal experience and a broad grasp of what is happening in the field as a whole as well as in cases like yours. Listen for an indication that the lawyer understands the realities of effort: that 20 percent of the effort produces 80 percent of the results. The art is in knowing what constitutes the 20 percent.

• *What is this lawyer enthusiastic about?* Trial-focused lawyers often lose interest when settlement becomes a real likelihood. Let the lawyer tell you some stories. If the lawyer enjoys playing the whole game, including developing and pursuing deft tactics to maneuver the matter to prompt resolution, that's a good sign.

• *How does the lawyer define success?* Do his successes include negotiated resolutions or the use of mediation? Does the lawyer understand how to use mediation or simply try to impress on you when not to mediate? Question the experience on which such conclusions are based. See if you can get a sense for when this lawyer thinks mediation is most effective in terms of what kind of work needs to precede the mediation.

The questions in Table 7.1 will help you make a determination about whether this is the right lawyer for you. Finally, ask if this lawyer personally will be doing the work on your case. If not, bring the lawyer who will do your work into the interview. The often younger, perhaps less personable lawyer who did not attract your initial interest may indeed be a good choice given adequate relevant experience. It is up to you to decide.

Table 7.1. Questions for Prospective Counsel.

Questions	Reasoning Behind the Questions
Tell me a little about your background.	Let the lawyer understand you are doing an interview.
Tell me about a couple of matters like mine that you have handled.	Check on experience. Be specific about results and methods.
How long did each one take?	This puts your situation in context.
What were the fees and costs on each of these matters?	This shows you are interested in cost considerations.
Tell me about your experience using mediation.	A lawyer who always finds others unwilling has little interest.
Have you initiated any mediations?	Is there any real commitment here?
When can I expect my situation to resolve?	Check for settlement as well as for trial.
What will it cost?	Write the reply down, and date it. Ask this question again every three months or so.
What are the key factors in determining when and whether we can settle?	Look for items within your control. It isn't always someone else's call.
What information do we need to be able to evaluate options for resolution?	Distinguish what is needed to try the case from what is needed to settle it.
What does the other side need in order to evaluate settlement options?	This tests collaborative thinking and a problem-solving mind.

AVAIL YOURSELF OF RESOURCES

Professional legal organizations have been little leavened as yet by the new paradigm that rejects the objectifying of self (into an archetypal role) and others (into either problems to be solved or instrumentalities for accomplishing one's own purposes). Nevertheless, one organization, the International Alliance of Holistic Lawyers, which was organized in the mid-1990s, provides a directory and resource location assistance. Its intent is to:

Acknowledge the need for a humane legal process with the
  highest level of satisfaction for all participants;

Honor and respect the dignity and integrity of each individual;

Promote peaceful advocacy and holistic legal principles;

Value responsibility, connection and inclusion;

Encourage compassion, reconciliation, forgiveness, and healing;

Practice Deep Listening, understand and recognize the importance of voice;

Contribute to peace building at all levels of society;

Recognize the opportunity in conflict;

Draw upon ancient intuitive wisdom of diverse cultures and
  traditions; and

Enjoy the practice of law

[International Alliance of Holistic Lawyers, 2000].

This is right in stride with an extraordinary movement within
the legal community that includes therapeutic jurisprudence,
restorative justice, and victim-offender mediation, which is based
on the Hippocratic admonition to first do no harm. This movement recognizes that "legal procedures . . . constitute social forces
that whether intended or not often produce therapeutic or
antitherapeutic consequences." By recognizing the impacts of what
judges do, jurists, lawyers, and scholars are beginning to work to
tailor the system to allow humanization of the individual's experience with the legal system and refocus on the importance of fairness and listening. Therapeutic jurisprudence does not trump
other considerations. Rather, it involves "the use of social science
to study the extent to which a legal rule or practice promotes the
psychological and physical well-being of the people it affects"
(Slobogin, 1995, p. 196). On the criminal side, in drug cases, for
example, the judge is no longer a detached arbiter of an offender's
fate. She is the head of a team focused on that individual's sobri-
ety and accountability. Sanctions are viewed not as punishment but
as tools for achieving compliance in order to lead to treatment and
recovery. The judge may be a stern parent or a cheerleader who
both attends to lapses and encourages and rewards compliance.

This change is important for consumers of legal and mediation
services to understand, because it points the way to a thorough
overhaul of how business is done in the formal management of

conflict. It reflects a profound change in thinking about what lawyers do and what courts do. Mediation attached to a court dedicated to therapeutic jurisprudence has a far greater chance of being the transformative tool it really is rather than a glorified street corner bargain over "this release" for "that money." Quality is the essence in this new paradigm.

There is evidence that lawyers with these kinds of values have a rising clientele. In *Transforming Practices—Finding Joy and Satisfaction in the Practice of Law,* American Bar Association Journal writer Steven Keeva relates many stories of lawyers who have broken down the isolation engendered by trying to live life without feelings and without an inner life. He tells of a lawyer whose holistic approach to the practice of law was written up in her metropolitan daily newspaper, after which she was besieged by calls from individuals wanting her to talk with *their* lawyers.

Keeva reports on a study done by sociologist and urban planner Paul H. Ray that identified a growing subculture in America that he calls the "cultural creatives." Estimating this group at 44 million people, or 23.6 percent of the population, he reports that they are characterized by high levels of education, a median income of $47,500, and a median age of forty-two (Ray, 1996). "They are seriously concerned with psychology, spiritual life, self-actualization and self-expression," writes Keeva (1999), and their values lead them to seek appropriate legal representation.

You do not need to park your values at the door when seeking competent legal representation.

You may very well be one of these people—people who by their choices are changing the way things are done in the world. And it is important to know that you do not need to park your values at the door when seeking competent legal representation.

The principal dispute resolution professional organization, the Society for Professionals in Dispute Resolution[1]—now known as the Association for Conflict Resolution (ACR)—has had a spirituality track for its annual conferences since 1995. Spirituality is used to designate material with an inner focus rather than an outer one. So much of what lawyers and other dispute resolvers feed on is substantive material—as if, Riskin points out, what the professional brings to the work from within is of no consequence. That is old-paradigm thinking. There is no reason to settle for less than the whole person of the lawyer you engage.

DO YOU REALLY NEED A LAWYER?

There can be risks to negotiating without counsel. Among them is the risk that stems from your own lack of experience in the subject area. You may lack experience as a negotiator. Also, you may be emotionally involved and give up too much, thinking it necessary to reach agreement. You may be blind to the weaknesses of your position or the strength of the other side's position, leading you to take unrealistic positions because you are too personally involved. There are times, particularly in relationship negotiations such as with partnerships or marriages, when one party is incapable of negotiating. In marital mediation, it is often (but not always) the woman. It may be the man—perhaps a former combat soldier struggling to live a normal life. Or perhaps one of the parties simply withdraws, feeling unable to fight without inflicting unacceptable wounds or perceiving that fighting is contrary to deeply held values. Mediation without adequate representation is not an option in such situations.

To some extent, these risks can be addressed through the assistance of those who are not (and never have been) lawyers—for example, labor negotiators; independent claims adjusters, who regularly negotiate claims disputes; and social workers, who often advocate for those less able to speak for themselves in settings such as special education conflicts and problems with social service agencies. In construction conflicts, sometimes experts initially brought in to fight one another become effective champions of conflict resolution. Accountants are licensed to represent people before the Internal Revenue Service and before state taxing agencies, as well under exceptions to laws governing the unauthorized practice of law. To date, the organized bar has successfully resisted most such incursions on its turf, but many feel that it is just a matter of time until specialized arenas carve out more and more exceptions to this general prohibition. The loss within the bar itself of a strong sense of professionalism in what it means to be a lawyer undercuts the primary rationale for giving lawyers exclusive rights to representation.

In a negotiation, there is plenty of opportunity to make mistakes. If you are an experienced and successful negotiator, you may be able to assume the risk. But if you are not or if you recognize that your stake in the situation imperils your flexibility and ability to respond rather than react, find someone to take this role. Negotiating artfully is a rising star in the firmament of conflict management skills. If you are in a field where lawyers are not always the negotiators, consider using a nonlawyer negotiator, perhaps an accountant or financial planner or a consultant in some specialized field who has particularly outstanding negotiation skills. You may still find that you need legal advice going in, so that you know you are standing on solid ground when it comes to your assessment of the alternatives.

OTHER CONSIDERATIONS IN ENGAGING A LAWYER

Still, the involvement of a good lawyer is a sound investment. The best value in legal services is advice. Even if you do not bring your lawyer to your mediation, you and the lawyer should discuss the situation and the possibilities beforehand. And during the mediation, you should be able to reach your lawyer by telephone. Your lawyer's involvement can be as little as initial and follow-up advice, it can be participation in working out a resolution through mediation or direct negotiation, or it can be more than that.

The more adversarial the process is, the less efficient is the lawyer's time. Even with court appearances by telephone conference call, there is often a lot of wasted effort in ordinary litigation. One hour rather than two days of deposition of a key witness may provide all the information you'll ever need to inform your settlement evaluation.

Cost-benefit ratios are important in the decision whether to engage a lawyer. This is especially true when lawyers become involved in adversarial processes. More than a few lawsuits cannot be won (it costs too much to win them), so you end up losing more than you ever could have won. Realistic cost assessment includes your own and others' time and the resources of the organization that are tied up by litigation and negotiation activities. Most people prefer to spend their time, energy, and resources running their businesses and living their lives rather than litigating, a poor way to do either one.

Sometimes a particular lawyer rises above mere advocacy or brings special expertise to the discussion, which all sides welcome. Such a lawyer may transcend the custom that brings all lawyers in if one lawyer is present and can help get your story out without becoming personally invested in the rhetoric.

On the other hand, there are times when party negotiation makes sense. If one or more counsel have been the source of friction, the other counsel may encourage his client to talk directly to the other side, taking himself out of the picture in order to take the opposing counsel out as well. Each situation must be evaluated on its own merits.

LAWYERS' SPECIAL CONTRIBUTIONS

Lawyers can do many things to make the mediation process productive. Lawyers can provide a level playing field for the parties in a variety of ways:

- *They can establish a range of outcomes at trial.* This is one of the most constructive uses of a lawyer's expertise and brings the matter down to the possibilities in a hurry. It lets us know what will happen if we don't settle, and especially the worst case. A lawyer who overestimates a case early in the representation may find it difficult to get the client to buy into a less optimistic outcome when problems emerge. Mediation addresses this dilemma.

The risks of going to court are always significant. There are no guarantees. In order to make a realistic decision to go forward, we need to accept the real possibility of total defeat. This does a lot to reduce surprises. Although lawyers have an ethical duty to consider alternatives to litigation,[2] the decision to fight or not to fight is always the client's, not the lawyer's. And it is the client who must take responsibility for the decision.

Some clients try to waffle on this decision so as to be able to hold the lawyer responsible if it does not work out. That is not the way to get a good decision, and we end up mostly hurting ourselves. Lawyers in such a bind can become pretty tough on their clients, forcing them to settle for what is available at the last minute. Clients who can face losing may be less risk averse than counsel, who may want to settle because they do not want to risk losing at trial the money they have advanced on the case. For other clients, some kind of recovery is crucial. For them, statistics are meaningless. If their case is unsuccessful, it doesn't matter that they had a 99 percent chance of succeeding. Mediation tends to clarify the client's commitment to settlement or trial, once and for all.

• *Lawyers can work out their own differences.* Lawyer animosity in litigated disputes can be high, and it is always expensive. Civil litigation is often frustrating. We may hear about it when our lawyer complains about how the other lawyer is causing all the difficulties and delays. In such situations, focus on ways of reducing the antagonism. One lawyer I know went over to an opposing counsel's office one day. After a quiet talk, the opposing lawyer became much less obstructive. It is highly constructive to take an interest in eliminating unnecessary frictions.

• *They can work with the mediator.* Lawyers and mediators who work together can form an effective team to encourage clients to end their fighting, control difficult personalities and aggressive or violent behavior, and start to get on with their lives. In the heat of battle, it is not always obvious that one's self-interest includes reaching agreements through collaborative negotiation and compromise. Nothing is more disruptive than the loser who needs to retaliate, robbing the victor of the benefits of victory. Studies have found that mediated agreements requiring monetary payment are roughly twice as likely to be complied with as when the obligation was imposed by order or judgment. (See Chapter Sixteen.) A way of improving your chances of achieving satisfaction is to see that everyone can claim success, even if it is intangible success. The need to retaliate depends on perceived injustice.

• *They can remove you one step from the negotiation.* Particularly in complex and highly charged situations, having a lawyer or another skilled negotiator negotiate for you is a way of ensuring that there is private caucus time between offer and demand and the response to these. There are strategic advantages in negotiating with this approach.

• *They can reduce right-wrong thinking habits.* Insisting that one side must win and the other side must lose is part of right-wrong thinking. It also creates a very large hurdle to getting what we want. It is a war metaphor, not a peace metaphor. In order to keep the

peace, each side must have something worth protecting, even if it is solely one's self-esteem.

In one wrongful-termination mediation, it turned out that the plaintiff had no case because a witness was mistaken. The case was set for trial, and the defense lawyer pointed out to his client that it would be costly for the defendant to seek dismissal formally without the plaintiff's cooperation. As part of the settlement here, the defendant paid $200 to help defray the plaintiff's costs. This token settlement led to a quick, final, and binding resolution. It involved a simple acknowledgment that the employee had acted with integrity, not maliciously, and so allowed not only the case to be dismissed but the sense of having been seen as someone unworthy laid to rest.

USE YOUR LAWYER EFFECTIVELY

The relationship between client and lawyer or other negotiator requires attention. The best return on your investment comes from periodic telephone calls or letters to check on any developments, get advice, and discuss strategy. The poorest return on the money spent on lawyers is for litigation activity.

Nevertheless, avoid frequent lengthy conversations and long letters, which are often evidence of an unhealthy infatuation with the situation. If you find yourself obsessing about the situation, let a therapist help you with that. Then partner with the lawyer to get your legal work done. If you find yourself avoiding calling your lawyer and letting things drift, you may be in denial about some aspect of the situation. In this case, consider getting a second opinion about the quality of your representation and perhaps the reasonableness of your expectations.

From time to time, review the situation to check your comfort level with the lawyer. There is some duplication of effort in changing lawyers, but if the relationship is not working, the sooner you get out of it, the better off you will be. Be open, however, to the possibility that it is your own unrealistic expectations that are causing the disappointment with the lawyer.

Lawyers have much more to offer the field of conflict resolution than is apparent from their work in litigation. More and more lawyers are developing skills in collaborative and holistic lawyering. Watch for this trend to grow, replacing the industrial model—the gun for hire mentality—that was so common in the latter half of the twentieth century. In these days of the Internet, you may find such a lawyer through a quick search of the Web or by contacting one of the associations of such lawyers, for example, the International Alliance of Holistic Lawyers (IAHL). Most professions seem to be under pressure to legitimize their members' use of nonstandard skills and aptitudes, such as intuition, sight, and healing capacities through an open heart. The legal community is likewise touched by these broader trends. So keeping an open mind may secure for you a far richer resource in your lawyer than you ever imagined. Naturally, even lawyers with such unusual gifts need to be evaluated, and clients need to be aware of how able they are to evaluate information from such sources. The presence of unusual gifts in an adviser does not signal that you should lay down your own wit, wisdom, and common sense. As with all advice from whatever source, consult your own interior, checking for resonance or the lack of it with the individual and any advice given to you.

Part Three

Putting Principles to Work

My cat Tink used to climb an eight-foot ladder from time to time looking for mice in my storeroom. One day the ladder had been pulled away and was leaning against a chest. The cat climbed up with great difficulty, as the ladder was nearly vertical. She pawed the air in disbelief, looking for the missing shelf, and then swung down head over heels, step by step, as cats do.

Sometimes when we think we are doing our best to resolve a matter, we too are bound by habit, pawing the air and looking for resolution where it cannot be found.

Chapter Eight

Evaluating Mediation

And we, light half-believers of our casual creeds,
Who never deeply felt, nor clearly willed . . .
Who hesitate and falter life away,
And lose tomorrow the ground won today.
MATTHEW ARNOLD

The decision to mediate is a low-risk one. It requires a small amount of time and effort, and costs are modest. Yet you will likely learn something important. The decision to mediate is also simple. The question should be, "Why not mediate?" rather than, "Why mediate?" The standard for decision may be a function of what it will cost to continue to pursue litigation for the next six months or more if you do not mediate. This approach aligns the burden of the argument with the probabilities of success. In this chapter, we look at some of the factors in evaluating the use of mediation.

Mediation is a personal way of handling lawsuits and other disputes. It affords more choices about ways in which a matter may be resolved. It provides a way of addressing the distortions in perception that accompany conflict: the creation of the "bad guy" image of an opponent that impedes progress toward resolution. It curtails the tendency of the mind to manufacture scurrilous motives to "explain" every move.

"Where else but in mediation do you have a chance to speak persuasively to another lawyer's client?"

Mediator Michael Lewis asks, "Where else but in mediation do you have a chance to speak persuasively to another lawyer's client?" (1995, p. 7). And where else but in mediation do you have significant support in handling the human side of the situation? The intimacy of mediation allows the mediator to monitor and support a party's ability to participate effectively.

A Cup of Coffee

In a medical malpractice mediation, the oncologist and the hospital were sued for blinding the plaintiff, a woman in her late fifties. The doctor acknowledged responsibility; the hospital expected to contribute only a token amount of the settlement. As the day wore on, it became apparent that progress depended on promptly obtaining a fair and reasonable demand from the plaintiff. But the plaintiff had spent much of the day alone in the library of the law firm hosting the mediation. She had a headache, was feeling stressed and miserable, and gave her lawyers no firm guidance, deciding first one way and then another.

With everyone's consent, the mediator took the plaintiff out for coffee. The break took about an hour. They walked down the street to a good coffeehouse, discussed what it meant to be blind, chatted about children and grandchildren, and enjoyed the fresh air. The mediator provided an attentive audience—recognizing the enormous distance that this woman had traveled and still needed to travel to let go of this last connection to the cause of her blindness. When they returned, the plaintiff was ready to resolve the problem and could talk with her lawyers in a meaningful and effective way. Shortly after, the plaintiff made a demand, which both defendants thought was fairly reasonable, and the case settled that evening. The plaintiff wept silently as the doctor tendered his heartfelt and profound regrets.

THE LESSON

It is this personal quality that allows mediation to open doorways to larger transformational potential. The mere settling of a malpractice claim does not even begin to lay to rest the complex and often poisonous reaction to being hurt by one who purports to care for you. Reconciliation is healing to everyone it touches.

It is helpful in developing an effective strategy to tackle an impasse to apply the questions in Table 8.1, both to your own perspective and that of each other person involved. In this way, you

Table 8.1. Questions to Address in an Impasse.

Questions for the Other Side	Questions for Yourself
How does the other side see the conflict?	How do *you* see the conflict?
What assumptions is that view based on?	What assumptions is that view based on?
Who are the decision makers?	Who makes your side's decisions?
What are the decision makers' interests?	What are your decision makers' interests?
What other interests might be brought to bear to influence their perspective?	What values other than those being advanced might be neglected in the existing strategy?
What might change their perspective?	What would it take for your perspective or your decision makers' perspective to change?
What would promote healing of the actual or perceived injuries?	What would promote healing of the actual or perceived injuries?

begin to recognize areas of common interest to build upon to secure cost-effective negotiated resolution.

As you seek to understand the situation at these subtle levels, you begin to free your perspective of those assumptions that so often turn out to be wrong, particularly about the other's presumed intransigence and evil motivation. Any judgment of another is felt by that other person, even if not at a conscious level. This reality—the judgment and its consequences—colors everything that happens between you and the other party. As you let go of judgment, you develop a new style of advocacy: you expose your own thinking and the assumptions behind your views. This invites others to do the same. Communications automatically improve as a result of your lack of judgment as well as your increased attentiveness and the sense of interest and curiosity you convey. Gradually there is an erosion of the other person's sense of the judgment and resistance you were perceived as carrying. There is a respectfulness conveyed through the mere act of truly listening—listening to understand.

A NEW APPROACH TO CONFLICT

Mediation, particularly reflective mediation, promotes under-standing difficult to achieve in unaided discussions. It helps you define and implement a strategy to head off far-ranging formal, legal investigation, the discovery that most of the time will prove unnecessary.

In early mediation, you have an opportunity to communicate that what you are interested in is a fair and just result based on the realities of the situation. Some lawyers effectively disarm the oppos-ing counsel by saying (and meaning), "If my client doesn't have a case, I want to know it now, and we'll go away. There's no point in putting us all through a lot of work if it's going to be in vain." This can do away with a lot of game playing in counsel communications.

Direct communications such as these shake the foundations of the stylized form of advocacy where posturing and fencing, smoke and mirrors, have been developed to an art form. By the values lawyers were taught, these are part of the tool kit. Without effec-tive communication, negotiation is ignored until the case staggers and falls of its own weight into some kind of settlement, close to the trial date.

The truth is that the dispute is at one level a problem to be solved. At another level, there is a higher order of wisdom in the existence of the dispute and the opportunities each is offered to hold on or let go. At still another level is a higher order of con-nectedness, in which what we think and what we do influences the present and future of the whole human species. It is never a war to be won. By approaching the problem in a spirit of inquiry and curiosity through a collaborative process such as mediation, we open the doors to substantial additional value that can be created:

- Better understanding and the will to use it to address root causes, where the problem is of a repetitive nature
- The beginning of a recognition and correction of constricted and nonproductive thinking when problems of this kind arise
- Release of past guilt, blame, and pain, recognizing our contri-bution to keeping it alive
- Release of anger, and even rage, that has infected relation-ships during the pendency of the dispute

- Softening of encrusted beliefs and judgments and recognition of assumptions that are long overdue for retirement
- Improvement of conflict management skills of ourselves and those around us who are touched by the changes in us
- Improvement of problem-solving skills and abilities
- A slight widening of the path to a culture based on mutual respect

The will to accept the reality of these possibilities is a first step in dissolving the impasse. Most of the time, a matter can be settled on reasonable terms at almost any point along the road. By thinking adversarially, we miss myriad opportunities to reach a negotiated resolution. We also miss all of the gold—the transformative potential—that the conflict has generated.

REMOVING SEEMINGLY IMPERVIOUS BARRIERS

Sometimes in litigation and far more often in mediation, a kind of camaraderie develops. This can provide an opportunity to explore possible agreement by counsel for a joint discussion with, for example, a key physician in a personal injury case. When the plaintiff's injuries refuse to stabilize, agreement on the extent of injury and medical needs becomes nearly impossible, as the plaintiff takes the pessimistic view and the defendant the optimistic outlook. Meanwhile, there is a negative effect on healing sustained by having the matter remain unresolved. A plaintiff, fearing to damage his case, postpones taking steps to train for and get started on a new life. In situations where injuries have not yet healed and may never completely, the best estimate of the physician, tested in the intimacy of a private conference with both counsel, may come to be accepted by both sides, making such difficult cases easier to settle.

MEDIATION FOR SHOWCASING IMPORTANT EVIDENCE

Using mediation to enhance the impact of significant evidence and convey that impact to the parties that need it is far more productive than planning the big bomb for that unlikely day in court.

The Silver Bullet

The executives and counsel for a manufacturing company reluctantly agreed to mediate when the mediator informed them of the plaintiff's invitation. They knew the case should resolve, but they were not going to pay any significant amount on what they saw as a false claim. The day of the mediation, the plaintiff, alleging sexual harassment leading to constructive discharge and a nervous breakdown, arrived with her husband and two lawyers.

The case manager came into the mediator's office and said, "The plaintiff is just coming into the building."

"How do you know?"

"There's only one person out there smoking, drinking coffee, and shaking like a leaf."

The mediator went out to greet the plaintiff, her husband, and her lawyers as they emerged from the elevator. She took the plaintiff's hand in both of hers and asked, "How do you feel?"

The answer was obvious, but having the mediator visibly aware of her situation began to build rapport. As the mediator left to greet the other parties, their lawyers, and the claims professional, the plaintiff handed her the remains of the cup of coffee and agreed to begin drinking water. They agreed she would use a signal if she needed a break and to try some relaxation techniques if she found herself feeling panicky during the mediation.

The company had been defending this case for some three years, believing fervently that the plaintiff was lying. The plaintiff's counsel finally got a silver bullet: the testimony of a psychologist now living two thousand miles away who had happened to be in the local bar and observed the foreman making advances on the plaintiff in a highly sexual manner. The lawyers knew that this testimony could dramatically change the other side's view of the case. Nevertheless, they sat on this information for months, believing that its impact would be wasted unless saved for trial. They sought mediation after successfully resolving another case in mediation.

At the mediation, the plaintiff's counsel held back the silver bullet in the joint session. In the second caucus, they shared it with the mediator. Little by little, they authorized the mediator to share it in the defense caucus, which in fact maximized its impact as the afternoon progressed. It was not easy for the defense, its insurance carrier, and counsel to change a view they had held so firmly and so long. But they found this new evidence compelling.

Using the caucusing process to present the evidence gave the defense team time before they had to respond. They also had an opportunity to evaluate the evidence with their own investigator, whose earlier call to this witness had triggered his memory. Having all these interests present at the mediation saved months of negotiating who would contribute, and how much, toward an overall settlement. The defense revised its estimate of the value of the case, and the case settled at the end of the day with what is called a structure, a long-term payout much like an annuity, which can have periodic and lump-sum payments. This satisfied the plaintiff and reflected a mutually satisfactory value of the claim.

THE LESSON

Because there is such a tiny chance that one's case will actually be tried, mediation is far and away the best forum for showcasing important evidence. As counsel and mediator dance the intricate steps—at times in flow—that give weight to this information, the information comes alive in the awareness of those with reason to resist it. This provides all participants with the opportunity to settle into a new understanding of how things came to be as they are and how they might best proceed from this point on.

TIMING CONSIDERATIONS

The appropriate timing of mediation depends in part on what kind of mediation is used. (This is discussed in Chapter Nine.) In facilitative mediations, it is safe to use the procedure at any time. Assuming the mediator uses caucuses or in some other way gives you control over how information is shared, any mediator reactions adverse to your side will be shared with you only confidentially in private caucus during the mediation. It is useful to have this opportunity to test your theories of the case on this disinterested party fairly early in the process, whether or not you settle (see Figure 8.1).

A more refined look at timing allows you to play off scheduled court or discovery activity to give added incentive to settle. Reaching agreement in mediation, for example, might avoid some impending unpleasant or risky event, such as a party's deposition or the hearing on a motion for summary judgment. Such deadlines are not necessary,

Figure 8.1. Dispute Resolution Flowchart.

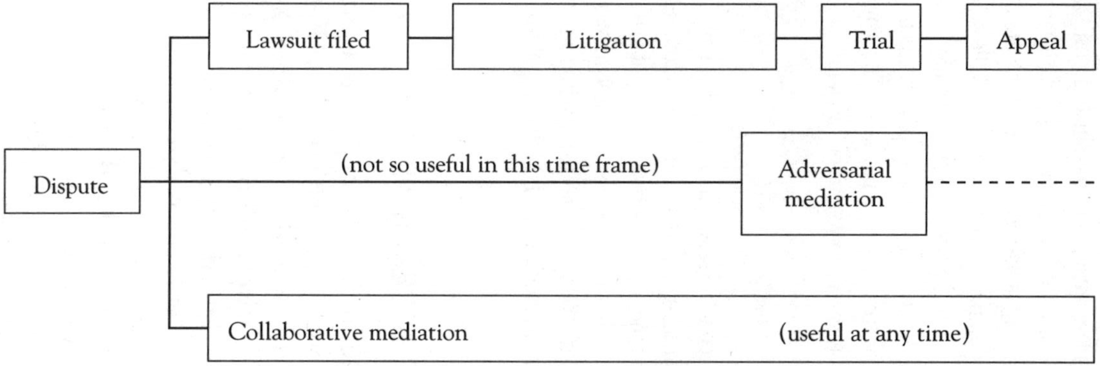

however, to make mediation effective. The mediator's skill builds commitment to the joint endeavor to reach agreement *now*.

Late Mediation

The most widely used timing for mediation is days or weeks before trial, an end-game strategy. Probably due to the residual effects of old-mind thinking, this is the easiest time to get counsel to agree to mediate. It is encouraged by court programs often addressed to meeting the courts' needs for fewer cases requiring trials rather than the parties' needs for cost-effective resolution. End-game mediations do resolve cases, but the majority of benefits that mediation could secure are lost.

Early Mediation

Early mediation is a way of heading off the tendency to manage the conflict through litigation instead of through collaborative processes. It offers an opportunity to capitalize on whatever flexibility remains with the parties, before they become polarized by litigation activities. It can significantly lower the transaction costs for cases that are frivolous and thus not worth the effort to defend. It is also often used in cases where the litigation costs border on astronomical, such as toxic torts, wrongful termination, and construction cases. By approaching early mediation with an open mind, the parties can save on preparation costs, pending an assessment of what really is needed (Novich, 1991). Cases frequently settle in early mediation, because it turns out nothing more is needed.

One product of early mediation is the *procedural agreement*. In cases that do not settle on the first round of mediation, procedural agreement describes what the parties will do, and when they will do it, to secure the information they need to reach final agreement. In a subsequent mediation or through subsequent mediator telephone follow-up, the case usually settles.

Following are some examples of the way people have used early mediation:

Investigatory mediation. Regardless of the stage of discovery, mediation allows balanced and candid exploration of the perceptions of witnesses. Witnesses may be gradually offered on both sides as questions arise during the mediation. The mediator conducts the questioning in person or by telephone. This procedure may narrow differences sufficiently so that parties can negotiate.

Mediated discovery. With or without counsel, experts and principals may have a detailed discussion of the information each party becomes willing to give concerning a key issue. The mediator keeps information-giving in balance, records progress, isolates hot issues, and identifies areas of agreement. This may generate statements of agreement and disagreement and show where more information is needed. The parties may negotiate a plan for addressing essential concerns. This type of mediation narrows the dispute so that settlement discussions can be productive, and it saves months to years of formal discovery effort.[1]

Pretermination mediation. When an employment relationship is in trouble, mediation enables those involved to discuss the situation and develop options in the face of likely termination followed by a complaint. It may involve counsel for the employee, otherwise in the background. It diffuses the emotional charge implicit in the situation.

Keeping the job going. When a construction project is faltering, early mediation among principals often affords perspective on responsibility and creativity in devising needed fixes. Usually it enables the job to carry on.

Joint inspection. When physical circumstances are significant, mediation has produced an agreement for joint inspection of sites, sometimes including the mediator, where a prompt return to mediation and further negotiation is planned.

Even with mediations on the courthouse steps, information critical to the parties' evaluation of options for resolution is often missing. With few exceptions, litigation usually fails to get the information needed to evaluate settlement options until the often bitter end. It is not true that you need to wait until all discovery is complete to use mediation effectively. And when you know almost everything about the dispute, mediation helps everyone focus on what is critical in all of that information.

COMMON QUESTIONS AND ANSWERS ABOUT MEDIATION

The following questions and answers will help dispel some of the uncertainty about just what mediation is and how best to use it.

What Is Mediable?

Almost anything is mediable (see Table 8.2). You can profitably mediate anything requiring a decision by two or more people. Mediation has been introduced into schools, where trained young-

Table 8.2.   Examples of Mediable Disputes.

Debtors and Creditors	
Collection claims	Bankruptcy matters
Foreclosures	Lender liability
Business Relationships	
Real estate	Licensing agreements
Product liability	Franchise agreements
Employment and workplace	Intraorganizational disputes
Almost all contract disputes	Intellectual property disputes
Construction disputes	Condominium owners
Trade secrets	Professional liability
Copyright and trademark	Partnership disputes
Landlord-tenant	Product disputes
Insurance coverage disputes	Patent disputes
Personal Relationships	
Marriage and divorce	Disputes over inheritance
Child custody	Neighbor disputes
Elder care issues	Prenuptial agreements
Family business disputes	Land use disputes
The Larger World	
Toxic cleanup issues	Regulatory negotiations
Personal injury suits	Public conversations
Disputes over disasters	International trade issues
Resource allocation fights	Matters pending in litigation
Resource management	Matters pending in arbitration
Solid waste siting conflicts	Property damage disputes

sters use a form of it to help their classmates resolve differences. Remember when you were a teenager and you wanted to use the family car on Friday night?[2] Dad might have said something like, "Hell, no. The last time you used the car, it had so little gas in the tank, I couldn't even back out of the garage. Did you think you could wean it?" Mom may have mediated, or rather conciliated, the discussion: "Perhaps you two could agree on how much gas would have to be left in the tank." Mom was a conciliator because she had an interest in the outcome: she wanted peace. A mediator technically has no interest in the outcome. The Federal Mediation and Conciliation Service, for example, is mandated by law to help keep industrial peace. By this definition, its mediators would be considered conciliators. For a mediator, it is the parties' business to decide whether the outcome will be war or peace or something in between. In Canada, the term *conciliator* describes someone who works for reconciliation of parties who do not meet face-to-face. However, in the United States *mediator* and *conciliator* are often used interchangeably.

When Is It Unwise to Mediate?

The decision to mediate must be made in the context of other options, including litigation. Is litigation a preferable forum? How costly is delay? Is there a business relationship to preserve or restore? If litigation proceeds, how will costs balance against both possible and probable returns (Singer, 1990)?

Court resolution may be needed for political reasons. For example, some issues are so controversial that at least one side does not want to take responsibility for voluntarily participating in its resolution. Examples include the school desegregation cases and high-stakes corporate disputes.

A truly nonmediable situation is one in which the other party is absent. Certainly there can be no mediation with an absent party unless the absent party has an authorized representative (something small businesses desperately need when something goes wrong with an offshore contract). Litigating is more attractive in this situation since you can take a default judgment and try to find some assets from which to collect it.

Since about 1980, many matters characterized as nonmediable have done very well in mediation. Moreover, the decision about whether to mediate must be made in context: how attractive are the alternatives to mediating? Sometimes they are so poor that mediation can become desirable even if it had nothing else to recommend it. Lawyers not broadly experienced in mediation may still caution against it because of their investment in the argument culture, which privileges criticism and disables inquiry.

Nevertheless, experience has taught that most disputes are mediable. When you find yourself in a doubting position, check to see what your reservations are based on. There may be some old assumptions underlying your view that on examination no longer prove useful. In fact, virtually every reason for *not* mediating is in fact a reason *for* mediating. Still, there are situations when mediation might not be the best option. Following are some of these situations:

- *When a party is marginally competent.* One example of a highly questionable situation is mediating with someone whose legal competency is in doubt. And yet, although mediation may not be an attractive option, it may be better than litigating with such a person because those who are marginally competent are better to deal with and get a more respectful audience in mediation than in the courts. In mediation, they may have representatives and advisers and family members involved. There is no time pressure, so that they have the fairest, most complete opportunity to evaluate their options and decide what to do. The mediator is there to be sure their concerns are heard and understood and that they understand their options.

The rule governing mediator practice in a case of marginal competency is that a mediator must terminate a mediation if a party is not competent to negotiate. In questionable situations, the presence of counsel may make it possible to continue, although the counsel then has the problem of deciding to what extent the client is aware of what is happening.

The Fragile Plaintiff

The plaintiff, a member of the college women's swimming team, alleged that her coach had engaged in long-term sexual harassment of her. She was extremely fragile. Her counsel, working closely with her therapist, did an excellent job of piloting her through two days of mediation in an effort to settle the case. Still, the plaintiff could not stick to any decision about what relief would be acceptable. A trial, hard as it would be for such a fragile person, was the only alternative.

The matter was eventually tried, and the plaintiff won a large verdict, only to have it reduced substantially later by the court's discretion.

- *When you want to delay things as long as possible.* Another reason often given for not mediating is that one party wants to delay a decision for as long as possible, as, for example, in collection matters. Parties using litigation to delay could as easily use their ability to delay as a bargaining chip in a negotiation where it might be traded for something of value impossible to get in litigation. Moreover, as filings go down and courts get on top of their calendars, the ability to delay is diminishing. One might well ask whether and to what extent delay for delay's sake is an ethical response. It may be, but it may not be.
- *When you want to set a legal precedent.* It is true that mediation cannot set a legal precedent, but precedent setting as a goal is always a gamble. In *Borel v. Fibreboard* (1973), the company seeking to set a legal precedent appealed a Texas jury's award of $80,000 to the widow of an asbestos worker in a wrongful death action. But the Fifth Circuit *affirmed* the award, writing a landmark decision applying strict liability to asbestos (thereby igniting the asbestos litigation explosion). Given the risks, mediated discussion is worth considering.

Not infrequently, the precedent-oriented party decides this is not the right case to try to establish the precedent, and the alternatives to judicial resolution are attractive enough for the matter to settle. There are many opportunities for derailment of principle-oriented litigation, which also may afford opportunities to resolve through mediation. At times, enforceability can be secured through a mediated stipulated order or judgment.

- *When you want a declaration that you were right.* Would you want to mediate a matter when you simply want a declaration that you're right? You might say, "Absolutely not," but this response misses the point. Yes, you may win at trial. But wouldn't you rather win at the table, where you have complete control over the outcome? If you do not mediate, you will never know what your alternatives to trial really are. Defendants who are clean, that is, without blame, and who look clean can and do walk away without paying anything in mediation, particularly in multiparty mediations. Plaintiffs often prefer the certainty of outcome when given a chance to consider all the options.

In the black farmers' class action against the U.S. Department of Agriculture alleging systemic racial bias over decades, mediation served to take this politically embarrassing story and turn it into something of a win for the government and many of the plaintiffs, although it did not satisfy the more extreme leadership that spearheaded the action. Continued rancor is not unusual in matters where making the problem visible has been especially difficult for the plaintiffs. A mediation with transformational potential is more likely to stimulate the parties' creativity to the point where that hunger can be satisfied. Sometimes it will not be. When creativity is needed, it is important to remember that the quality of the mediation process is something that the mediator and the parties can mold to their liking. It is only the limits of people's imaginations and their relative openness that limits the outcomes.

• *When someone's reputation is at stake.* Some have used as an example of nonmediability the situation in which one of the parties wants to clear his wrongfully tarnished name. In truth, a quietly mediated agreement to secure favorable counterpublicity might do a great deal more for one's reputation than media reports repeatedly raising the malignant accusation before the public while the libel or slander litigation is pending.

• *When you want to gamble.* Would a party bent on rolling the dice want to mediate? They might, as plaintiffs hit the jackpot or as defendants win a defense verdict. Such people assume they will get less by mediating than by trying their case. This may be true in some cases, but it is not true across the board. Defendants have refused to pay what turned out to be a fraction of what a jury later assessed against them. Some plaintiffs have turned down much more in mediation than they eventually recovered at trial. They also lost the chance to structure the settlement in financially advantageous ways.

• *When one side is unwilling.* Many insist that mediation is not an option when one side is unwilling. The barrier, in fact, is often not the other side's unwillingness but the *belief* that it is unwilling.

It is so common a misperception that the rule of thumb should be to ignore it. If you have not been able to get the other side to agree to mediation, use a convener—a mediator, for example, with skill in drawing reluctant parties to the table. Parties learn to want to mediate through the patience and skills of the convener. (See Chapter Ten.) Turning a "no" into a "I'll give it a try" is challenging and productive work. Tactically, the focus is to work with the interests of the reluctant party so that a "no" does not become final. Consider enlisting the aid of the court in encouraging attendance as well. (See Chapter Ten.)

• *When a serious crime is involved.* For a long time, it was thought that a matter in which a serious crime was involved could not be mediated. But the criminal justice system offers little to victims. Victim-offender mediations began in Canada and were brought to the United States in 1977 with the help of the Mennonites (*Wall Street Journal*, Oct. 28, 1993, p. B1). Research by Mark S. Umbreit, professor of social work at the University of Minnesota, shows that victim-perpetrator mediations are productive in many ways. For example, the victims lose some of their fear, perpetrator recidivism goes way down, and restitution is made much more often.[3]

If there ever was a need for a protective arena for the discussion of terribly painful events, it is in cases of rape, incest, robbery, and murder. Convicted perpetrators can most often realize the depth of the pain and grief they have inflicted. Victims can let go of the victim stance and move on with their lives. It is a very delicate mediation, and each side needs support, either present or just outside the mediation. There may need to be a premediation evaluation of the parties to ensure suitability and also screening to ensure that the mediator or mediators are compassionate, highly skilled, and experienced in such matters.

• *When cost is a big issue.* One lawyer well versed in mediation recommends mediating if the parties know enough to negotiate (Wulff, 1990). I would add that other important factors include knowing what you would like to negotiate for and if both sides have a good-faith interest in the discussion. Some observers worry about mediating prematurely, as it might be unnecessary.[4] I consider it a low-cost insurance policy protecting against the far greater wasted litigation expense. Considerations such as cost must be weighed against what you will accomplish with the same money if you do not mediate. What will likely happen if you do not mediate now? Is a 90 percent chance of success good enough?

How Confidential Is Mediation?

The vast majority of states have some confidentiality protection for mediation and mediators, but these are effected through some 250 different state statutes, frequently differing in such areas as the definition of mediation, the subject matter of the dispute, the degree and scope of protection, the exceptions, and the context of the mediation to which the statue applies (National Conference of Commissioners on Uniform State Laws, 2001).

The problem of conflicting legislation, the fact that mediations can be and are conducted multistate, and the felt need for strong protection of confidentiality has led to the effort to provide coherent and uniform protection for it in the form of a uniform act. The proposed Uniform Mediation Act (UMA), scheduled for release in 2001, will, for those states that adopt it, provide a common set of understandings and provisions to build on. Legislation already limits the extent to which private agreements may afford more protection to mediation confidentiality than is provided by law. New legislation will likely use a privilege structure (as attorney-client, priest-penitent, and doctor-patient relationships are now governed). This is the approach taken in, at the time of writing, the two most recent drafts of the proposed UMA. (See UMA, Sections 5 through 8, Draft of February, 2001.) Privilege is also the route taken by most of the states already extending such protections.

Confidentiality is unavailable under the UMA February 2001 draft for mediation communications:

- In a mediated agreement (Sec. 7 (a)(1)) and any communication in a mediation required by law to be open to the public (Sec. 7 (a)(2))

- When a participant uses or attempts to use the mediation to plan or commit a crime (Sec. 7 (a)(4)) or there is a threat to inflict bodily harm (Sec. 7(a)(3))

- When it is offered to prove or disprove abuse or neglect, abandonment, or exploitation under certain circumstances (Sec. 7(a)(5))

- Regarding a claim or complaint of professional misconduct or malpractice filed against a mediator in a proceeding (Sec. 7(a)(6))

- Where there are issues of professional misconduct or malpractice filed against a party, a non-party, or their representative based on conduct occurring during a mediation (Sec. 7(a)(7))

Also, where the validity of the mediated agreement is in question with allegations of fraud, duress, or incapacity or the like (Sec. 7(b)(2)), the court can apply a balancing test and waive the privileges and prohibitions, except for the mediator's. It also can apply a balancing test in a felony proceeding (Sec. 7(b)(1)) with no reservation of the mediator's right to choose whether to testify. This proposed uniform law is intended merely to provide a minimum level of confidentiality in mediation. Stronger state legislation should remain controlling, even if this provision is adopted, according to National Conference Reporters Nancy Rogers and Richard Reuben.

A hotly contested provision has concerned whether a mediator could be compelled to testify. An important decision in confidentiality is the ruling of Magistrate Judge Wayne Brazil in *Olam v. Congress Mortgage Co.* (1999), where, on agreement of both parties to the mediation, the court *compelled* a mediator to testify concerning whether Mrs. Olam, a sixty-five-year-old widow, was physically, intellectually, and emotionally incapable of giving consent to the mediation agreement reached in the early hours following the day that mediation began. The February 2001 draft of the UMA rejects this position.

This is an important case from another perspective. Olam alleged that she had been kept alone in a conference room all day, that she had not participated in any negotiations, that she was suffering from the effects of a preexisting condition, and that she fainted more than once. Her counsel were undoubtedly doing what they thought was best for her, but she was not a participant in the proceedings. Nor did the mediator apparently tune in to what was going on for her, so that there could be greater kindness shown and inclusion offered. Yet it was her case and her decision. (Another way of handling the human side of mediation is described in the section "A Cup of Coffee," p. 126.)

Let those who think that disputes are just about numbers take note. It is and always will be about people. There is some recognition of this in the draft UMA: parties have the right to have an attorney or other individual whom they designate to attend and participate in the mediation. For years, I have made this explicit in mediations, sometimes including parents of adult parties as well as significant others. Never once has that backfired. When people who are significant to a party attend, the mediation has a chance to work on them and their perspective. It makes a party feel less vulnerable and therefore enables him or her to be more effective in making wise decisions. This is the greatest and most certain protection for confidentiality in mediation—addressing the needs of the human beings who participate.

To secure the level of confidentiality you need, it is always wise, given the fluid status of confidentiality and privilege issues, to check on the laws of the state where the mediation is to be held to be sure that all requirements are met. Look for windows where private agreement may control and take advantage of them with a simple mediation confidentiality agreement. (See Appendix F.)

How Final Is Mediation?

Finality is a buzzword in dispute resolution. As a practical matter, a mediated resolution has a quality of finality unapproachable in adjudicated disputes. The dispute receives a decent burial, and the resulting agreement is nonappealable. (You would have to file a whole new lawsuit to attack it.) The parties have invested both time and effort in reaching this agreement. They reached it voluntarily, believing it served their best interests, and they have come to terms with the end of the conflict. This is what is called a *secure outcome*. The matter is at rest because the parties have become invested with ownership of the process *and* the outcome. (See Figure 1.1.)

There are times in any mediation when finality through court action may need to be added in order to provide for enforcement of the private agreement. For example, the parties may decide to make their mediated agreement the heart of a stipulated judgment in the pending action, so that judicial enforcement is available. The proposed UMA would provide an additional mechanism for turning a mediated agreement into an enforceable judgment, which appears not to require a pending lawsuit.

Another way of ensuring finality is to have the mediator, after a mediated agreement is reached, become an arbitrator for the purposes of making the agreement an arbitration award. This is probably the ultimate finality because there is little that can upset an arbitration award.

Court judgments in litigated cases may make one or both sides feel they were not heard. Mediation lets them know they were heard and that they controlled the outcome. This leaves little reason to attack the agreement of settlement.

If no agreement is reached, mediation is a milestone along the way, producing other desirable outcomes, such as lowering hostilities, clarifying focus, and learning what needs to be done to resolve. There is value in knowing that this matter must be tried—that the investment of time and resources required to prepare for trial is necessary. Given the enormously high rate of resolution of lawsuits other than by trial, this is an extremely valuable bit of information.

What Are the Preconditions to Mediation?

The only preconditions to mediation are those needed for any negotiation. Do those on the other side know they have to deal with you? Do you have their attention? Do they know that your claim or defense has substance?

Substance is established automatically in most cases, because the existence of a viable claim or defense is obvious. Even in situations where the weight of your position comes from *procedural advantage* (your ability to require or delay action by the other side), there can still be enough substance on your side to win agreement to mediate.

When the theories of recovery (the legal underpinnings of claims) are new, when liability is slim and damages are heavy, a prospective defendant may not believe he has to deal with you. Often, in addition, a party may be misinformed. Based on what this person has been told, he or she may see no merit to the claim or defense. Mediation usually exposes these errors and tests the plausibility of difficult theories once you can get the other side to the table.

When someone is not listening to you, *you* can still offer to listen to him or her. This is in accordance with the mechanical view of human communication: "To open ears, operate mouth." You might say something like, "You seem pretty convinced of your position. Let's spend a few hours in mediation and see what we can accomplish. Maybe there's something we've overlooked." It is easy to hear this statement as an admission that *you* have overlooked something rather than that *both* may have overlooked something. No matter. The object is to get an opportunity for serious discussion, and this will often accomplish the purpose.

Agreeing to mediate does not mean agreeing to resolve.

Does It Make Sense to Mediate a Frivolous Case?

When you believe there is little substance to a claim or defense, should you mediate anyway? In mediation, you can check on what the other side has. You may be missing something—or they may be. In mediation, you may test your assumptions; if you're still convinced there is no merit on the other side, impress the other side with your determination to resist or persist. *Agreeing to mediate does not mean agreeing to resolve.*

Is It Necessary to Litigate First to Get the Other Side's Attention?

Lawyers often use litigation activity to impress opposing counsel with the need to give a claim or defense serious attention. In large cases, after perhaps a year and a half of discovery, when tens of thousands of pages of documents are produced and copied and indexed, you have the other side's attention. This is often gross overkill.

A lawyer with a great trial record automatically commands the opposing party's attention. Some lawyers' names on the file may have the opposite effect. Clients simply need to be alert to the situation. Today the tactic of hindering and delaying just claims has risen to an art form, which makes litigation far riskier and mediation far more compelling.

Filing a lawsuit usually gets someone's attention, but at considerable price, particularly if there are allegations the defendant will see as insulting. In mediation, at least you can find out where the problem lies. Is it counsel or client? If client, who? And why? All of this information will be useful in designing your long-range strategy.

How Trustworthy Is Information Secured Through Mediation?

Information made available through mediation can have the same marks of trustworthiness as that elicited through formal discovery. For example, it can be submitted with a declaration as to its nature and extent under penalty of perjury. That simply needs to be an item for negotiation. Fisher and Ury point out in *Getting to Yes* that in a negotiation, it is unwise to trust the other side. This is sound advice. Meaningful trust builds gradually from experience. You will learn to recognize how far to trust, if you do not already know. Ultimately trust is essential, but it must be earned. We earn trust ourselves by being reliable and giving our attention to the other side's concerns.

What Does Mediation Cost?

Overall, the cost of using mediation is about 10 percent or less of the cost of relying exclusively on litigation. Some community dispute resolution programs and some court programs still provide free mediation. For private mediations, the cost is often split at least two ways and is usually less than the cost of a deposition. In round numbers, it might cost from $300 (for a small claims or support payment mediation) to $5,000 (for complex or sensitive commercial mediation) per day of mediation. In rare, high-stakes mediations, certain mediators, perhaps those whose connections are essential to resolution, might charge as much as $25,000 per day. The cost is meaningful only in comparison to what the alternatives are. It may make sense to pay $2,500 for a day of mediation if you would otherwise spend $150,000 or even $15,000 on the litigation before the year is out.

Some mediators work by the hour, some by the day. Some charge higher fees for more sensitive and complex matters and lesser fees for smaller cases to remain competitive. Contingent fees (those based on the outcome) are not available, to my knowledge; to be effective, the mediator needs to be free to allow the parties to fail to reach agreement. Occasionally, where the parties' tempers are frayed and getting started is nearly impossible, mediators will allow the parties to pay what they think the service is worth, after the mediation. At times, even in commercial cases, the parties will mediate the division of the fee.

What About Fee Sharing?

Compared to litigation, the cost of mediation is very small. Sometimes parties get upset about who pays what part of the cost. There is a value in having all parties contribute, but no particular advantage in having the contribution be equal. I suggest that it is unwise not to resolve the fee split, if any, before mediation. How and whether the fee is split is not a topic that addresses anyone's underlying concerns, and it gives the mediator two things to think about when there should only be one: how you and the others are going to accomplish what you came together to accomplish.

To be of any use, the mediator must be neutral. Unlike an arbitrator, the mediator makes no decision. Everything he does happens in plain view of one or both parties. Equal sharing is important only if a party thinks it is.

How Long Do Mediations Last?

Most civil lawsuits are resolved in mediation in a few hours to a day. Particularly complex cases such as business contract disputes and some construction disputes may extend to two days. And particularly when there is very early use of mediation as the container for the conflict, there may be two or even three separate mediation sessions of varying length as essential steps are agreed on and carried out. Some court-annexed programs allow as little as two hours for the mediation. Popularly referred to as McMediation, this model seems to be justified primarily by the inability of the institutions involved to fund their programs adequately. It will pick off those matters that will simply settle once people have a chance to talk face to face. To be credible, it should also identify those that require longer intervention and provide additional resources for them. If you find yourself in such a program, consider arranging with the mediator for a continuation if you feel one is needed.

Generally even a complex mediation is unlikely to last more than a few days, although there are situations where mediation is used to facilitate technical discussions in which the mediation can go on for weeks. In these situations, litigation is likely to go on for years. In public policy and environmental matters not in litigation, the mediations are still measured in days, but they often occur over months. In such matters, preparation time is key, and the number of mediation days is relatively few.

These estimates of duration assume that facilitative mediation is being used. Evaluative, advisory mediation can take much less time (an hour or two instead of three or four) or much longer (two weeks rather than two or three days). I believe these differences are inherent in the nature of the processes. Evaluative mediation can be shorter when the facts are simple and known, since the adviser's focus is on giving his opinion. Facilitative mediators take the safer tack of building the parties' awareness of where justice lies, but without giving advice. In complex matters, the facilitative mediator's expertise in what is *not essential* saves a great deal of time. This mediator will check with the parties regarding his views on the question of relative importance of issues, but part of his job is to help sort the wheat from the chaff. The evaluative, advisory mediator is burdened with the responsibility of giving sound advice and therefore labors much harder to be sure all arguments are heard and understood.

What Is the Level of Principal Participation in Mediation?

In some mediations such as divorce, only the principals are present as a rule. In business mediations, client and counsel work together as a team during the mediation. Sometimes the client just listens, saving comments for private meetings with counsel, with or without the mediator present. Sometimes the principal is an active, if not leading, participant. This is a strategic decision based on maximizing the benefits of mediating.

Does Mediation Satisfy the Need for Your Day in Court?

In good mediations, participants, regardless of their level of active participation, tend to experience the process as having their day in court. Their side is presented. Their counsel is at their side and visibly on their side. The bad news—the downside—is delivered by the mediator whose perspective they can evaluate for themselves. There is often more complete examination of disputes in mediation than in trial due to rules of evidence and greater formality.

Mediation is simple and straightforward. Why not mediate? There is little to lose and much to gain. If no settlement is reached, the parties often agree on what is needed so that the next meeting will make resolution possible. The process of resolution has begun.

Mediation literally turbo-charges negotiations because the parties drop the defensive, adversarial, distrustful stance they took on as part of litigation and become more the problem-solving, justice-seeking, open, and compassionate human beings they have been all along.

Chapter Nine

Selecting a Mediator

Education consists mainly in what we have unlearned.
MARK TWAIN

The choice of mediator is a delicate decision with many consequences. This choice determines what style of process you may
have. The mediator helps the parties do what they came together
to do, such as reaching their own resolution. However, the term
mediator has been used loosely to include advice givers and even
decision makers (Singer, 1990). In selecting a mediator, it is well
to bear in mind the view of ADR pioneer Lon Fuller:

> The central quality of mediation [is] its capacity to reorient the
> parties towards each other, not by imposing rules on them, but by
> helping them to achieve a new and shared perception of their rela-
> tionship, a perception that will redirect their attitude and disposi-
> tions toward one another [quoted in Riskin and Westbrook, 1987,
> p. 210].

This quality is just as important in a personal injury mediation as
it is in a partnership mediation.

SERVICES BEFORE YOU GET TO THE TABLE

A mediator may perform many functions, but not all of them as a
matter of course. To the extent the following apply to your situation, be sure to ascertain that a prospective mediator does in fact

offer them. There are several things a mediator may do prior to an actual mediation. They include negotiations coaching, conflict assessment, process design, convening, stabilizing the situation, and helping you to focus your preparation.

Mediator as Negotiations Coach

You can learn about your hurdles by engaging a mediator to give a reaction to your side of the case even without benefit of a mediation. Facilitative mediators serve as settlements experts; their job is to look for weaknesses in a side's position with possibly overlooked options for resolution. They are often expert negotiation strategists as well. Expect them to bring a global perspective to your deliberations because of their habit of mind of looking for mutual benefit.

Conflict Assessment

In complex matters, even before the mediation can be convened, the mediator may need to prepare a conflict assessment, one of the most overlooked services of the mediator. That assessment encompasses the following considerations:

- Identifying the issues, needs, and concerns to be discussed
- Developing a tentative plan for approaching the situation and the people involved in it
- Identifying those whose presence is necessary for the good of the whole
- Devising a flexible and tentative design for the process: whether to approach the situation as a mediation, a facilitation, a consensus-building process, or some combination of these; whether to use caucusing; whether to have principals present; and the nature and extent of their participation
- Developing an understanding of what kind of product or output is needed from the process
- Planning the role of the neutral

Each of these considerations is key in complex and difficult matters presenting themselves for mediation. If the matter you are handling is not fairly routine, engaging a mediator who is familiar with these considerations can be very helpful. This is work for mediators familiar with environmental and public policy mediation. It is not common to find awareness of it in mediators primarily engaged in routine civil dispute mediation. Still, those who practice largely civil mediation and even divorce mediation may have these skills. It bears inquiry in the right case, where such skills are important.

There can be an enormous increase in the effectiveness of mediation when it is set up in a salutary way. More ground can be covered, more effectively, and with greater ownership of the outcome. A mediator whose skills include consensus building and facilitation may see opportunities for using these approaches to good effect, whereas one who mediates only civil disputes may not. A mediator with experience in training may be able to seed the discussion with some useful skills and techniques in multiparty negotiations particularly, without necessarily making training a separate step.

Process Design

The mediator designs the process, at least initially, and then develops a strategy for how to carry out the recommended process. The mediator determines the following:

- Timetables
- The manner by which people will be informed of the gathering and provided with time and tools to respond
- How questions and concerns in the preprocess period may be dealt with
- Whose absence would impair the credibility of the process
- Whether any representative status needs to be recognized among those whose participation will most obviously be needed and how that might be managed
- What kind of preprocess caucusing with diffuse stakeholder groups might be needed
- What the output of the process might look like and how to communicate and disseminate it

There can be huge impacts from taking careful steps in laying the groundwork for the process. Sometimes the hardest battles are fought before the parties even sit down at the table to discuss the matter at hand. Parties and their counsel may have very differing views of the situation and the possibilities. There is often a need to narrow the focus to one simple step at a time: having the best meeting, the best facilitated discussion possible, and often as soon as possible. Then you learn what is really possible and what more complicated, time-consuming, and expensive steps are really necessary.

Convening

In ordinary civil mediation, the mediator, mediation firm, or mediation case manager is worth considering as a resource in sensitive matters to entice the opposing party to the table. Good conveners succeed in this more than 80 percent of the time. (Eighty percent is a common figure that mediation practitioners use to describe convening and mediation successes, so long as their actual success rate equals or exceeds that figure.) Even if they do not succeed, there will have been some improvement in the quality of communications because of the intervention, provided it is done skillfully. A skilled convener's intervention carries the message, "Someone wants to listen to you." Questions and concerns that would not be brought up to you are often raised in a confidential discussion about convening. Although these likely cannot be disclosed without prior consent, there may still be some feedback that may deepen your understanding of what it will take to have the discussion that you seek. If communication has been hostile, if you are distrusted because of your role, there is good reason to reach out for this resource.

You do not need to have an agreement to mediate in order to file a matter in mediation. Some of the techniques professionals use to convene a mediation are set forth in Chapter Ten.

Stabilizing the Situation

One important role the mediator may play is to help hold the situation together until the parties can meet on the common ground that mediation may afford. When people feel helpless or hopeless, they may do things that will have bad, if not dire, consequences, all in the name of protecting themselves from someone or something they feel cannot be tolerated. Such desperate feelings are not uncommon in conflict situations that have deteriorated significantly. By listening to people's concerns, providing some coaching in the preparation phase, and offering tangible evidence of progress toward a civil discussion, a mediator may head off such difficulties. Using a mediator in this phase helps the gradual building of the trust essential to any agreement. It allows the mediator to begin to establish relationships within the participant group, which will increase the mediator's ability to be effective on behalf of the whole. None of this is wasted effort.

If your situation involves such volatility, you may want to secure a mediator who has the capacity to perform this function at a high level of competence.

Focusing Preparation

Another often ignored function of the mediator is to focus the parties in their preparation, either jointly or in separate caucuses, as they may agree. (This subject is discussed in Chapter Ten.) By confidential communication between and among parties and counsel, the mediator can help ensure that everyone's preparation is focused on what will most help others understand their perspective. Needless preparation can be avoided in this way. By offering a neutral mirror showing how some tactic or strategy might be seen by others, the mediator can offer insights into its effectiveness, enabling the parties to avoid destructive approaches while strengthening constructive ones.

MEDIATOR QUALIFICATIONS

A bundle of skills and personal characteristics becomes visible in what a mediator does in mediation. There has been a substantial effort among mediation practitioners, teachers, and scholars to come up with an experiential way of demonstrating competency rather than having to rely on formal degrees (which only recently have even been available) or credentials from other professions. It is important for consumers of mediation services to be somewhat familiar with this effort, for it teaches much about the core competencies and what makes for excellence.

The Quest for a Measure of Competency

Mediation, despite its ancient antecedents in tribal cultures, is still in its childhood as a modern approach to dispute resolution. To date, it has afforded little insight into its subtle and powerful process. Yet court-annexed mediation programs, community dispute programs, and many others have for years recruited and trained people to be mediators without a clear understanding of mediation's requirements and promise.

In 1985 Christopher Honeyman, then at the Wisconsin Employment Relations Commission, began to develop criteria for evaluating mediators and tests to check performance against them (Honeyman, 1988). Not long after, the Massachusetts Office of Dispute Resolution worked with Honeyman's criteria in a court-annexed mediation program for a court of general jurisdiction, made some modifications, and found them useful in developing a quality mediation program.[1] At about the same time, the Society of Professionals in Dispute Resolution (SPIDR) established the Commission on Qualifications. Its 1989 report concluded that in general, the marketplace could be sufficiently discriminatory as to quality. But with mandatory programs and those in which the parties have no effective means to influence the selection of mediators, the report suggested that standards should be established to ensure consistency and quality in the delivery of services. In 1993, the Test Design Project group, chaired by Honeyman, developed Interim Guidelines for Selecting Mediators, which was published by the National Institute for Dispute Resolution (Honeyman and others, 1993). The subject was reviewed at length and from many angles in a symposium published in the October 1993 *Negotiation Journal.* That issue was a factor contributing to the replacement of the Interim Guidelines by the "Performance Based Assessment: A Methodology for Use in Selecting, Training and Evaluating Mediators" (Honeyman and others, 1995). This is commonly referred to as the Performance-Based Methodology, which may be found in full at the Web site http://www.convenor.com/madison/performa.htm.[2]

The problem with the concept of marketplace screening is that in many, if not most, states, the marketplace is ill informed about mediation. Even in states where a great deal of mandatory mediation is taking place, there is reportedly a dearth of awareness of the potential of mediation. Rather, mediation is viewed as more of a jazzed-up court settlement conference, with zero-sum bargaining as its principal focus.

The Importance of Selecting Wisely

It is only after one has experienced a variety of mediators and mediation styles that one's ability to discriminate develops. Some years ago, a lawyer told me that a well-known mediator had "mediated on him" two years earlier. "My arm still hurts from the experience," he said. What one author refers to as "Attila the Mediator" (Schrader, 1992) is often far less skillful than his quieter sisters and brothers and may use dominance to define the outcome rather than making it possible for the parties to design their own. The overwhelming consensus within the mediation profession is that such behavior is abusive and that the process is not mediation. One of the fundamental shared views—and indeed the keystone in mediator ethical mandates—is that self-determination, that is, voluntary and uncoerced agreements made by parties free to leave at any time, is an imperative of quality mediation. As one of the most reflective scholars in the field, Robert A. Baruch Bush, puts it:

> [T]he real challenge mediators face is not how to gain control of the agenda, but how to keep control in the *parties'* hands. The temptation for the mediator is to take control, rather than remaining committed to the principle of party control over the definition of the dispute [Bush, 1993, p. 343].

In reaching this type of resolution, the ability to contain difficult and even barely controllable discussions can be an art form. Those lacking experience in using mediation may be misled by appearances. In one situation, a mediator was criticized in a *Wall Street Journal* article for allowing the parties to a farm credit dispute to get into a shouting match. The lender's representative, however, conceded that he ended up with a reasonable settlement (Lambert, 1993). Was it because the farmer could at last vent his feelings or in spite of it? There is nothing about a shouting match that indicates the mediator is not competent. In fact, one indicator of mediator competence is the ability to allow the honest expression of feelings, while keeping discussions on track through virtually transparent controls. Suppression of feelings is not considered good practice.

During the Mediation Process

While for years mediation has been considered so personal an art, not a science, that it defied analysis, Honeyman and his successors are proving otherwise. They found that although styles differ widely, good mediators have several characteristics in common. From these efforts, I have culled a list that seems most useful for our purposes here:

• *Information gathering* (Honeyman and others, 1995). Good mediators engage in intensive factual inquiry early in the case. It may be general or highly focused on what the participants and mediator see as the critical facts. It may be done in joint session or in private caucus, or both. This is the foundation for everything that follows. The mediator's effectiveness in devil's advocacy—showing you the weaknesses of your position—depends in large part on being seen as knowledgeable about the dispute. An important multifaceted mediator tool for communicating that one has been heard is the reflective read-back—giving the speaker a concise and insightful recap of factual statements and non-judgmentally reframed reflections of emotional material.

• *Empathy.* Good mediators win trust by being willing to hear and discuss what concerns you, whether or not it is strictly relevant to the dispute. Through empathy and compassion, they may come to some understanding of the situation from your perspective and let you know that. Their ability to sift what is important from what is said and cast doubt on overstated positions—by reframing and by applying their appropriate sense of humor—will gradually win your belief in their competence. A good mediator will be motivated to find out what your most fundamental desires and interests are and to see whether and to what extent these can be addressed through the management and resolution of the conflict. More important, she will be there to see and understand you, for you are the context for your fundamental desires and interests. Most important, a reflective mediator will see you, with no agenda or

reason at all. And you will know you have been seen. When someone really *sees* you, it is a profound experience.

• *Impartiality*. The term *impartiality* is defined in the drafting of
the proposed Uniform Mediation Act to mean free from favoritism
or bias, in word or by action, and committed to serve all parties. A
mediator who is untrustworthy can spoil the process. Impartiality is
one of the touchstones of trustworthiness, but not necessarily at all
times and in all cases. At times mediators who are seen as having an
interest in a particular type of outcome—for example, peace—can
be extremely helpful, as we often see in international diplomacy.
However, a mediator seen as favoring one side is a liability. As one
lawyer said after a successful mediation, "I thought I wanted a mediator who was favorable to our side. I learned that I needed one who
was favorable to all sides. If I had gotten my wish, the other side
would never have trusted enough for us to be able to negotiate this
settlement." If the parties select a mediator who favors a particular
outcome, it is important only that they do so knowingly.

The *perception* of impartiality is a somewhat different element.
The mediator owes it to you and all other participants to be perceived as being impartial, in addition to actually *being* impartial.
However, in order for this to occur, you and the others owe it to
the mediator to let her know what you think she needs to know—
for example, if you sense that her impartiality is torqued in some
way. She cannot do her job unless you do yours.

• *Persuasion*. Often mediators take steps early to obtain small
concessions. Agreement on ground rules can be such a small step.
This builds a pattern of agreements that helps you believe the discussions will be fruitful and helps you suspend your disbelief for
the period of the mediation. This is subtle persuasion, not argument for a position or outcome. As the mediation progresses, the
mediator's intensity may increase, creating a sense of urgency
about getting the matter resolved now, if that is appropriate. Some
people think only loud or controlling neutrals are persuasive.
Experience suggests the opposite is true. You often make the quiet
mediator's voice your own, persuading yourself. As master mediator Tom Colosi says, it takes only a tiny seed of doubt to motivate
someone to truly reconsider the options (Katzeff, 1996).

• *Generating options*. A mediator cannot contribute much to
devising options for resolution until the parties believe she is

knowledgeable about the situation. Early attempts at resolution, however brilliant, may be seen as condescending and can prevent the parties from reaching their own agreement. Good mediators are not ego invested in their ideas or proposals and will make it as easy to reject them as to accept them. This may be done by how they are offered—as a "What if the others would . . ." rather than labeling an idea as the mediator's idea. When they do that, acceptance has far more impact, for it is uncoerced. In addition, good mediators are creative and not afraid to repackage ideas that were passed over previously. They are also a source of ideas about how to overcome significant hurdles.

Prior to the work leading to Performance-Based Methodology, the term *intervention* sparked intensive debate over the tilt toward a proactive model of mediation. The phrase *generating options* does not imply the mediator should be launching proposals under his or her own banner. Using "what if" questions—"What if the other side would agree to X?"—to surface ideas is a good way of allowing the parties to reject the proposals or make them their own. When an idea or proposal comes from a mediator's agenda, it has momentum or energy. Look for a mediator who is willing to have his or her ideas tested without such momentum or energy, who will offer thoughts of his or her own devising without imprimatur. That most deeply protects everyone's ability to decide for themselves.

• *Distraction.* Mediation is hard work. You are called on to challenge your assumptions and recognize your fantasies about how the matter may resolve. You labor over your side of the negotiation process. Good mediators provide distractions to ease the tension. These may be stories of other mediations with similar difficulties, appropriate humor, or doing something unexpected, such as acting completely out of character.

• *Managing the interaction.* This encompasses maintaining appropriate control over the process. Some mediators are expert at keeping counsel and parties at the task, creatively and productively, without seeming to exert pressure. They prevent bullying and create space for a party to speak, an opportunity that can get lost when counsel are the major carriers of the argument. They respond constructively to pressure tactics, including personal attacks, for in part their role is one of lightning rod. Distraction helps in this. This process skill begins with establishing the contract. Mediators who are expert in managing the process might well establish early agreement about the objective of the meeting. They may carefully lay the groundwork for the operational "contract" of the mediation: what their view of their role is and what they need from the parties to enable them to be effective. This is particularly important when there is suspicion of the mediator by one or more parties. Being completely transparent about the understanding of the mediator's role draws into the open hidden concerns about this and invites participants to articulate their concerns to the mediator, when there is a perception that this commitment has been neglected. A role, for example, might be, "The mediator is here to help you." What the mediator might need in order to do this at a high level of competence might be an agreement to "tell the mediator what we think he needs to know." (This was the basis for the contract in the "Vulnerability Works" case in Chapter Two.)

A second component of this process skill is drawing ground rules from participants. Ground rules can be one-size-fits-all or custom-made. I tend to prefer the latter, allowing the ground rules to arise organically from the situation. A ground rule committing the participants to respectful communication might be agreed on after one or more incidents of rudeness or slight, when everyone can see the cost of not following such a rule. If the situation is complex, the mediator might ask for a ground rule stating, "It's okay to make mistakes." She might wait until she made a mistake to do this or might ask for it up front. This rule makes it safe for everyone to make mistakes and disarms those who lie in wait to find someone else's imperfect expression. Such rule building wins heartfelt support, not just formal support. In complex matters, sometimes many of the ground rules will be developed during the design and convening stage. But there is advantage in devising or modifying them during the process.

• *Strategic direction.* It is one thing to juggle a lot of balls. It is another to give that activity direction, purpose, and meaning. With this skill, the mediator works with the parties' real agendas, their underlying interests, and the pivotal issues needing exploration in order to keep all efforts productive. Without it, mediation can bog down, and much of its potential can be lost. A good mediator tests his or her assumptions about the importance of certain issues in deciding what questions to ask and what avenues to privilege. This gives the parties a chance to correct his or her direction, if it is not serving their purposes. If the mediator's own agenda has crept into the mediator's thinking, this is one way of smoking it out.

Mediator Qualities

In addition to the aforementioned capacities (Kolb, 1983, 1994), a good mediator works under several important professional and ethical constraints. How a prospective mediator thinks of her role is important in the vetting. A good mediator will be comfortable with these guidelines:

- *Humility.* The first injunction is to do no harm. Hippocrates stressed that surgeons should foster and use the healing power of nature rather than interfere unnecessarily. This is good counsel for mediators today, for the parties are the most knowledgeable about what it will take to resolve their differences and serve the larger interests involved. Humility dictates deference to the parties' wisdom, however hard it may be to bring it into play.

Many beginners use techniques that work sometimes but carry a significant risk of prejudice to the negotiations when they do not work. Proposing one's own idea to one side, without having a very good sense that it would be acceptable to the other side, is an example. Some mediators reject the whole notion of making their own proposals. Others, advisory mediators in particular, see this as central to their role. My preference is for the mediator to use open-ended questions aimed at clarifying understanding in private caucus to develop the parties' thinking on the subject. And when the mediator's ideas are surfaced, they are not so labeled.

- *Patience.* A second rule of good mediation practice is never to attempt to work beyond the parties' trust level. Trust ebbs and flows during a mediation. It is often lowest when the mediator says something you do not want to hear. You feel pressured and disrespected when a mediator ignores your distrust. Good mediators stop at this moment and come back and work to rebuild trust, so that the arena for collaborative problem solving is big enough to allow for productive change. Ask a prospective mediator what his or her approach might be to the loss of trust.

- *Self-awareness.* A third rule is that the mediator has sufficient self-awareness that he or she is able to function without personalizing anything that happens in the mediation or at the least to be aware when this is starting to happen. The mediation is not about the mediator. It is about the participants, counsel, and the situation. Qualities listed in the Performance-Based Methodology include sensitivity, emotional stability, integrity, maturity (not chronological age), impartiality, and insight into themselves and their clients. The mediator's technical skill pack should include skill in reasoning, analyzing, problem solving, reading comprehension, writing (sometimes mediators draft agreements at the conclusion of mediations), and oral and nonverbal communication skills. It should also include a capacity for openness and vulnerability.

• *Endurance.* Tenacity is a big part of mediator effectiveness. A good mediator's tenacity can be characterized as seeing the glass half-full rather than half-empty. A mediator who helps the parties focus on *what is there* rather than *what is not* can help the participants begin to believe in the possibility of success. It takes very little of that to carry the ball across the finish line. At some point, this is perceived as "believing in us" rather than merely wishful thinking.

THE CONTINUING INQUIRY

The work of Christopher Honeyman beginning in the Test Design Project, the Massachusetts program, and the many critics and commentators drawn into the discussion are demystifying mediation in a significant breakthrough.[2]

Many in the mediation field are also passionately committed to avoiding setting up one model of mediation as the standard against which all are measured, thereby stifling the innovation and creativity that are such an important part of mediation. Testing is itself an arcane science, but performance testing, particularly if it is combined with some form of peer review process, is highly promising. To date, the studies done on mediators have not been validated to standards recommended by the testing industry generally (Honeyman and others, 1995).

There is ever-increasing legislative interest in the certification of mediators. Most professionals are certified by some authority. Why not mediators? But in these discussions, it is easy to forget the burdens that a wider awareness imposes on the definition of a profession. Today we are acutely aware of the sexual, ethnic, racial, and cultural biases that sneak into the establishment of norms. Professions depend for their existence on exclusivity, often hard to square with these important considerations. A critical conclusion of the SPIDR Report and Performance-Based Methodology recognizing these needs is that, "No single entity (rather a variety of organizations) should establish qualifications for neutrals" (Honeyman and others, 1995, p. 2). So it is unwise to hold out hope that essential screening will be done by a third party any time soon. Court and institutional programs mandating mediation conduct only the most superficial screening. You are the one who must develop the expertise in what the possibilities and opportunities really are.

Mediation is a good field in which to move beyond paper-and-pencil tests of mental abilities, which ignore emotional intelligence.

As a user of mediation services, you may be interested in the inevitable growth of legislation governing the field. Heavily affected, for example, is the ability to maintain confidentiality, as with the new proposed Uniform Mediation Act. Perhaps you will see the risk of setting harmful limitations on the evolution of the profession and the power of the resource if we rush to legislation on mediation without learning more about it first. Like teaching, mediation is a good field in which to move beyond paper-and-pencil tests of mental abilities, which ignore emotional intelligence and the ability to think on one's feet, among other things, and to strive to identify professional excellence. Despite the pressures from mandatory programs, our conclusions will need to be tentative for some time to come.[3]

WHAT PAPERWORK CAN TELL YOU AND WHAT IT CONCEALS

Our culture's tenacious commitment to expertise leads us to overvalue two aspects of mediator qualifications: (1) non-mediation experience and recognition, and (2) substantive knowledge concerning the subject matter of the dispute. Before joining the herd in overvaluing these aspects, consider the following conclusions based on in-depth research studies.

Mediator Experience

A mediator's track record tells you far more than paper qualifications. A long resumé of experience in other work, such as law, engineering, or accounting, speaks volumes of scant mediation experience. Nor does the number of cases handled say anything about the quality of this mediator's work or the breadth and depth of his other experience. Here as elsewhere, objective criteria have their limitations. As your experience with mediation grows, so will your ability to find precisely the type of mediator you want for a particular case.

There is no best mediator. In the realm of professional qualifications, it becomes obvious that different mediators are better in different situations. You may be looking for breadth but not depth, for depth but not breadth, or for both breadth and depth, or for neither one. There are mediators to fit every situation.

When you want a mediator to be an expert in the mediation process, you will be looking for a facilitative mediator. Or you may be looking for a mediator who is more than facilitative—one who bridges the problem-solving and transformative—that is, a reflective mediator. You want the mediator's reactions and observations in confidential caucus if a caucusing model is used, but you want it to be more informative than advice giving. You already know that once the mediator's mind is set on a particular way you should go, that mediator will (like all of us) marshal information to support that view, while generally ignoring conflicting information. You want someone who finds agreements in the cacophony of the dispute when no one else can. And you want someone who can hold the center when chaos threatens, while allowing what is needed to happen.

Substantive Knowledge

A mediator must have sufficient knowledge of the subject matter to allow him or her to work effectively. For individuals who are quick studies, a short briefing from a colleague experienced in that area or an expert in the field may be sufficient to develop a vocabulary and a sense of the context for the particular dispute. For others, it may require years of work in the subject area. There is an advantage to having a mediator whose mind is still open on the subject—something that is not always easy for those with a career investment as an expert in the subject area. This is one of the characteristics you may want to evaluate in the mediator you are considering.

The tendency is to choose a mediator with outside credentials, since credentialing in the field is still in its infancy. It has been most common for conflict resolution firms to provide mediators selected for their subject area expertise. For example, if you have an agricultural dispute, the firm will assign a lawyer or other technical expert practicing in that subject area rather than an expert mediator with experience in that field.[4]

Among mediation services are two influential organizations: the American Arbitration Association (AAA) and the Center for Public Resources (CPR). Both have contributed significantly to the education of lawyers and the consuming public about mediation. Both pay attention to quality issues and are aware of the public's increasing ability to discriminate among mediators. Both are beginning to put facilitative mediators on their panels, presumably because of their effectiveness. Both have done much to advance the use of litigation alternatives, AAA by focusing on arbitration and CPR by focusing on mini-trial. (*Mini-trial* is the highly compressed presentation of a case by counsel, often to a panel consisting of a neutral and top executives from the opposing sides, followed by a facilitated negotiation.) CPR's Jim Henry wrote years ago of mediation as "the sleeping giant" (Henry and Lieberman, 1985). Both organizations have been instrumental in awakening that giant.

CPR's policy also has been to get lawyers to serve as mediators as part of their law practice. Lawyers can and do excel as mediators. However, not one of the studies discussed in this book shows that being a lawyer is a predictor of success as a mediator. In fact, in the Massachusetts program, where mediators handled cases valued in excess of $25,000, researchers found that lawyers did not perform better than non-lawyers. The mediators needed only to be comfortable working with lawyers and the law, the study concluded. The mediators in this study were trained in facilitative mediation, where the essential skills are in the mediation process, not in giving advice. In such mediation, the mediator's nonmediation training and experience are not so relevant as his or her current skills and abilities (Honoroff, Matz, and O'Connor, 1988).

The preference of organizations for lawyer-mediators has somewhat limited access to the market for those who are not and never have been lawyers. This means that those who are looking for such a mediator may need to search diligently.

From the sometimes heated debate in the Test Design Project over professional standards, several themes emerge. First, the findings from Wisconsin and Massachusetts concur with SPIDR's Commission on Qualifications in a surprising conclusion: no particular type or degree of prior education or job experience is an effective predictor of success as a mediator.

Our society is vastly overinvested in the culture of expertise. The best conflict resolution work is not about that. In desperation, we have used degrees and experience in law, accounting, therapy, and a variety of other fields as proxies for process skill. And we stubbornly refuse for the most part to look at process skill, which is vital to effective work in mediation. It is time to lay down the papers and reflect on what it is that we have to do and how best to do it. Evaluate mediators on their performance as perceived by their clients and by observers in their field. You will not be sorry you did. You may become the exception to the rule, learning to look first for process expertise, since a mediator is not there to tell you or anyone else what to do.

A mediator must be reasonably conversant with the language and context of the conflict.

To be effective, a mediator must be reasonably conversant with the language and context of the conflict. That is all. That is a far cry from expertise in the subject area of the conflict. With an understanding of what mediators do and how mediation works, you will be far more successful in finding the mediator who will do the best job for you.

TYPES OF MEDIATION

Generally the choice of mediator will determine the type of mediation process you are offered. For this reason, it is important to know about what's out there in terms of models. Then your choice will be better informed.

Evaluative Mediation

All mediation takes place under the umbrella of broad acceptance for the nonbinding Model Standards of Conduct for Mediators. A product of the joint efforts of representatives from SPIDR, the ABA, and the AAA between 1992 and 1994, this document represents the best thinking available on what was considered necessary to allow this radical new approach to conflict resolution to become established and to realize something of its potential. The keystone of the Model Standards is the requirement that mediators "recognize that mediation is based on the principle of self-determination by the parties."

Coerced agreement is clearly inappropriate. But as the mediator's power has been recognized, considerably greater refinement has infused the inquiry into just what it takes to ensure self-determination. For example, serious questions have been raised over the years over whether advice giving by the mediator is consistent with this insistence on self-determination.

To some extent, the advisory capacity of mediators may be curtailed by ethical considerations. *Advice* as used here is not simply providing information. It carries a value judgment and expresses an opinion. However, the information giving–advising dichotomy is not easy to recognize, as lawyers themselves are now finding out. For years, it has defined what was and what was not the practice of law. Lawsuits have been brought successfully against nonlawyer neutrals for what is called the unauthorized practice of law, based on this distinction. But now that lawyers are faced with having to apply it to themselves, they are finding that it is far too vague to be realistic, so the end of that story has not yet been told.

There has been a long debate over the past decade concerning whether evaluative mediation is actually mediation. Advisory mediation, the name given to mediations by subject area experts (not necessarily mediation experts), is evaluative in nature. Its purpose is to get a fix on the merits, sometimes of some technical issue, should the matter be tried. Evidentiary and technical arguments can be evaluated in this setting better than people problems. Advisory mediation is not to be confused with "muscle mediation," in which the mediator becomes an advocate for his position. Muscle mediation is clearly not mediation at all.

One of the biggest problems in treating evaluative mediation as mediation is the confusion of the public. By the late 1980s, courts had come up with a process called *neutral evaluation*.[5]

In the hands of an experienced trial lawyer or jurist, neutral evaluation, sometimes called evaluative mediation, also provides information about the disposition of local judges and juries. If the best way to resolve the dispute is to get an independent opinion, you may want what amounts to a neutral evaluation. If crafting remedies, putting people in touch with their own best judgment, or dealing with difficult people is the goal, facilitative mediation is more productive.

In the typical time-limited, court-type settlement conference, the neutral informs the parties of his expectations of the outcome at trial and may well tell them what he believes the case is worth. This approach requires the parties to have their information reasonably well in hand so that this advice will have meaning.

A particular subset of evaluative mediators is mediators with an apparent bias, which includes lawyers specializing in work for just one side, such as defense or plaintiff work. They fill a useful niche in the mediator offerings and are often engaged specifically for the benefit of their experience. Such arrangements are used by defendants who see many doubtful claims, such as the California State Automobile Association. They will select recognized plaintiffs' lawyers as mediators. When one of these lawyers says a plaintiff's case is weak, the plaintiff's lawyers are likely to listen.

Due in part to the pressure of court programs mandating cases into mediation, many lawyers now serve as mediators, although what they bring to mediation is still a practicing lawyer's mind: his way of envisioning the process and his view of his role. Notice I do not say *lawyer-mediator*. Many lawyers who do mediation are not lawyer-type mediators and are excellent mediators. A lawyer-type mediator is more likely to offer an opinion about the merits and what the parties should do.

The lawyer-type mediator has not yet changed his or her mind: it is still a lawyer's mind, focused on advice-giving and matters of substance, not a mediator's mind, focused on process and party control. There is nothing wrong with advice giving, provided that is what a client is seeking. Still, it would seem that the advice-giving role of lawyers can be far better invoked when only advice is specifically sought, as in neutral—and early neutral—evaluation. Sometimes neutral evaluators have some training in mediation skills and can help move counsel toward areas of agreement. But by the nature of their approach, they do not have the capacity to draw deep creativity from the parties or to potentiate the transformation of perspective, attitude, and even relationship that a skilled facilitative mediator can.

Mediation, if well managed, has the capacity to build awesome trust—something that the adversarially oriented lawyer-mind has no training and little or no experience dealing with. There are great opportunities within true mediation for creative outcomes for the parties. This lawyer-mind is not likely to bring these out. Those with lawyer-minds do not know what they do not know, for their mental maps may prevent them from recognizing that there is something more to know. Thus, there is greater potential for harm; a person with such an orientation who discovers the enormous capacity of mediation for building trust may lack skill in managing it for the benefit of the parties.

Much of the transformational potential of mediation can be lost if the mediator conceives of his or her role as primarily a deal maker. There is more likely to be a strictly bargaining quality to the mediation. Disputants and sometimes even their lawyers are more likely to experience their role as peripheral. Even when settlement is achieved, the pain and frustration of the conflict may continue to fester, poisoning everything participants later touch surrounding the conflict. It is not uncommon for this to leak into the rest of their lives as well. Just about everyone—lawyers, litigants, and judges—ends up feeling used and abused. Ask yourself whether this is necessary. Why not engage a mediator with some emotional intelligence and transform the baggage as well as resolving the formal conflict?

Facilitative Mediation

This mediation is generally free of advice. Facilitative mediators usually have significant experience mediating the type of dispute in question, unlike evaluative or advisory mediators, whose expertise most often comes from practicing law or some other profession (engineering, for example) in the subject area of the dispute.

The essential expertise in facilitative mediation is in the process—in mediating. If particular technical expertise is required, the mediator will often suggest bringing in a neutral expert or will bring in a technical co-mediator as needed. It is helpful if this expert has mediation training and skill.[6]

Facilitative mediation requires greater skill and more experience than advisory mediation. I have observed a small trend for advisory mediators to become facilitative mediators as their skill and experience grow. Once exposed to facilitative mediation, some evaluative mediators simply make it their own. It is a lot more fun and offers a lot more room for growth. The parties are treated more gently and more respectfully than in evaluative processes, and this is empowering to them. Facilitative mediators are more likely to have expertise in dealing with interpersonal problems. They may mediate in one field only, such as family law, where they develop an understanding of the field, or they may be generalists. Generalists offer opportunities for cross-fertilization, bringing to the situation techniques and strategies used in other types of disputes.

Lawyer-mediators (whether lawyer-mind or mediator-mind) have special issues and concerns that other types of mediators do not have.[7] Lawyers may be required to report something—lawyer misconduct, for example—while as a mediator, they must keep this confidential except under certain circumstances (Model Rules of Professional Conduct, 1997; Sub, 1994). Under the Proposed Model Rules of Professional Conduct of the Lawyer as Third Party Neutral (Center for Public Resources–Georgetown Commission, 1999), there are also numerous ethical restrictions placed on mediators' subsequent engagement by parties to mediation.[8] While these are not presently binding, they carry great weight with legislative drafters in several states.

More than a few commentators are observing that what the mediator does in mediation can determine whether what is happening is law practice or mediation. Thus, the evaluative mediation style carries the lawyer-mediator into even more difficult territory than simply being a lawyer who mediates would do. It is here that the role of a lawyer most overlaps the role of a mediator.

There are conflicting ethical obligations, the lawyer's being primarily to the client and the mediator's being primarily to the process (Nolan-Haley, 1999). This is something to keep in mind as your experience with mediators broadens.

If the mediator you select displays qualities you do not trust or care to work with, you have the option to stop the proceedings and go for another round with a mediator more to your liking. In most jurisdictions, even the fact that the matter was court referred does not tie you to any particular mediator after the preliminaries.

Functional Differences in Types of Mediation

Facilitative mediation is useful at any stage. In matters mediated too early to settle, parties may seek agreement on what is needed and how to get it, so that both sides may evaluate settlement options. One doesn't have to write ten letters or make twenty telephone calls to get what is needed. Little or no preparation may be needed in a facilitative mediation because there is more control. Settlement efforts may be halted at any time and the agenda turned to what each side needs to know to be able to resolve and get it.

The need to know is greatest in fact-finding processes, somewhat less in evaluative mediations, and much less in facilitative mediations. Facilitative and reflective mediators are experts in recognizing what they do not need to know. They know or quickly learn the language and the context of the dispute and help focus everyone on the issues seen as crucial to agreement. These issues, identified by the mediator and tested with the parties to ensure concurrence, may become the entire focus of the mediation. At times, some issues can become proxies for more or larger issues. Sometimes problems that infect a number of issues can be resolved for all issues when dealt with in one issue.

There is a story told of a test given to two men. Each was shown a particular field with uneven terrain. "Where does the water flow in this field?" each was separately asked. One took up a shovel and began turning over the earth in the field, looking for signs of the presence of water. One looked at the field first from one angle, then another, and then another and another. "There," he said, pointing to a faint trace of difference in the color of the green mantle clothing the field. Some people need to know everything about everything before they can do anything about anything. Others do not. That's the difference.

In evaluative mediation of cases with complex facts, such as construction, the parties must often go into detail in order to make the advice meaningful. Thus, processes that can take many days with advisory neutrals may take only a day or a few days with facilitative and reflective mediators.

In the end, most people want to make their own deal, not the mediator's deal, although they may want the mediator to develop a range of options with them. With several options on the table acceptable to each side, the intensity of feeling about a particular outcome is lessened.

As a general rule, well-mediated negotiations are secure from subsequent attack, although there may be a lot of arguments along the way in particularly contentious situations, and some of these may last for a while. Particularly in the political arena, nonmediated negotiations *do* blow up, bringing chaos where order is desperately needed. Consider the spotted owl controversy in the Pacific Northwest, where proposed regulations drove private landowners to harvest their timber way ahead of schedule, for fear of being prohibited from doing so through government regulation to protect the endangered owl. The government, acting without consultation and perhaps with little consideration of the likely consequences of its actions, rattled its saber, only to discover that its own actions had led to the situation it was trying to avoid. Each side would have been better off if it had tried a facilitated discussion first. The landowners might have remained with their long-term plans for their timbered properties, and the habitat for the spotted owl might have been increased gradually over time. No one will ever know.

How Mediators Use Pressure

An example of the different ways in which mediators work is their use of pressure. Mediators use varied techniques to pressure parties. To me, the issue is not the use of pressure but its direction. Some people advocate aggressive mediating that will pressure the parties toward settlement. Although many believe this is the most powerful approach, many highly skilled mediators think otherwise (Matz, 1994; Boskey, 1994). If the mediator pressures parties toward an outcome that the mediator has decided is best (contrary to ethical mandates governing mediation), the parties' control of their dispute is threatened. Yet the mediator is usually called in because the parties are at impasse. This is where mediator tenacity pays off. It is tenacity itself that can be a form of pressure.

Whether mediators should pressure the parties is not the question. The real issue is, pressure them to do what? Pressuring parties to buy into the mediator's view of a proper outcome is entirely different from pressuring them to release their grip on the short-term view, think of long-term interests, and take other steps that contribute to their power to make a wise decision. If the parties feel pressured by the mediator, there has been a coarse use of pressure, more likely perhaps in advisory processes than in facilitative ones. If the parties feel no pressure from the mediator, that mediator likely applied pressure skillfully and with great respect for the participants. There *are* pressures on the parties to a conflict. How awareness of these is managed by the mediator is a function of skill and the mediator's own awareness. Mediators coming from a facilitative frame are perhaps more open to moderating the effects of pressure than those who believe they have the answer people are seeking.

Deployment of Expertise

One key contribution of effective mediation is the mediator's ability to help position the parties so they can tap into their own wisdom. This ability requires not only human relations skills but a high level of mediator maturity as shown in his or her emotional, mental, and spiritual development.[9]

In the early days of construction mediation, many mediators received their training from nonlawyer mediation professionals.[10] They learned that it was the parties' dispute and ultimately the parties' responsibility to resolve it. Lawyers steeped in the culture and mental models of mediation think differently than do lawyers who are still thinking that what they are doing is practicing law. By virtue of their role as professional information givers and advisers, lawyers encounter built-in hurdles in shifting to a more facilitative role.

The kinds of complaints that Florida has received, for example, show common concerns that are unique to mediation: "failure of the mediator either to allow the parties to exercise self-determination, to act impartially or to refrain from providing professional advice" (Press, 1997, p. 913). That plus the very small number of complaints—fifty total between 1992 and 2000, out of approximately 100,000 references per year—suggests that little will be lost if party-selected mediators are not made subject to court-imposed standards (Sharon Press, interview, Jan. 23, 2001). The risks of standardization to the vitality and effectiveness of the mediation process may outweigh the benefits of having standards, but there has been some controversy on this point (Press, 1997; Brazil, 1991; Nicolau, 1988).

Formal ethical standards seem to be moving toward discouraging evaluations in order to protect the parties' right to self-determination.[11] It is widely viewed as improper for a mediator to give legal advice. The ABA Section of Dispute Resolution and SPIDR *Model Standards of Conduct for Mediators* (1994) states:

> The primary purpose of a mediator is to facilitate the parties' voluntary agreement. Mixing the role of a mediator and the role of a professional advising a client is problematic and mediators must strive to distinguish between the roles. A mediator should therefore refrain from providing professional advice. Where appropriate, a mediator should recommend that the parties seek outside professional advice [p. 3].

Nevertheless, there still is much room for mediators to express perceptions in ways that do not constrain the parties. It is important that they do so in situations where the parties are unrepresented and the problem of vulnerability to influence is compounded significantly. For example, the American Bar Association Standards permit mediators to "define the legal issues" but not to advise the parties based on the mediator's understanding of the legal situation (American Bar Association, 1994).

Duration of the Mediation

Facilitative mediations may take longer in smaller cases and be faster in complex cases. This is because in simple disputes, giving advice is faster than helping the parties to reach their own resolution. In complex disputes, the opposite is true. The beginning sessions must build trust and develop language, tools, and strategies for approaching the issues and concerns for there to be a high-quality negotiation. But once this foundation is laid, it may be followed by rapid progress, so that sometimes the mediation may end way ahead of schedule.

MAKING THE DECISION

The choice of mediator carries with it the choice of types of mediation. The following questions are useful to ask before choosing a mediator:

Is the problem a people problem? If so, facilitative mediation is best.

Do you want an expert opinion? Evaluative, advisory mediation combines the role of mediator and opinion giver. Another option is use of a facilitative mediator with an advisory co-mediator or neutral expert.

Are you ready to listen to advice? It is a mistake to use evaluative, advisory mediation to persuade the other party, because advice givers are not all that persuasive. Often when people say (without knowing the result) that a particular issue controls, if the opinion giver comes out against them, their minds quickly shift to a new ground for justification. A better test for the appropriateness of advisory mediation is, Are you ready to seek advice? If your mind is open, there is a better chance that the other side's mind will also be open.

Are you primarily trying to get a handle on the case? Facilitative mediation is safer.

Do you want a tough-minded mediator? Both facilitative and advisory mediation offer these.

Do you want a compassionate mediator? Facilitative mediators are perhaps more likely to fill this bill.

Do you want an evaluation of your arguments and positions? Both facilitative and advisory mediation offer these, but with different emphasis. A facilitative mediator is likely to present your weaknesses in confidential caucus as hurdles. An advisory mediator is perhaps more likely to question your view from the point of his or her expertise.

Do you want to address relationship concerns—business or personal? Select from the pool of facilitative and reflective mediators.

Are there downstream consequences of not healing the wounds inflicted by or exposed in the conflict? Seek a facilitative or reflective mediator.

No single mediator makes all clients happy, and that is all right. The question is whether the detractors' complaints raise concerns that might be important in a particular situation.

Mediating is a highly complex activity. When it is well done, it seems easy, even effortless. Poor mediators are very expensive, even if their services are free. Ask broadly experienced users of mediation what is the single most important factor in the power and potential of mediation, and they will reply, "It's the mediator." Good mediators are always a bargain.

Chapter Ten

Preparing to Mediate

Everything an Indian does is in a circle, and that is
because the power of the world always works in circles and
everything tries to be round.
NICHOLAS BLACK ELK,
BLACK ELK SPEAKS, JOHN J. NEIHARDT (2000)

Mediation preparation begins with an analysis of objectives. There will be objectives that address concerns in every aspect of your life and that of the organization involved. Dollars are likely a part of that, but rarely are they the whole of anyone's objectives. By acknowledging your deeper concerns, you enhance your ability to address them. Whatever they are, it helps to hold them lightly, keeping them subject to review based on new information and fresh perspective.

The decision to resolve or not should take into account the hazards of litigation. Most often, frustration and aggravation do not translate into the bottom line.

After your analysis comes implementation: what will it take to address the concerns you have identified? What information and people and what kinds of presentation and negotiation strategies are needed to ensure the desired outcome? Think mutuality. What goes around, comes around.

WHO SHOULD ATTEND THE MEDIATION

Having the right people present at the mediation is key to success. Sometimes lawyers and others make themselves more available for court procedures than for mediation. That is a mistake because it says litigation is more important than mediation. In fact, nothing is more important than for decision makers to be present at a mediation. This is one of the clearest rules about mediation.

The need for counsel in mediation varies. Family mediation, for example, is often done without lawyers present. However, this has become controversial where there is any question of a party's ability to negotiate (Grillo, 1991). In commercial mediation, where litigation is in the picture, there seems to be general agreement that lawyers should participate or at least be close to the negotiation process.

If you decide not to have lawyers participate, then it is important to ensure that any lawyer whose advice you are listening to at the time be kept informed on the mediation. This means allowing the lawyer to advise you going into the mediation and perhaps having the lawyer on standby during the mediation, available to take your call if needed. It may mean having the lawyer attend when an agreement is reached, so that a proper memorandum can be drawn up. (See Chapter Six and Appendix B.)

Others whose presence is desirable may include spouses and perhaps other members of the decision maker's family, if they have substantial influence. Claims supervisors might be needed. Experts whose information or reactions are important may be needed in person or on telephone standby. Sometimes key witnesses are held in reserve, for possible telephone interview.

With the decision about whose presence is needed comes the decision about whose presence is likely to be destructive. Sometimes a party's negotiating team includes an individual who will lose face if that side's position is compromised. To increase the chances of success, assess the liabilities as well as the assets of potential negotiating team members from your own and the other side as well.

Making and unmaking a negotiation team is delicate business. Often the team is assembled based on unexamined values and assumptions. When you seek to influence another side's choice of participants, learn to listen for those unexpressed interests, as a contractor did in the following case example.

Unmaking an Enemy

Owhy Corp. had a contract claim against a federal government agency. The official who made the adverse decision was the principal decider on the company's appeal. He had again denied its claim, and claims litigation was begun. This individual still had weight with the agency. What could the company do?

If Owhy had an enemy, this man was it. But everyone was powerless to get rid of him. At the suggestion of a mediator who was serving as a settlement consultant, company executives began to ask themselves exactly what value this individual represented to the other side and looked for a higher value that would permit them to get paid. The obstacle was studied from the perspective of "How does this person serve the other side's values?"

Could it be, for example, that the value this person represented was that of not paying excessive and unjust claims? Everyone in the agency would agree with that value. So long as that individual was seen as speaking for that value, he would continue to have influence. If the company could identify another important value that would be threatened by that individual's participation in the mediation, it might get a fairer hearing.

In casual meetings with agency counsel, the company's counsel emphasized that value—the value of paying just claims promptly—as part of making agency counsel aware of the depth of his preparation and the strength of his case. When it came time to identify the most constructive negotiation team members for each side, the name of the person presenting the obstacle was not mentioned. The claim was successfully negotiated at the ensuing mediation.

THE LESSON

Frontal assault creates a push-resistance dynamic. Adroitly avoiding this, the lawyer in this case used a collaborative strategy to engage opposing counsel by working to define and then to commit to mutual objectives. Looking at the values that motivate a player in a conflict situation and then aligning one's expressions of concern with those values is an effective way of accomplishing this.

CONVENING THE MEDIATION

A mediation does not just happen. It is the end product of steps taken by counsel, parties, and the mediator or mediation firm. Each is a co-creator of the mediation itself. The first stage is convening.

Attracting People to the Mediation Table

Some view convening as insignificant. The preliminaries are not as glamorous as the mediation itself. In the early years of modern mediation, new firms in the ADR market offered convening services, sometimes called "bringing the parties to the table," for free. They quickly found that there was a lot more to it than they imagined, and very few cases ever got to the table; they languished in the ADR firm's file drawer. As one claims adjuster in Minneapolis observed wryly, "I wish someone would pay *me* $100 a case [the filing fee then] to keep these cases in *my* file drawer."

The quality of the convening bears fruit in the mediation itself. It is true that attracting people to mediation is more complicated than relying on compulsory attendance by rule or order of court. It is also more beneficial. Mediators and others who write the letters and make the telephone calls to convene the parties open participants to creative approaches. They become hopeful about reaching resolution, an advantage when the sessions get tough later on.

Convening requires listening and speaking skills, and both a goal and process orientation. Frontal assault sets up resistance, even among those who are favorably inclined. This compromises the voluntariness that allows mediation to deliver on its promises. This is one of the reasons that court-ordered mediation often seems so burdensome to parties. Energy is invested in resistance, not in exploring the possibilities constructively.

Using the Mediator to Convene the Mediation

You do not need to get the other side to agree to mediate. Convening is often done by the mediator you select or the mediation firm's case manager. A third-party invitation sidesteps impasses that have already developed between the parties. The success rate in convening using professional mediators or case managers is above 80 percent, so the odds are good if you choose this course.

Doing Your Own Convening

When you convene a mediation, you are inviting others to participate in a remarkable process. It is unstructured but can be given structure as needed. It is personal but not dangerously confrontational, by virtue of the mediator's presence and role. It is sometimes helpful to think of convening as inviting people to a party or game. Yes, goes this reasoning, this is a serious situation, but let's be a bit more tolerant of each other and give it our best. In game mode, it is less stressful to handle the rejection and any stray verbal shots. Think of rejection as only an initial rejection, signifying no more than that something else needs to be done before mediation can take place.

The skills of a convener are those of a negotiator, for convening is itself a negotiation. The objective of convening is simply to bring the parties together with at least enough interest to stay a while. The only commitment is to show up. It works even if people come just because they are curious.

Convening Skills

Careful listening helps one hear between the lines. Many people are word oriented and take words at face value. When someone says she is not interested in mediation, that is viewed as a final statement.

In one joint telephone conference with two counsel during a convening, a mediator had occasion to talk to one of them after the other got off the line.

"You see," the lawyer said, "no dice."

"I wouldn't be so hasty," the mediator said. "I believe the proposal will fly; it simply needs some fine tuning."

"But I heard him say no," the lawyer insisted.

"I heard that too," the mediator said, "but it wasn't a final no. You have room to maneuver."

The case settled in mediation not long after.

Skilled negotiators look beyond the words to the context in which they are spoken, the tone of voice, even the assumptions on which the statements are based. They seek to understand the underlying cause of resistance.

Listening with a judgmental attitude is worthless for this purpose. Destructive self-talk, such as "They'll never listen," sets up a self-fulfilling prophecy. The need to be right is often so strong that people would rather lose the opportunity to mediate than be wrong about their opponent's resistance. Not surprisingly, they

Destructive self-talk, such as "They'll never listen," sets up a self-fulfilling prophecy.

often do lose. Listening skills and strategic thinking are tools of the negotiator. An example of how they are used is this mediation of a construction case.

Winning the Judge's Support

One of the parties in an eight-party case was reluctant to commit to mediating. The case manager talked with other key counsel in the case about how they might use the upcoming court status conference. They decided to mention the interest in mediating to the judge. The strategy worked. The judge took a substantial interest in the proposed mediation and set the next status conference for one week after the mediation date. "I want to hear all about the mediation," the judge concluded. After that, the reluctant party agreed to participate.

THE LESSON

There was no need to accuse the reluctant party before the court. That strong-arm tactic would have been a weaker strategy, since in this instance the court could not have compelled attendance at mediation. Mentioning the upcoming mediation to the court put pressure on the reluctant lawyer. He did not want to have to explain at the next status conference why his client did not participate. Although he left the hearing with his options intact, he was persuaded that it was in his client's best interests to participate.

Verbal Strategies and Skills

The verbal skills used to convene a negotiation are quite different from the verbal skills of advocacy. In negotiation and mediation, words are used to acknowledge feelings and affirm factual assertions and arguments. Verbal skills help give back to the speaker a version of what he or she said that minimizes any dead-end, destructive comments and emphasizes those that were creative and constructive.

You respond to the dead-end observations at the feeling level. You acknowledge the feelings the speaker is expressing rather than the words of the communication. This tells the speaker that he or she has been heard and understood.

When you respond directly to the words by arguing, this convinces the speaker that you are not capable of hearing what he or she is saying. To reason with a person who does not listen will be fruitless, and so the discussion goes nowhere.

Following are some sample exchanges that might occur during an invitation to mediate. The comments that follow provide insight into the dynamics of these telephone communications. Test your own reactions to what is being said on both sides.

Here is the initial invitation:

I've been thinking. Maybe it would be useful to try mediation at this point. We know the rough outlines of the situation. It's going to take a lot of work, time, and money to do the needed discovery to refine this very much more. What if we sit down with our counsel and a mediator and see what we can accomplish?

Take the invitation apart, piece by piece:

I've been thinking.

> This indicates an interest in working creatively toward resolution. It can catch an opponent off-guard.

Maybe it would be useful to try mediation at this point.

> You sound tentative, though your resolve may be made of steel, by inviting a productive discussion rather than an argument.

We know the rough outlines of the situation. It's going to take a lot of work, time, and money to do the needed discovery to refine this very much more.

> This general justification for the idea of mediating invites a discussion about where the parties are. It puts you both on the same side, with a mutual interest in the efficient resolution of differences. It establishes the area of common interest. From there you can pick off issues that divide you.

What if we sit down with a mediator and see what we can accomplish?

> "What if" is the classic way of forwarding an idea without ownership. This enables the listener to make it his or her own idea and gets authorship off the table as a possibly divisive issue.

That's a good start. But the real work begins with what follows.

Response 1: Rejection Based on Perception of the Merits

There's really nothing to mediate. I just don't think you have a case.

There are many ways to respond to what is wisely considered the *initial* rejection. Here are some of them.

Initiator: Acknowledgment, Opening the Discussion

I know you really believe in your position.

> This responds to the feeling of frustration but avoids an argument about whether there is something to mediate.

And you know I've been committed to mine. Maybe there's something we've overlooked. If one or the other of us is wrong, I'd sure rather know now than later.

> There are several things here for the opposing party to agree with. One of them is the idea that you may have overlooked something. You also follow up with a practical observation that if someone doesn't have a case and finds out early, a lot of wasted effort is saved. This reinforces the idea that you are open to reason.

What have we got to lose by spending a few hours in mediation?

> Discussion is still open. You have provided food for thought; if you do not get agreement now, you may get it later. You've also put mediation in perspective by showing that few resources are involved in trying it out.

Response 2: Rejection Based on Personal Considerations

I think your side isn't being honest. What's the use of talking when there is so little trust?

Initiator: Opening the Discussion

Well, we can agree right now to try this case and forget the possibility of resolving it ourselves at a lot less cost in time and money.

> This is the consequence of holding the view expressed. Often a person does not realize that views such as this mean literally that there will never be anything to talk about.

Or we can see what the possibilities are. With mediation, it's a lot easier to deal with people issues like this. And whatever certainty is needed to conclude an agreement, we can negotiate about.

You discuss the implications of this serious lack of trust specifically to see if you can get behind the categorical statement to a place where reason will prevail.

We're only talking about a few hours of our time.

Again you put mediation in perspective.

Response 3: Rejection Based on Timing

This case isn't ready to settle yet. What's the point?

The assumption is that mediation is useful only when it's time to settle. Yet much time and money can be saved by using mediation to secure agreements on procedures that will lead to settlement. And a surprisingly high proportion of mediated matters do settle, even though one or another party thought things weren't ready to settle yet.

Initiator: Acknowledges, Gives New Information, Lays Groundwork for Follow-up

You may be right.

This is one of your most useful phrases. It admits nothing but is read by your listener as a sure sign you are hearing and understanding what he or she is saying.

But I've been surprised in several situations in which cases I knew wouldn't settle in mediation in fact did.

This shows empathy with the other side's viewpoint yet provides new information about how these perceptions are often erroneous.

Also, we've got these expert issues on the horizon. If we just got together to look for a better way of handling them, it would be worthwhile.

This gives the other side something specific to focus on rather than generalities. Also, you are in prime time to persuade. Those who know they have been heard and understood are far more receptive to what is being offered.

I don't know about you, but I would rather not make a career out of this case.

In litigation, the other side is often convinced that you want to drag out the case. It is a strategic decision whether and when to disabuse them of this idea. In discussions around mediation, this impression can serve as additional reason that mediation might be helpful. Also, it serves to remind opposing counsel of his own client's needs and interests, something it is all too easy to overlook in the pressures of litigation.

It would be a waste to keep slugging it out, only to discover on the courthouse steps that we could have resolved this ages ago.

This cuts to the chase. Everyone gets hurt by delay for delay's sake. And it helps everyone to know for sure whether a case has to be tried.

STRATEGIC PREPARATION

If you are using mediation rather than litigation as the envelope or container for the conflict, you can relax in the preparation phase. Review what you know of the other side's thinking; then go behind and beneath it. What assumptions and what values are driving it? Consider how you could approach these while you look around for more congruent assumptions and values. Always bring a draft memorandum of agreement, since settlements often happen even in the earliest mediations.

Because mediation works to secure agreement on what you need and how you are going to get it, you need only prepare appropriately. In a 1994 survey of the use of mediation in the construction industry, more than 60 percent of the respondents favored mediation, even in the absence of discovery (Stipanowich and O'Neal, 1996). There is an orchestral quality to a group of architects, engineers, contractors, subcontractors, and occasionally owners coming together in mediation. As the mediator draws out the story from the varying perspectives, participants are moved to contribute what they know. I have felt at times that I was conducting an orchestra and only the players knew the score and I did not. When it was time for information from the engineers, they would step forward and provide it, like the trombones. When the subcontractors' contributions were needed, they would fill in the essential pieces, like the wind instruments. The architects might come in with the overall picture, like the string section. And when the contractors speak, it can sound like the brass section. Discovery, with its adversarial quality, cannot do anything like this. Moreover, it takes a lot of time and is very costly. In construction mediations I have done, huge misunderstandings were cleared up in just a few hours to a few days, and a whole picture was put together with areas of agreement and disagreement duly noted for follow up.

With almost no preparation, you might take a run at settling a case you consider worth little more than nuisance value or one in which you feel the parties are not so far apart. If this does not result in resolution, you could agree to resume at another date, after identifying what each side will do to prepare for further mediation. Nothing is lost, and indeed much is gained, by setting the negotiation process in motion.

On the eve of a trial or in a situation where you anticipate there will be no opportunity for another mediation session, you might want to prepare more extensively. Or you may prepare strategically, focusing on what you think will be most important and having the rest of the information accessible. On the other hand, you may want to save the expense of preparation, as one San Francisco lawyer does who handles a lot of construction disputes and is experienced in the use of facilitative mediation. He advises his clients: "You should prepare for the mediation as little as possible. The reason for this is that you conserve costs and you can control the mediation process anyway. If an issue comes up that you're not prepared for, you can break and go do the necessary work to deal with it" (Novich, 1991). (For situations where extensive preparation is always required, see Chapter Fifteen.)

Advisory mediation is less amenable to this flexible approach, but it could still be used to improve cost-effectiveness, with the advance concurrence of the mediator. Forewarned, the mediator will not be expecting to give his opinion before it is timely.

Use the Mediator

A major resource in the preparation phase of the mediation is the mediator. Some mediators offer confidential discussion opportunities to each side before the mediation, in person or by telephone. Often in a relatively short time, perhaps half an hour, you can get a host of useful perspectives on how to use the mediation most effectively.

If you have been immersed in adversarial processes, you may think initially that the one you prepare to persuade is the judge or jury or the mediator. In facilitative mediation, it is the other side you must persuade. Each side must find some benefit in the outcome, or they will not buy into it. The mediator's experience is extremely useful in helping you to shift your thought processes to persuading the other side.

Another use of the mediator is to build congruent expectations on both sides about what will happen in the mediation. He may help ensure that where the parties so desire, each side is prepared to meet and receive what the other is saying. For example, if one side will bring an expert, the other side better have an expert present or on telephone standby to help evaluate the presentation.

Plan to use the mediator or mediation firm for all discussions about what will happen in the mediation. Either in private or joint preliminary session or by telephone, you can talk with the mediator about what type of presentation and approach will be most effective and what you and the other side need to know in order to evaluate settlement options. This discussion may touch on experts, audiovisual aids, and witnesses who could be useful either as part of the presentation or in reserve. The discussion will help establish the critical focus on persuasion and on quality discussions rather than argument.

Negotiating without the mediator about what issues are to be discussed can consume a great deal of time. Counsel with little mediation experience have a tendency to overstructure the discussions rather than take advantage of the flexibility of mediation. The benefit of the mediator's experience is also lost in these pre-mediation skirmishes.

Suspend Disbelief

You can improve your odds of success in mediation by being willing to believe, however briefly, that you will succeed in reaching agreement. A good mediation causes this to happen spontaneously.

Within a short time, you begin to act and speak as though it were going to succeed. You can see the mediator deal with difficulties and notice that a pattern of agreements is being developed. You will help to devise a framework for working out differences and see the benefit of the parties' receiving positive reinforcement for their successes. You and the others become more creative and more reasonable, and the discussion becomes more a problem-solving exercise than an exercise in futility.

Evaluate Information Needs

A key item on your premediation checklist is information. It is part of your mediation tool kit. If you are going to a mediation to settle the matter, be sure to bring the information you will need to support your arguments and calculations. Look at the information needs of both parties, and determine whether you have what you need to evaluate settlement options. If you do not, should you try to get it before or during mediation? Ask yourself the same questions about the other side.

Seek Mutuality

One's own readiness is useless if the other side is not adequately informed. This is a key strategy. Once again, things have to work for all, or they work for none. Too many times I have heard one counsel say, "Yes, he was calling me about those documents all the time, but they weren't very important to me, and it was a lot of trouble. I was too busy." Often those are the very documents that would have enabled the other side to evaluate settlement options and were crucial to getting the requester to agree with the foot-dragging counsel's view of the case.

Use Surprise Sparingly

Surprise needs to be carefully evaluated. If the surprise relates to something that stands on its own and does not invite inquiry, it is good to use it in the mediation. (As an example, see "The Silver Bullet" in Chapter Eight.) If, however, it is something that cries for further investigation, think carefully about whether to disclose it in advance so that the other side will be prepared to respond to it. It is fine to use surprise, but have in mind that insurance carriers in particular react poorly to surprise. The more complex the decision-making structure is on the other side, the greater the risk is of using surprise. It can grind the process to a halt until appropriate decision makers on the other side are consulted.

When insurance carriers are involved in big cases, the person with authority to increase the reserves on a claim substantially may be back at the home office. Many of these close at 4 P.M. eastern time. If you wait until the afternoon to introduce new information that substantially raises the ante in a case, particularly in the western states, you may have lost the opportunity to have the mediator work on both sides' perceptions of the value of that information. There is a sense of urgency that builds in mediation. Take advantage of it.

Assess the Timing and Extent of Disclosure

In planning premediation or mediation session disclosures, there are degrees of openness. You have exceedingly fine control over the flow of information in mediation. Information can be presented, insinuated about, leaked, or withheld.

Decide the timing of providing information in the mediation itself based on what is going on. What is to be gained? What might be lost? How receptive is the opponent? Does the mediator need this information to penetrate the other side's approach to the issue? The tendency in mediation is to inform rather than hold back because most information is truly necessary for the parties to close the gap in their views sufficiently in order to reach an agreement. You make these decisions moment by moment as the mediation proceeds.

Construction mediations, for example, usually involve active participation by the principals so that some joint understanding can be built, piece by piece, out of the experience and recollection of the parties. The mediator keeps this information giving in balance. A party who feels that he or she is giving all of the information sees it as giving up power and feels taken advantage of. This destroys trust and threatens the viability of the negotiation.

FORMS AND MODES OF PRESENTATION

There are many ways of presenting information in mediation.

Oral Presentation

The chief way of presenting information is orally. And for a forum, you need a joint session. I do not support the trend in some areas toward a mediation process that is strictly caucusing. That is cutting off both legs in a misguided attempt to cut to the chase. There is great opportunity in joint process—both to show another that they have been heard and to actually be heard yourself. All this is lost in a purely caucusing model.

Mediation is an oral process. Enjoy it. Think of yourself as a good storyteller. Since the story ultimately must persuade not the mediator but the other side, be gracious and generous in your story, and be relevant. Venting is all right, but dumping is not. In Greek mythology, the Augean stables were owned by Augeas, king

Mediation is an oral process.

of Elis, in Greece. Three thousand oxen occupied the stables, which had not been cleaned in thirty years. One of the labors of Hercules, son of Jupiter and a human mother, was to clean them in a day. He did so by diverting and joining two rivers to run through the stables, leaving them entirely clean in only one day. If your side's situation resembles the Augean stables, cluster and group items so as not to seem to be presenting a litany of grievances. (See "Building Trust Through Sharing Control" in Chapter Two.)

Your oral presentation is the way you position yourself in the mediation. It is important to organize it either chronologically or in some other logical fashion. When making the statement, include all important parts of your position. Do not assume that your listeners remember everything in your written presentation. Even if they did, they would not give it the emphasis you do. If some points are covered in detail in a written submission, briefly summarize them in your oral presentation, so that the flow and meaning of your presentation are clear.

Remember that your audience is the other side. The mediator is a translator and interpreter of your position to the other side, and vice versa. Give her something to work with, even if you believe the other side knows every bit of it already.

Your opening may run from a few minutes to several hours, depending on the case. As you finish, some mediators concisely and elegantly summarize what you have said, so be prepared to determine whether that summary is accurate and complete.

Verbal Information

Information from witnesses or those responsible for the operation of systems can be very powerful. Sometimes, as in construction mediation, this information is given by individuals through their ongoing participation in the discussion. But even nonparticipants have a chance to tell what they know in a coherent and orderly fashion.

The mediator sets the stage as a quest for information. The qualities of an adversarial process are minimized. When an opposing party needs additional information, the mediator usually asks the questions. This eliminates the adversarial crafting of the questions that can turn a simple inquiry into a much more difficult process. An expert may be required to state his qualifications, and any reasonable question is fair. The neutrality of questioning allows the witnesses to look as good as they can so that the mediator's reactions, given privately and later, will be meaningful.

Another way of offering information is to have a witness available on telephone standby. Offering a witness for an off-the-record interview shows openness as well as confidence. Imagine that you have negotiated to a point where it is obvious that someone to whom you have access has the key information everyone needs to be able to move forward. You lean forward and say, "If you like, you can find out right now. So-and-so is available on telephone standby. We have a speaker phone here. Let the mediator make the call, and ask the questions. Let's see what happens."

Sometimes the opposing side refuses what seems to be a golden opportunity for fear it is being set up or because it does not feel prepared. The point has been made perhaps better than the witness could make it. When the questioning does proceed, a lot of erroneous supposition can quickly be laid to rest. If you are the one surprised by such an offer and are fearful of accepting it, ask for a caucus, invite the mediator, and go along with the interview if you can. You can always put what is said in context if you don't like it. And you may find it not so bitter a pill as you fear.

Documents and Summaries

When you anticipate that the mediation will be fact intensive, it is good to have key documents or important summaries at hand. People rarely see the same thing in documents, so your ability to pinpoint the support for your assertions can have great weight. This is particularly true when the evidence is unequivocal. If multiple parties are involved, it is sometimes useful to have key documents on transparencies, so that everyone can see them by overhead projection at the same time. This gets everyone looking in the same direction and makes it easier to spot areas of agreement. When everyone is looking in the same direction, there is a certain rhythmic quality to it as well, which improves receptivity in the group.

Rules, Regulations, and Decisions

When a rule, regulation, or decision is important to your side, have the full text available. Highlighting of particularly relevant passages may be helpful. Let the mediator review it before plunging into extensive argument about its meaning. Then you will get more benefit from the mediator's confidential reaction.

Written Submissions

At times it is helpful to make a written submission to the mediator in advance of the mediation. If the facts are unduly complicated or a new or novel issue requires briefing, by all means do so. Sometimes providing the mediator with copies of pertinent papers already filed in court is sufficient, or you may want to prepare new material. Any submission may be shared with the other side or at your option be entirely confidential—something the other side has not seen and will not see.

These submissions may run from a few pages to several bankers' boxes. Remember that mediation is an oral process. Oral presentations provide a common ground for negotiations. The litigants get to hear their story told, and the mediator has a lot more material to refer to when discussions become more intense. (See Chapter Eleven.)

Settlement Agreement Drafts

Many kinds of settlements fall into well-defined patterns for documentation: a dismissal with prejudice by the plaintiff of the lawsuit; a full release of the defendants and a fairly spare settlement agreement, outlining who has agreed to do what and when, perhaps with required statutory language. It saves a great deal of time later on to bring drafts of the *boilerplate,* legal language commonly used, drawn in as neutral language as possible, with appropriate blanks. Laptop computers also are valuable, particularly in settings where a fully equipped office is not available. (See Appendix B.)

PREPARING YOURSELF

Disputes create a kind of stress or compression in us. Common phrases like "he's sure wound up" and "she always works under a head of steam" speak to this stressful compression. Most people bring this right into the mediation. The mediator will do everything possible to allow it to be safely diffused, but you can help with this process. (For an exercise to relieve the stress or compression of the dispute and become far more effective in negotiation, see Appendix A.)

If at some level the mediation fails to achieve the resolution you feel you need, be prepared to explore what information each side might need to be able to evaluate settlement options better. You need to be able to listen well, to reflect wisely and to make decisions.

Convening and preparing for a mediation offer many opportunities for strategy. Keep the strategy constructive by focusing on mutuality—making common cause with the other side, looking for mutual gain, like Black Elk, who understood the circularity of everything we do. If you are not ready to do this, put the matter aside and come back to it when you're fresher. Your perspective is crucial to your success.

Chapter Eleven

The Art of Mediating

Why not go out on a limb? That's where the fruit is.
WILL ROGERS

Until now, you have been seeing the game of mediation somewhat from the grandstand. Now let's look at the inner life of mediation, what is happening beneath the surface. Mediation is much more enjoyable when you do your part. It is not just about settling a dispute. It is about changing people's relationships to the problem and to each other. The people side of the equation is as important as the legal and factual sides.

Mediation is the process, but satisfaction is the goal. We often make the mistake of defining our goal as battlefield victory, assuming that this will satisfy our interests. We keep plugging away until we achieve the goal, even if it is a pyrrhic victory. Dogged determination of this type is not appropriate in mediation. In mediation, there is an opportunity to reexamine goals as well as strategies to see if the way they have been defined ignores realities and imposes needless burdens on securing satisfaction. Goals need adjustment from time to time until achieving them satisfies our true interests.

The goal of satisfying underlying interests—even some that are not in our minds when we approach mediation—is a worthy one. To achieve it, we entertain various hypotheses about what it will take, without being captured by them. Success is more likely when we are open to the myriad forms in which satisfaction may come rather than being locked onto one form only.

THE MEDIATOR'S BALANCING ROLE

Some critics fear that a party will enter mediation with a strong hand, only to have the mediator bail out the weaker party. One experience with facilitative mediation will put this fallacy to rest. Mediation is too dependent on trust to get very far with high-handed tactics, although complaints about pressure tactics are more common in evaluative mediations, where the neutral gives an opinion and then is seen as overly enthusiastic about having the parties accept it. The term *power balancing* is not entirely accurate. It is not positions that are balanced in mediation, but the ability to participate equally in a negotiation. Power in most marriages, for example, is exercised differently but is nonetheless balanced. While one spouse has the power of speaking, the other has the power of silence. While one understands finances, the other understands emotions. The divorce arena provides considerable insight into the concept of power balancing.

Good divorce mediators, for example, generally work to balance negotiating power between the parties. This tends to produce agreements that are voluntary rather than coerced. With a stake in keeping the agreements, both sides are more likely to live up to them. The mediator may therefore encourage the silent party to speak or the speaking party to become silent, to educate one about finances and the other about emotions. This breaks the power system on which the marriage or business relationship was based and empowers the parties by moving them out of their dependency.

Sometimes a party is unaware of the power he or she wields and fails to take responsibility for outcomes. Good mediators frequently have an understanding about where real power lies, and they use this awareness to ensure that we look at the long- and intermediate-term consequences as well as the immediate effects of our position (Haynes, 1988).[1]

In advisory mediation, the adviser's expertise automatically balances the parties' positions to some extent. A weak negotiator is protected since there is an external measurer of fairness. Power balancing in certain other situations may be necessary when the parties are unrepresented or counsel are not personally present. Without two parties capable of negotiating, mediation must be terminated.

Experienced negotiators want to be sure there is someone on the other side capable of negotiating. In one case, a distraught plaintiff in a wrongful-termination case fired her lawyer midway through a mediation. She then asked to meet privately with the lead defense counsel. There was a risk the mediation might have to be terminated because of the plaintiff's distraught condition. The mediator, the plaintiff's former counsel, and defense counsel discussed ways of helping the plaintiff see it was in her own best interest to continue using her counsel, who had been doing a good job under very difficult circumstances. A lawyer is not free just to walk away when his client fires him under stress. He is ethically bound to act in the client's best interests, even though he no longer may speak for the client. This can be very tricky, as it was here. After a brief, private conversation with defense counsel, the plaintiff asked to meet with the mediator and agreed to the reinstatement of her lawyer. The mediation proceeded to a conclusion that satisfied both the plaintiff and her former employer.

Mediation may reveal that power is not where we suppose it is. Sometimes the apparently powerful party is utterly dependent on the seemingly weaker party. The weaker party refuses to take responsibility for the power he or she holds, and the parties remain deadlocked.

In commercial mediation, power balancing may be addressed to either side or both. For example, in one wrongful-termination case in Chicago, the plaintiff, a bright, older black man, was mentally disturbed and had managed in his brief time with the company to humiliate most of the top brass and threaten shareholder relations by disruptive behavior at the annual shareholders' meeting. He came to the mediation with his third lawyer, having discharged the previous two. The company felt it held all the cards. Nevertheless, the plaintiff had caused and was continuing to cause a lot of embarrassment.

The mediator began balancing the power by first suggesting to the corporate defendant that beating someone who was mentally impaired was not much of an accomplishment. The company might better satisfy its interest in justice by working for a compassionate resolution. It turned out that an employee mental health benefit program was available, so the company began to be willing to move toward settlement. The mediator then appealed to the plaintiff, the apparently weaker party, to put the fight into the context of the rest of his life and decide how much to sacrifice now in pursuing revenge. He finally began to let go of his vendetta, and his counsel and counsel for the defendant worked out a settlement that met his needs.

Because resolution requires mutual approval, people eventually put aside the one-sided view that for them to win, the other side must lose. (See Appendix C.) This is the beginning of problem solving and often the beginning of a negotiated resolution.

THE CONTAINER

Good mediators can create and, with the parties, hold the quality environment needed to make rapid progress in any kind of negotiation and to enable people to go as deep as they want to go. It is more than an atmosphere. It is a crucible, this quality of space, which allows the most difficult and emotionally substantive concerns to be dealt with in a safe way.

A high-quality space feels safe. It invites honest expression of feelings and open exploration of assumptions and other underpinnings of perspectives and postures. When a high-quality space has been created, the parties become absorbed in the process of transforming this conflict. They may begin taking responsibility for maintaining the quality of space—that is, the container—as we saw in "Vulnerability Works" in Chapter Two. Some mediators give few breaks and no time for lunch (or dinner for that matter); food is brought in for working sessions. The intensity and focus promote resolution without hardship, because everyone's attention is fully on the subject.

Creating and maintaining a safe, high-quality space requires mediator attentiveness to subtle shifts in power balance, confidence, a participant's trust in the process, feeling states, an ability to present one's side or to hear and comprehend the other's. Mediators use many tools to allow this to happen. One is the now familiar read-back, the succinct reflection on the essence of the information given by a party together with acknowledgment of the feelings conveyed.

An expert read-back acknowledges the constructive portions of a party's presentation but responds to the feelings behind angry or destructive words. In it, the mediator shapes his own observations, responses, and wording in such a way as to allow the parties to hear what has been said and to clarify the focus. A half-hour presentation can be summarized in a read-back as a clearer and more cogent synopsis in perhaps two or three minutes. The technique is an art form in the hands of expert mediators and sets the tone for the entire mediation. It also promotes mutual understanding.

Another tool is the *check-in*. With large, multiparty conflicts, it is difficult for the mediator to have any kind of meaningful understanding of where people are—that is, how comfortable or uncomfortable they are, where the difficulty is in the way they are seeing the possibilities, and what concerns them most at any given stage. The check-in is a way of assessing whether a person is participating effectively. One simple check-in is to ask, "How do you feel? What do you think?" This invites feelings to be expressed, so it serves a balancing function, putting people in touch with their emotions as well as what is going on in their minds. (This tool was used in "Vulnerability Works" in Chapter Two.)

The container is what allows people to relax, to put the accumulated hurts aside and become constructive. It encourages the transformation of the parties' relationship from adversarial to problem solving, and it sets the stage for such healing as may occur at that time. Parties who are absorbed in the conflict may not recognize it early in the mediation. At times, they never do, but they nevertheless get the benefit.

The greatest resource in the mediator's hands is the participants. You as participant, as you emulate and amplify the respect, open-mindedness, intensive listening, and unpretentiousness that characterize good mediators, are contributing to the safety and reliability of the container that the mediator created. Also, by giving the mediator the feedback you can—whatever it is you think the mediator needs to know—you draw the greatest abilities and skills from him or her. You are no passive observer, unless you choose to be.

GETTING TO FEELINGS

Mediation is the time to bring out the best that is in us. This does not mean to put on a false front. Nothing is more transparent than smiles that fade the minute the other person takes their eyes off us. Courtesy, consideration for others, compassion (feeling with), dignity, and presence (attention) are all qualities that lead to good results. The power of attention is greatly underestimated in our culture. In negotiations, real listening that is open and nonjudgmental changes the nature of the interactions so that discussions may become fruitful. The same is true in health and healing. Physician Deepak Chopra writes:

Real listening that is open and nonjudgmental changes the nature of the interactions so that discussions may become fruitful.

> When you "pay attention" to something, you shift from passive to active awareness. Attention exerts far more control than people ordinarily realize. That is because we are victims of passive awareness. A person in pain is aware of the pain but not that he can make it increase, diminish, appear or disappear. Yet all this is true. People can walk on fire, for example, because they can control their level of pain; more remarkably, they can control whether their feet actually get burned—that, too, is under the control of attention [Chopra, 1989, p. 237].

Inevitably there are gaps in the process when the mediator is caucusing with another party and we do not have a specific or general assignment. It is tempting to fall into storytelling, running down the opposition, or getting on the cell phone to deal with other matters. Such activities may be interpreted by the other parties as lack of commitment to the process, no matter how hard everyone has worked previously. Keeping your present attention on the situation, realizing how things might be when a mutually satisfactory resolution is reached, letting go little by little of the pain and frustration of the conflict—all this helps strengthen the container and promotes greater healing through the process.

People start working harder—shifting into low gear—to see if there is some way to reach a mutually satisfactory resolution. One side's serious consideration of proposals and alternatives is a sign of respect for the other side and vice versa. Good mediators will be acknowledging the sincere efforts of all parties to make progress, in part because there is such effort and in part to encourage deeper commitment. It is usually a self-fulfilling prophecy: by expecting the best, they draw out the best.

All sides may have a lot of feeling tied up in the dispute. Mediation allows this to be expressed in joint session, private caucus with the mediator, and private talks with counsel. The key to success in joint sessions is to honor those feelings by acknowledging them. No matter how angry the words are, considerate response to the feelings underlying them will let the person know that he has been heard and understood.

Counsel may also have a lot of feelings tied up in a matter. Tensions between counsel encumber the entire process. By keeping calm, we can seize the opportunity we might otherwise have missed. Consider this example, which demonstrates how appropriate humor can change the atmosphere.

Counsel Wrangle Resolved

This seven-party California construction case involved two counsel who truly hated each other. One defense lawyer had filed motions to have the other removed from the case, citing that this person had been a witness to some of the events under consideration. The plaintiff property owner's lawyer had retaliated with complaints to the bar association about this counsel's conduct. Their warring was poisoning everyone's efforts to make progress toward settlement.

The mediation got off to a rocky start, and the main agreement was to convene a second day of mediation in the plaintiff's home town. The plaintiff's chief counsel was host. All the other lawyers had to travel some distance to get to the second day of mediation. The morning session went slowly, in part due to the stormy atmosphere contributed by the two battling counsel.

At lunch, the group was taken to a nearby club. When the two arrived late, there were only two empty seats, side by side, at the round dining table. During the lunch, they managed to stumble through passing the salt and pepper, the butter, the rolls, and the coffee, to the others' well-masked amusement. As the group walked back to the conference room, a gentle humor broke out, and the two began to let go of some of their hostility.

During the afternoon session, the two began to be constructive. The mediator drew attention to everyone's good efforts. Momentum to settle began to build. The case settled in a third day of mediation.

It's always darkest just before dawn. In the nature of things, hurdles in mediation sometimes appear insurmountable. You are tempted to walk out. What reason could there be for staying, with the other side being so intransigent? Watch and wait. The mediator knows where the discussions are hung up and may become blunt with one or both sides. Allow time for that all to take effect. People and perspectives change, but this takes time. The mediator equivalent to a body block is to step between you and the door and plead for a little more time to allow the process to work. This is how President Carter brought about the Camp David Accord. Menachem Begin and Anwar Sadat were prototypical protagonists in matters of personal style—one a generalist, the other a "details" person with less concern for the overarching form. Yet one of the most difficult frameworks for peace was negotiated in just thirteen days, through the skill and tenacity of President Jimmy Carter and his team (Kahn, 1988).

OPPORTUNITIES FOR RECONCILIATION

Once agreement is reached, counsel will often work to hammer out the terms of the written agreement. (This process is described in Appendix B.) While counsel are drafting agreements, the clients may be getting back on speaking terms. The mediator may sit in at these casual moments, to get the discussion going or simply to provide a stable, warm-hearted presence that sometimes makes it easier for people to talk. At the conclusion of one construction mediation, the parties, both businessmen, gave the mediator a standing ovation. It is not unusual for former employees who sue their employers to become constructive members of the employer's loyal alumni after a successful mediation.

There is time for talk about plans for the future. Future thinking is often blocked by the weight and demands of the dispute. This kind of talk is a healthy sign that the dispute is being left behind, so each person can move on to new things.

BUILDING POWER

Power is often thought of as manipulating or as synonymous with force. And certainly force is a crude form of power and underlies much of our collective bargaining processes (Ury, Brett, and Goldberg, 1988). It is based on the assumption that for one side to win, the other side must lose, an odd operating guideline for a relationship. In fact, *power is the ability to get results.* Authority is the coercive force that depends on one's position to get people to do things whether they like it or not. As pointed out in the Introduction to this book, it is far weaker than true power, which inspires people to join in common cause and become their own leaders for mutual benefit.

Mediation plays into the important new-mind value of taking responsibility for both creating and resolving the conflicts we find ourselves in. The remedies available in mediation are limited only by the imagination. Often the items with little or no monetary value prove critical to final agreement. People routinely agree in mediation to do things no court would compel them to do, for they see that these agreements serve their own underlying interests as well as satisfy the other side.

Interest satisfaction determines the quality of the resolution. Interests are what lie behind what people say they want. Both a plaintiff's demand for a seven-figure settlement and a spouse's demand for a new car spring from underlying interests, not necessarily greed or ostentation. This means that satisfaction can often be secured by something different from the demand, provided those underlying interests are met.

We battle under banners proclaiming rights, yet these are rarely clear. Often they are contradictory. It is the quality of our legal system to maintain many separate and conflicting threads of decisional law and practice simultaneously. Rights are determined by a tribunal that considers the facts of the situation and decides which body of authority applies to it. When rights are agreed to, however, they provide a shorthand way of making decisions. Problems then arise only at the periphery of the rights.

Negotiating to resolve a dispute always takes place in the context of rights and power that are both defined and undefined. Perhaps it is because rights are fuzzy, once the factual situation emerges, that people so overwhelmingly choose to design their own resolutions. Or perhaps certainty is a sufficient motivator for most of us.

Mediation empowers us to satisfy our underlying interests. Mediators often influence parties to drop strategies that jerk others around in favor of those that serve mutual needs. This does not diminish that side's power. It enhances their ability to get something they want. Mediators thus help parties to understand that apparent power is different from real power and to see how they are participating in perpetuating the problem.

We always have a choice about whether to resolve. If there is no agreement, the mediation has not failed. The mediator has not failed. To paraphrase William F. Lincoln of the Conflict Resolution Research and Resource Institute in Tacoma, Washington, one of the legends in the mediation field: The mediator never fails. It is the parties who reach or fail to reach an agreement. When they exercise that choice, they are doing exactly what mediation was created to allow them to do.

Chapter Twelve

Mediating Employment Matters

It is well to remember that the entire population of the universe, with one trifling exception, is composed of others.
JOHN ANDREW HOLMES

The employment relationship is one that virtually all of us have experienced—for better or for worse. In Western cultures, employment is the principal staging area for relationship problems outside the family. Employment is often one of the most important relationships in a person's life. Relationships require mutuality—not necessarily equality, although commitment to equality is nourishing to all relationships, employment and otherwise. At a minimum, however, there needs to be commitment to mutual gain and an acceptance of each one's "right" to be wrong once in a while.

Without mutuality, it is just a matter of time until something goes seriously wrong. It happens at times that the apparently weaker party, the single employee, becomes the manipulator of the employer, rather than the other way around. Although typically it is the employee's needs that are not met, at times the employer is virtually powerless to have its needs met.

THE TENDENCY TO ESCALATE

The employment relationship in the United States is heavily legislated and heavily lawyered—a situation that can make problems difficult to resolve. There is a tendency to name the action of another in terms of some legal right or responsibility. *Discrimination* might be the label for rudeness, *sexual harassment* for inappropriate behavior, and *management right* for a basic lack of consideration. This is not to say there is not real discrimination and violation of rights in the workplace. The issue is how and when problems get resolved. Early, low-level resolutions that satisfy underlying interests and concerns are far better than lawsuits over the failure to resolve those concerns. Most employees, given the chance, would rather not suffer the hurt needed to establish a viable legal claim.

In today's charged employment environment, employees more easily perceive violations of statutory protections. They may see a lack of responsiveness in internal procedures as discriminatory. On the employer side, employee relations professionals (personnel or human resource staff) may virtually be required to label complaints according to legal theory (disability discrimination or sexual harassment, for example) to comply with accounting mandates from company and government. This has an escalating effect. Lawyers for both employees and employers create entangling webs of strictures on their clients, trying to ensure the benefit of some legal remedy in case it is needed. These are only a few of the forces pulling toward escalation rather than de-escalation of the problem.

Escalation causes the loss of many opportunities to resolve matters at a low level. Those involved become defensive and reactive. Defense attracts offense; a lawsuit is filed, and from then on, communication stops. What could be resolved in a day or two by a quality discussion in a safe environment takes on a life of its own, consuming time, money, energy, and attention, while returning only grief. For every all-star victory, there are thousands of defeats.

THE FRUITS OF CONTENTIOUSNESS

Employment lawsuits tend to be long, drawn-out affairs. One or both parties are likely to rely on the observations and testimony of the employee's coworkers, and the testimony of supervisors and managers will inevitably be involved. By the time the matter might be tried, key witnesses have moved away or disappeared. The depositions, document productions, and trial may create or exacerbate problems between coworkers, between employees and their supervisors, or between various levels of supervision and management.

Resolution of the case may be achieved only at substantial cost to those involved, as well as to the productivity of the workforce and the profitability of the enterprise. Unjust-discharge cases in California were reported in 1988 to cost the employer routinely from $81,000 to $208,000 in attorneys' fees per case (*Daily Labour Report*, 1988, p. A-10).

The lawsuit often obscures the important questions to ask: Is this necessary? Where are we going, why, and at what cost? When can we expect resolution, and what can be accomplished? Our thinking is dominated by the wrongdoing of the other side, which translates into an unwillingness to talk until all other options have been exhausted.

Disgruntled former employees have done everything from buying a share of stock and disrupting shareholders' meetings to shooting up the place. Legal remedies often fall short of meeting the parties' needs: back pay may be small or inordinately large, due, perhaps, to the hazards of the job market and delay in reaching trial; a plaintiff may not want reinstatement, and compensatory damages for pain and suffering are available only in certain actions. Punitive damages to teach the offending employer a lesson may be very hard to get. Claims for compensatory or punitive damages as well as the Racketeer Influenced and Corrupt Organization Act of 1970 (RICO), a common claim in many actions filed, may cause the employer to defend as if death itself were the alternative.

LOW-LEVEL RESOLUTIONS OF EMPLOYMENT CONFLICTS

Mediation is a low-level, low-impact method of airing concerns too touchy for conventional in-house treatment. It provides a safe place for venting emotions while the calm discussions that predominate move the parties ahead. It is safe to broach difficult topics without fear that things will blow up. With a skilled mediator, highly charged situations move from accusatorial to problem solving and even beyond to transformative.

Offering mediation to an employee implies respect. The vast majority of employees respond with respect for the employer's integrity and willingness to problem-solve. The USPS REDRESS program, for example, is voluntary, but it garners approximately 95 percent of all EEO complaints (Kevin Hagan, interview, Jan. 24, 2001).

Some employers too are beginning to respond favorably to offers to mediate coming from employees, at least where they are represented by counsel or a union.

The USPS REDRESS Program

The U.S. Postal Service has created the flagship program for resolving discrimination complaints in the workplace, based on the principles of Bush-Folger transformative mediation. Prior to piloting and later adopting this approach, the postal service dealt with discrimination complaints by resorting to the heavily backlogged Equal Employment Opportunity Commission (EEOC). At the time, the EEOC administrative complaint procedure was adversarial in tone, starting with an informal complaint that led to counseling. If counseling failed to resolve the dispute, the employee filed a formal complaint with the EEOC, which resulted eventually in a full investigation. The next stage was an adjudicatory hearing before an administrative judge that could result in federal court litigation. Half of the informal complaints were turned into formal complaints under this system (Bingham, 2000, p. 9).

The USPS mediation program, dubbed REDRESS (Resolve Employment Disputes Reach Equitable Solutions Swiftly), was piloted in 1994 to 1995 in the Florida Panhandle using outside neutrals. In this program, a neutral third party serves as a mediator to help complainant employees and respondent supervisors resolve the discrimination dispute. It is voluntary for the employee, but attendance is required for the supervisor, who however is under no obligation to enter into any agreement. The mediation session is scheduled promptly, within two to three weeks of a request.

The USPS was looking for a "form of dispute resolution that would contribute to improvements in communication between employees and supervisors. While constructive resolution of employment discrimination disputes was desirable, settlement was not the primary goal" (Bingham, 2000, p. 5). This is a rare and significant recognition of often overlooked by-products of a quality mediation process.

The USPS reports that "the average mediation takes just four hours, and the parties successfully resolve 61 percent of the cases at the mediation table. Overall, 81 percent of mediated cases are eventually closed without a formal complaint being filed. . . . Exit surveys . . . [from] 26,000 participants show that 88 percent of employees are highly satisfied or satisfied with the amount of control, respect, and fairness in the ADR process," against a traditional satisfaction of only 44 percent. "Moreover, both employees and supervisors are equally satisfied with ADR" (Interagency Alternative Dispute Resolution Working Group, 2001, p. 4).

The most important benefit enjoyed by the postal service and its employees is "that mediation seems to be changing how people relate to one another in the workplace. With the increased communication that mediation provides, employees and supervisors appear to be learning to get along better. In the first year after full implementation of the program, the number of complaints dropped by 24 percent [from] the previous year." By fiscal year 2000, there was an additional 20 percent drop in complaints. This reduction of complaints by several thousand a year means both cost savings and productivity increases. And it may well mean better postal service and greater job satisfaction with fewer stress-related complaints among employees (Interagency Alternative Dispute Resolution Working Group, 2001, p. 4).

This is a powerful success story. Because these mediations deal with people in the workplace who most often continue to be involved with each other after the mediation, the results are quick to see. How many road rage accidents and spousal abuse cases, suicides and shootouts will not occur as a result will never be known. And this is just the beginning of the breadth and depth of what can happen in mediation.

In her study, Bingham secured exit feedback from participants relating to whether there had been "acknowledgment of the legitimacy of one's own and other's perspective, views or interests." More than 50 percent of employees and supervisors agreed this had occurred. Apologies, which were used as proxies for recognition, occurred in the 25 to 30 percent range, with supervisors perceiving far fewer apologies (17 percent) than employees believed they gave (25 percent). More than 70 percent of the time, both employees and supervisors felt they had been listened to by the other. These results point to good questions to ask to evaluate mediation processes qualitatively.

Mediation works to facilitate a discussion when discharge is contemplated but no action has been taken yet. Typically an employment relationship that is not working for the employer usually is not working for the employee either. Both are unhappy. Before the situation becomes too adversarial, it is still possible to have a reasoned discussion in which each side can evaluate what steps make sense under the circumstances.

Mediation has been used in a number of situations. For example:

- To initiate discussions over an employee's claim to patent rights
- To sort out trade secret issues after an employee has voluntarily left
- To resolve inter- and intradepartmental conflict
- To reduce peer group frictions within a department and within an office, including among law firm partners

Mediation also has been used to improve the quality of contract negotiations, helping to ensure that people's expectations match. Its most common use in this field is to transform employment litigation into a mutually acceptable postemployment relationship, though at times even continued employment or reinstatement is agreed on.

Settlement rates in employment mediations are just as high for prelitigation situations as for disputes on the eve of trial.

Settlement rates in employment mediations are just as high for prelitigation situations as for disputes on the eve of trial. Mediating early thus means substantial savings, since in most cases, a lot of lawyering proves unnecessary and there is immense saving of upper-level staff time, among other resource impacts. In one class action case that had been pending for a year and a half, the corporate head of human resources in a Fortune 500 company said he had spent half his time the preceding year on that case. These indirect costs can mount up considerably.

Employers often authorize preliminary legal activities that can cost tens of thousands of dollars. This is called "erring on the side of caution," and cost justification is not considered. It is, of course, necessary for the employer to do a thorough investigation, headed by someone independent of those with a motive to cover up. It is not necessary that lawyers do this. In fact, using someone focused on building a defense may be counterproductive, for it may block understanding of the larger picture.

Some people equate softness with weakness. In mediation, it is easier to be soft on the people and tough on the problem. This avoids many of the hassles that lawsuits engender: parties or counsel snarling at each other and making work of the simplest tasks.

Consider the following common situation, often a prelude to a lawsuit.

Innuendoes to Sexual Harassment: A Study in Escalation

Margot has been working for her company for some five years. She recently requested and received a transfer into the key secretarial post in a new department. She has no problem with the work; it's the people. Some young engineers hired in the department have her running around bringing them coffee, and whenever she walks past one of them, there are audible appreciative sounds. Her boss loves his engineers and is unaware of what is going on. He thinks of Margot as a kid, although she is twenty-one years old. He is a busy man and seems never to have time to listen to any problems she brings him.

What might happen next?

Margot complains to her boss.

> Unlikely. She feels the deck is loaded against her, and the subject is not easy to talk about. Nor is he inviting talk from her.

Margot complains to personnel.

> Maybe, if the human resource professionals have a unique reputation for protecting confidentiality. Margot isn't one to rock the boat. She doesn't want to become a victim, but she's increasingly unhappy.

Margot doesn't complain.

> Likely. The situation becomes an accident waiting to happen, since it is causing her serious distress. It's just a matter of time until the situation festers into something bigger.

Margot complains to her fiancé.

> Likely. What she does may well be heavily influenced by family and friends. She believes she has nowhere else to turn.

One of the engineers goes too far.

> Likely. The situation is unstable in a downward direction.

Margot complains to an agency or a lawyer.

> A lawsuit or complaint is filed and served on the employer. Maybe, if someone she knows has had a decent experience with this approach recently. Still, that's more rocking of the boat. She's going to reach this point when she feels the situation is so out of hand that the company needs a lesson, so others will not have to suffer in the way she is. This generalizing is almost always present when a legitimate sexual harassment claim surfaces.

Here are the likely reactions of those involved:

Boss	Surprised, embarrassed, and angry he hasn't heard about the harassment earlier from Margot. Blame is often the first reaction.
Margot	Defensive and furious. Why didn't her boss notice? It was so obvious. Now she's a victim. She didn't want that. Rage is, surprisingly, a form of progress.
Engineers	Surprised, caught off-balance, defensive, and angry at Margot for "leading them on." Some are still in denial.
Human Resources	Missed this one. A new label on a new file. How far will this go? No other kind of case presents a bigger double-bind to an employer.
Management	Critical of lower management and personnel for "not being observant enough, not performing supervisory responsibilities adequately." Management is seeking advice from counsel, investigating, and justifying its position by its carefully choreographed response. The focus is on damage control and preparing the defense.

Legal offense and defense obscure the need for response. Such a response can lead to transformation, enabling both Margot and the employer to benefit from the whole affair. Lit-think dominates; just about everyone is blaming, defensive, and self-justifying. The stage is set for months to years of litigation, before anyone mentions the possibility of negotiating a resolution. Early mediation can stop the escalation in its tracks in the vast majority of cases. But who will propose it? Consider the situation from both sides' viewpoints.

THE PARTIES AND THEIR RESPONSES TO THE DILEMMA

Each one affected is likely to feel *they have no choice* about what they must do. This feeling of helplessness leads them to seek strength through rigidity, which only deepens as the adversarial proceedings labor onward.

The Employee's Dilemma

Lawyers for employees often counsel their clients through the steps of internal complaint procedures. Often they do so with a view to helping secure a resolution without formal proceedings. Sometimes it is also to build a record. With confidential counseling, the employee may gain the confidence to carry the matter forward inside, knowing someone is in her corner. It also keeps the matter at a low level. Lawyers who represent employees know that the mere appearance of a lawyer for the employee escalates the situation.

With the client's consent, the lawyer may contact company counsel directly. This requires a great deal of trust and confidence; the company can readily build a fence around the employee in the name of containing the problem. It can become just a matter of time until the employee leaves, often under adverse circumstances. Without a formal complaint or a clear understanding with employer counsel, the employee may be defenseless.

Employees who have collaboratively minded counsel in their corner are themselves offering to mediate, sometimes through counsel and sometimes not. Offering mediation usually has the effect of disclosing the employee's lawyer, who may have been in the background. Many counsel prefer to get some impact from making their presence known. This can be done by attaching a proposed charge or complaint to the offer to mediate. The implied threat of this approach simply needs to be evaluated.

Handling the Initial Rejection

Companies in the past, not understanding that mediation is simply a tool for productive discussions, have tended to respond that there is nothing to mediate. A plaintiff's lawyer or manager also may offer to mediate the same brush-off. If an offer to mediate is rejected, discuss how long it should take before a session might be productive. The strategy here is to keep the other party talking about *when* it will be useful to talk. In this way, the focus changes from whether to when, a major step forward. Eventually the employer or manager or the plaintiff's lawyer may see that there is no time like the present. When the days, weeks, and months go by, it becomes obvious that if a quality discussion were to take place, a lot more could be done, with less hassle, to everyone's benefit.

The Employer's Dilemma

Given many companies' hesitancy to use mediation, one might ask, "What is the risk?" Is it the risk that you did something (suggested mediation) when perhaps you might not have had to do anything? Is it the risk that by offering to talk in a neutral setting, you are admitting something or perhaps showing weakness?

Employers use early mediation to obtain new information and a fresh perspective. They may use it to telegraph a firm resolve to resist unreasonable demands as well as to make a just settlement. Employees and their counsel almost never see an offer to mediate as a sign of weakness. They may use the mediation forum to impress on the employer their intention to go forward if no agreement is reached. In the confidential environment of the mediation, these strategies can have considerable impact, but posturing tends to fall away under the intense light of mediation.

If you were the company, what would you want counsel sought out by your employees to do? Could you encourage early, direct contact by counsel for employees? How? The personal relationships that would enable counsel in smaller communities to let your lawyer know that they are involved in a matter rarely exist in a large urban environment, and so the matter festers until a complaint is filed. Yet most management lawyers and human resources professionals would probably prefer to do something about every situation in order to catch the one that otherwise would become a blockbuster with perhaps millions of dollars in legal fees and indirect costs and years in litigation—a true no-win situation. Early contact serves this strategy.

In some cases such as the example in this chapter, the company never has a chance to offer mediation because it "learns" of the situation only after it becomes public. The harassment label is applied and the adversarial process launched. One or more ADR resources might have headed this off. For example, a company could have a program to provide a mediation process at the employee's request. This puts the option forward formally but not confrontationally. One of the hardest things for employees to understand is the responsibility the company has to provide due process to an accused employee in sexual harassment cases. To the complaining employees, it feels as if they are not being believed. In mediation, the employee can gain some perspective into the employer's situation and vice versa and may help to devise an approach that resolves this difficult situation.

Mediation may also allow employers to act more decisively. In one sexual harassment mediation, the company was so convinced of the wrongdoing of one long-term employee that it terminated him immediately following the first day of mediation, despite the very real risk of having that decision set aside later by a labor arbitrator. It did so to demonstrate solidarity with several highly credible women—employees and former employees—and to emphasize its commitment to a decent work environment. Prior to the mediation, it was not willing to take that risk, even though it knew the facts.

Using an Ombuds

If the company had an ombuds practitioner, a confidential resource and skilled mediator outside of line authority and outside of human resources responsibilities, Margot in the case example might have consulted with that person and been willing to tackle the problem before any complaint was filed.

ADR resources within the system help employees deal with just such situations. To provide a workplace for people is to take them with all of their human frailties. The question is not whether there will be problems in the workplace but whether what is provided enables problems to be self-correcting.

The question is not whether there will be problems in the workplace but whether what is provided enables problems to be self-correcting.

Manadatory Binding Arbitration: Some Concerns

One resource that does little to address underlying problems is mandatory binding arbitration. Binding arbitration agreements, imposed as a condition of employment, are popular with many companies. According to the General Accounting Office, almost one-fifth of the national workforce is subject to them. The popularity of binding arbitration agreements is explained by employer groups on the grounds that arbitration is less expensive, time-consuming, and unpredictable than litigation. However, such agreements raise serious concerns. As the past president of the National Academy of Arbitrators, George Nicolau, has stated, "[m]any employers have adopted plans that are quite unfair" (Semas, 1998, p. 3).

The EEOC along with groups such as the NAACP and the Now Legal Defense Fund are opposed to binding arbitration. In a 1997 policy statement, the EEOC affirmed its support of voluntary employment dispute resolution programs while observing that mandatory arbitration usurps the court's role in enforcing civil rights and fails to provide public accountability for employment decisions. Another concern is that employees are disadvantaged by these agreements. They rarely have the experience and knowledge of the arbitrators that their employers do. And they often lack access to critical evidence.

The industry is responding to these criticisms of binding arbitration. Some companies have delayed plans to implement such agreements (Semas, 1998, p. 2), while others have changed existing binding agreements. For example, the National Association of Securities Dealers was one of the first to respond to EEOC concerns. They announced plans to eliminate mandatory arbitration of statutory discrimination claims for registered brokers and proposed a new policy allowing employees to choose between a private arbitration agreement and litigation (Van Duch, 1997, p. 2). The American Arbitration Association (AAA) has also responded to the concerns about binding arbitration. In a rare public statement, the AAA announced that employment disputes are best resolved when the parties "knowingly and voluntarily agree on the process" (Semas, 1998, p. 2).

The courts have examined the legality of such agreements. This issue has been litigated at various levels of courts, and while some decisions have been upheld, others have been struck down. The 2001 U.S. Supreme Court case *Circuit City Stores, Inc. v. Saint Clair Adams* involved an employee who was required to agree to binding arbitration before the store would hire him in 1995. He quit a year later and filed a lawsuit alleging that coworkers harassed him because he was gay and that the company did nothing when he complained. His lawyer, Michael Rubin, argued that the mandatory binding arbitration provision violated the Federal Arbitration Act. The Supreme Court held it was not, leaving it binding on the employee.

Worker's Compensation: The Broken Wheel

One of the problems about the way we approach systems is that once they are established, we tend to ignore them and assume that they are running fine—that is, until some disaster happens. We don't notice the little, daily disasters that cost so very much in both human and economic terms.

Worker's Compensation is one such institutional system that is filled with adversarial procedures and, in many jurisdictions, is barren of processes capable of opening those involved to reconciliation. Pennies are pinched in a variety of ways. Yet the physical and mental problems created when a person feels disrespected may generate far greater costs than many imagine. The true cost of the largely adversarial nature of the program is worth pondering.

Key classes of claims that might benefit from mediation would be *pro se* claims (in which people represent themselves), stress claims, and claims concerning physical conditions that are recognized as often being triggered by stress, such as lower back problems. If employers and carriers could see their self-interest more broadly, then quicker but smaller damages might be awarded in such cases. This is what Timothy Miller, a clinical psychologist and Qualified Medical Examiner in private practice in Stockton, California, writes: "In many cases, in my opinion, one-way or mutual apologies cleared up misunderstandings, and similar responses could be more beneficial than endless psychotherapy and vast quantities of Prozak. . . . Some of these cases just cry out for voluntary, confidential mediation" (Timothy Miller, personal letter, January 22, 2001).

Miller reports how unresponsive he's found people to be to his suggestion to use mediation: "I've raised this possibility a few times and tried to pitch it to claims representatives and applicants' attorneys, so far without any response whatsoever." How responsive would your company, your agency, your applicants' attorney, your claims adjuster be to a suggestion that mediation be used to address some of the underlying emotional and relational issues between the parties involved?

The Stake for Human Resource Professionals

There is most often a dual pull on human resource (HR) professionals, who are at once responsible for implementation and, sometimes, design of HR management systems and also for helping employees, supervisors, and managers to resolve on-the-job conflicts. In-house dispute resolution resources have to earn trust, which does not come easily.

The most common employee complaint seems to be about confidentiality: there isn't any. People are seen going to the HR office. The gossip mill hums. No matter how hard the HR professional might try to maintain confidentiality of information gleaned from an employee, all too often it gets right back to the manager or supervisor in a form that blows the employee's cover. Sometimes even the fact that the employee came to the HR office is enough to trigger this. HR is not a function that lends itself to maintaining confidentiality, given its dual role. There is no blame in this. It comes with the territory. For this reason, an aware HR head often will work to secure for the employer other resources besides its own that can meet the critical need for confidentiality.

The ombudsman is an ideal confidential resource to the workplace. Private companies and government agencies are increasingly realizing that it is good insurance to provide employees who are troubled with workplace situations with a confidential resource whose loyalty is to helping employees get back on track. Numerous organizations are available to assist other organizations in exploring this option, including The Ombudsman Association, which can provide a great deal of valuable information.

Thinking collaboratively—recognizing the common ground that employer and employee share—can turn conflict into a vehicle for strengthening loyalty and commitment on all sides. It goes hand in hand with a management style that seeks to engage employees' heads and hearts as well as their hands. Such management may view employment complaints as opportunities to deal with accumulated concerns in a mature and mutually respectful manner. Once management understands that what isn't working for the employer really isn't working for the employee as well, such mutuality can emerge. Trust is built with repeated demonstration that management can be trusted. This earned trust is money in the bank when it comes to handling change creatively.

By contrast, pursuing or defending a lawsuit becomes a consuming passion. The issue changes from what is good for us to what is good for the country—as we see our own position standing for justice, freedom, and peace. The courthouse is the place for this, but here's the catch—even cases fought primarily for principle rarely go to trial. And there is a terrible economic and emotional price for keeping the grievance fresh for all the years it takes to get to trial. The best protection against serving as cannon fodder for the litigation game is to keep looking for opportunities to talk, to mediate. As Winston Churchill said, "To jaw, jaw is always better than to war, war."

Chapter Thirteen

The Construction Industry

A Model to Ponder

For a long time it had seemed to me that life was about to begin—real life. But there was always some obstacle in the way, something to be gotten through first, some unfinished business, time still to be served, a debt to be paid. Then life would begin. At last it dawned on me that these obstacles were my life.
ALFRED D'SOUZA

Many industries know that obstacles are part of life, and many have become major players in the world of litigation. However, some—for example, manufacturing industries (steel, autos, refining) with organized workforces—have taken timid steps toward a more flexible adjudicated process, moving from trial to arbitration. Yet the idea of a business relationship as requiring *process* rather than formal *procedures* when impasse occurs has brought little real change to most industries. Few have extricated themselves from rights-based or power-based conflict management as a way of life. As we saw in the last chapter, employers still seeking to force arbitration in employment disputes are perpetuating the old-mind power-based, rights-based approach to the employer-employee relationship. New mind looks on in amazement.

One industry, however, has wiped the dust of reactive battle from its boots and significantly changed its mind. In the process, it is becoming a model others might contemplate when the burden of adversarial proceedings and its rippling negative effects on business relationships (with employees, customers, and suppliers, for example) grow too heavy. That industry is construction.

THE CONSTRUCTION INDUSTRY IN A NUTSHELL

Construction is the largest production sector in the U.S. economy, estimated at between $500 billion and $800 billion annually and roughly one-quarter of the world's total construction volume. It has been estimated to account for 13 percent of the U.S. gross domestic product. The complexity of construction has been likened to a three-dimensional chess game and is governed largely by a "transactional system representing a veritable minefield of conflict which is a fertile source of recurring, often unique legal issues" (Stipanowich, 1998b, p. 465).

The construction industry has taken mediation and other collaborative processes to heart and in a little over fifteen years has changed the way business is done around disputes. In one sense, the rationale is obvious. Construction projects are one-of-a-kind products, drawing multiple parties—owners, design professionals, contractors, subcontractors, and an almost infinite variety of suppliers—into an intricate dance. If one falters, nearly everyone else in the project downstream of the problem is affected. When the supplier fails to produce the needed materials on time, the entire job can grind to a halt. When an on-site subcontractor is not ready on schedule, other subcontractors and portions of the workforce may sit around, incurring additional costs.

Owners, contractors, and subcontractors seek to allocate this risk, often with the more powerful laying off risk on the less powerful. This power-based method of making decisions has adverse consequences. In this situation, if the less powerful falters, the more powerful is going to be adversely affected as well. An owner who lays off too much risk on the contractor may end up not getting the job completed. A contractor who pinches pennies on expenses for design professionals may end up with costly errors in design and job management to deal with. A subcontractor whose own subcontractor goes bankrupt or whose supplier fails to deliver on time is still responsible to the contractor upstream in the contract chain for that performance.

Workforces of both contractors and subcontractors and the contractors themselves approach the situation seeking control through rights-based methods, relying on adjudicatory procedures. These, however, are little adapted to making the best of what is actually happening on the project at any given time. It is backward looking, not forward looking, for the most part. It reduces flexibility rather than increasing it.

Taking even the smallest step backward to gain perspective, it is readily obvious that the whole project and everyone in it will benefit if an interest-based approach can be used—one that harmonizes interests rather than setting them against one another. All kinds of things can happen during the life of a project that are beyond the control of any of the parties—weather, earthquakes, supply shortages, and transportation strikes, to name just a few. With the inevitable uncertainties and interdependence of construction industry participants, adversarial processes just didn't make sense. Wyatt McCallie, general counsel of the international engineering firm CH2M Hill, told me in a telephone conversation in January 1997 why: "First, litigation is a poor way to make money; second, the construction companies hurt their relations with clients when they are constantly suing people."

INDUSTRIAL CRISIS

Litigation in construction typically requires a great deal of principals' time and effort. Construction projects involve a mass of detail and a web of interlocking activities, each dependent on the other for its timing and appropriateness. The complexity and the vast interdependency of activities on a job site militate against the lawyers' knowing all of this information until it is fairly certain a dispute will have to be tried. Thus, vast amounts of principal time can be consumed in any protracted conflict, making affected individuals unavailable for work in the business. The drain on industry resources from adversarial conflict is extensive.

Still, it took a crisis to bring change, even in an industry that greatly suffered from continuing along with the way things had always been done. As the 1980s began, construction was an industry with a habit of litigating and every reason in the world to find other ways of solving problems. Bad as it was, however, it seemed that things could still get worse.

In the first half of 1980s, one in three commercial construction projects ended up in litigation. In this time period, it was common knowledge that some contractors planned on making their profit through litigation of extra work claims instead of through proper bidding and efficient project management. Public entities that were bound by rule, ordinance, or law to take the lowest bidder were often targets for these unscrupulous buccaneers (Elliott Gleason, former senior vice president for claims, Design Professionals Insurance Company, personal communication, 1997).

Between 1981 and 1983, interest rates rose sharply, and there were tremendous cost overruns. The industry was in turmoil. Architects' cost projections were far surpassed by bids, which were surpassed again by cost overruns, so the architects looked bad to their clients. Litigation was exploding. In 1984, the insurance market got very tight, premiums skyrocketed, and firms became very serious about containing costs. For every one hundred insured firms, there were forty-four claims (Homer Sandridge and Victor O. Schinnerer, telephone interviews, Jan. 1996). Cheryl Terio, director of contract document services for Associated General Contractors, worked for the American Institute of Architects (AIA) at that time and remembers: "Members would call in, grown men in tears, saying they couldn't get liability insurance coverage. It was awful" (telephone interview, Jan. 1997).

THE TURNING POINT

Design Professionals Insurance Company (DPIC), an insurer of architects and engineers, spearheaded the move to mediation. In March 1985, Bernard P. Engels, then vice president of claims, and Elliott Gleason, then assistant vice president of claims, visited American Intermediation Service (AIS), a small mediation firm in San Francisco. The meeting involved a discussion of the mediation process and its benefits. At the conclusion of the meeting, Engels said, "I don't believe a word you've said, but we're going to do it anyway. We've got to do something."

Gleason identified the cases for mediation. AIS's assignment was to persuade the parties to agree to mediate and then to conduct the mediations. Gleason remembers his instructions well:

I asked the claims staff to pick cases that were at impasse for various reasons: perhaps our insured had no liability but needed a forum to convince other parties of this; perhaps the case was extremely complex technically; perhaps there was a party or lawyer with an attitude involved in the case. Whatever the reason, the situation wasn't going anywhere. We wanted to put mediation to the test. I told them to pick some tough ones. The only way we could find out what mediation could do was to try it.

Within six months, we knew we were on to something. The results of the test were amazing. Part of the reality of the 1970s and 1980s was that roughly one of three bid construction projects ended up in litigation. Construction litigation is uniquely complex, with interwoven issues of fact and law. Principals become actively involved in the litigation activity—something that takes them away from their business. Experts are commonly used and are expensive. Construction principals had every reason to prefer to spend their time pursuing their business rather than pursuing the business of litigation. Counsel, by and large, were sympathetic. There was, after all, a tremendous amount of construction litigation [Elliott Gleason, interview, 1997].

Part of the strength of DPIC's experimental use of mediation was that it avoided the pitfall of trying to pick the "right" cases to mediate. It used several mediation service providers and so began to develop some expertise in different styles of mediation and approaches to it. Within eighteen months, construction principals and sometimes their lawyers began to choose mediation to help handle disputes in their industry. Following this initial experience, these principals and their lawyers were convinced of the benefits of collaborative dispute resolution methods, and DPIC implemented a comprehensive claims management program using mediation. In 1991, CNA, the other major architect and engineer carrier, began responding to interest in mediation. By 1995, it had its own mediation program component in its loss prevention program.

In 1985 few lawyers and virtually no courts had any interest in mediation programs, fast-track programs, or laws encouraging or mandating mediation. Broad use of mediation in construction disputes developed when few, if any, such programs were in place. Thus, this is a fairly pristine example of what people themselves can do when motivation is high.

The transformative power of mediation showed participants that there is a better way to resolve disputes and that creative solutions remain possible even when matters seem at an impasse. More important, it became evident how much greater the returns could be if the collaborative experience tasted in conflict resolution could be drawn upstream by putting resources into building a project team, investing in a shared vision, nurturing a sense of mutual interest, and experiencing joint problem solving and even transformation right from the beginning.

FROM CHAOS TO COLLABORATION

Uniquely, the construction industry made collaborative dispute prevention and dispute resolution processes its own. The continuing vitality of mediation in the construction industry is demonstrated by the 1994 Construction Industry Survey on Dispute Avoidance and Resolution (Stipanowich and O'Neal, 1995, 1996). According to this survey of 2,300 ADR users, 84 percent of the ADR experiences involved mediation; while one-third were court initiated, two-thirds of these mediations were the result of agreement between the parties. Construction principals and lawyers are among the most experienced mediation users today.

The success and staying power of mediation were demonstrated by DPIC's results from the first four and one-half years of its program: 78 percent of referred claims were accepted into mediation by all parties; of these, 76 percent were settled. At AIS in those years, the statistics showed an 80 percent acceptance rate and an 85 percent settlement rate when the carrier initially proposed mediation through the firm (the most common way mediation occurred at that time). This is strong evidence of the power of a voluntary process backed by mediation professionals' extending the invitations to mediate.

The 1994 survey gives the benefit of mediation participants' views, collected from the responses of more than 2,300 contractors, design professionals, and attorneys. The survey found that 64 percent of the 459 responding attorneys had participated in at least one mediation. About 60 percent of these mediations had occurred within the two preceding years. Nearly 25 percent had five or more mediation experiences, and 14 percent had mediated at least ten times. Ninety-five percent claimed to be at least "somewhat familiar" with mediation, compared to only 62 percent in a 1990 survey. Dollar amounts in dispute were significant, averaging over $4 million, with a median of $1 million.

The attorneys responding to the 1994 survey were highly experienced, with 80 percent having practiced law for more than ten years and 33 percent having over two decades of experience. They also were highly experienced in construction law, with approximately 75 percent claiming that at least 40 percent of their practice was construction related. There also is evidence that these lawyers were willing to put their clients' interests above their own: 60 percent said they would recommend partnering, a process of dispute avoidance in which few lawyers ever become involved.

The survey found that mediation resulted in resolution of some or all of the issues in 67 percent of cases, and full settlement was reached in 59.1 percent of matters mediated. Interestingly, in DPIC's experience between June 1985 and January 1990, 75.8 percent of the claims mediated were resolved. Although DPIC submitted matters for mediation that were not yet in litigation, there is one other noteworthy difference between the two sets of results. In the survey, fewer than 10 percent of the mediators were professional mediators. However, DPIC used professional mediators from the beginning. In the survey, the majority of mediators were attorneys. Although attorneys often start out as evaluators, which is much closer to the experience of traditional law practice, they can develop significant mediation process skills if they have an aptitude for mediation and develop the essential mediator mind.

THE ADVENT OF COURT INVOLVEMENT IN MEDIATION

Interviews conducted with lawyers in Seattle, Portland, San Francisco, and Los Angeles support the findings of the survey and provide additional insight. A Portland, Oregon, construction lawyer notes the vast decline in construction litigation:

The percentage of routine construction projects going to litigation is more like one in twenty today. With major construction projects, it's more like one in eight to ten, nothing like the one in three of a decade ago [Richard E. Alexander, interview, Jan. 10, 1997].

In Seattle, another construction lawyer assessed the critical role of the mediator and the changes in how mediation has been used over time:

In the last seven to eight years, there has been a great increase in the use of mediation. At first, mediation was novel. It was warmly received and very successful. About four to five years ago, partnering and dispute review boards came along. The whole atmosphere in construction became more dispute prevention oriented. It seemed there was a lot less conflict. A lot more is happening in terms of prevention rather than conflict resolution. The vast majority still settle, but people don't believe as much as they used to, perhaps because being effective as a mediator is so very, very hard. What the mediator brings to the process is critical to success [Sam Baker, interview, Jan. 10, 1997].

Today's reality, in the words of Wyatt McCallie, is that in construction, "most sophisticated businesspeople do not litigate."

CONTINUED RESISTANCE AND EFFORTS TO ENLIGHTEN

All of the lawyers interviewed agree that major public works may be more prone to litigation because of potential political problems, such as the fallout from having to make a potentially unpopular decision. Even these, however, usually resolve in mediation, although sometimes after agreement is reached, the mediator turns into a technical arbitrator for the sole purpose of committing the agreement to the form of an arbitration order.

Construction law work regarding shopping centers, condominiums, and residential developments is also less likely to pursue mediation than litigation strategies, perhaps in part because of less sophisticated players and perhaps because of less expertise in the carriers who get involved in the litigation. In the view of one San Francisco construction attorney,

Much of this business is controlled by general liability carriers and today these are often defended by casualty defense lawyers rather than construction lawyers. They rarely get to mediation and tend to be referred to retired judges and wallow along in endless conferences. Often we just don't participate. That at least saves fees [Lee Novich, interview, Jan. 10, 1997].

Lawyers unfamiliar with mediation may resist as well. One San Francisco construction lawyer has a creative strategy for getting a mediation plan approved by opposing counsel and adopted by the court:

The retired judges don't insist on compliance with their orders and requests and let counsel and clients opt out of conferences. Those who go perhaps go to just be with the flow. But even general liability carriers get annoyed by being called to settlement conference number eight.

My strategy is to go to the presiding judge upon the first contact under Fast Track to persuade plaintiffs' counsel to proceed with a mediation plan, setting forth a time table of activities, culminating in mediation three months, six months, or nine months later. These plans only get through if we represent owners or general contractors, because the special master process is usually underway, when design professionals are brought in. The problem is that many plaintiffs' attorneys are uncomfortable without what they believe is the hammer of the special master. We then agree that if there are disputes under the mediation plan, the disputing parties may go to the special master at those parties' expense [Jane Pandell, interview, Jan. 10, 1997].

Insurers, particularly DPIC, undertook a massive education program for those it insured, teaching conflict management skills through, among other things, premium reduction inducements for reading books and answering questions about them. (The first edition of this book was among those they used.) Insurers report that the number of claims against architects and engineers has been reduced dramatically over the past four years.

COLLABORATIVE PROCESSES

The change in the field is solidly grounded in realities that old ways of thinking did not recognize. Wyatt McCallie states why:

There is a lot more partnering. The engineers and the contractors have figured out that it's in no one's best interest to be surly to one another. There is more understanding, more savvy, more common commitment to bringing in the project on budget and on time. Engineers also are trying to be more realistic about the demands placed on contractors. I believe that the change is largely permanent. It won't go away.

Confidence to develop and use conflict prevention processes such as dispute review boards (DRB) and partnering derives in large part from construction industry principals' and lawyers' experience with mediation.

DRBs were made famous by Boston's Central Artery Project (the Big Dig), begun in 1991 and due for completion in 2004. With more than seventy-five interrelated construction contracts (as well as design, insurance, eminent domain, and workers' compensation disputes), planners expected ten thousand to twenty thousand disputes. Around 1997, existing boards initially created for all large projects were consolidated into ten to fifteen DRBs—one for each large contractor. These panels consisted of two neutral technical panelists, subject area specialists, and a panel chair with significant dispute resolution experience, who might or might not be a lawyer. The panels were empowered to call for the information they thought they might need. They met quarterly to review the projects, even if there were no disputes—a practice that allows some informal resolutions to take place. Generally however, three or four less-formal levels of dispute resolution precede resort to a DRB.

Joe Allegro, director of construction, reports that of around 11,000 disputes, 80 percent have been resolved at the field level, thanks in large part to the use of partnering on the project. The remaining 20 percent have been resolved by DRBs, with only three disputes going to litigation, one of which was settled before trial (Joe Allegro, interview, Jan. 29, 2001). The most common observation—shared by Allegro—is that these boards serve primarily as a deterrent and motivator to resolve in the early stages. Generally, they seem to be rarely used but often provided for.

The greatest gift from the construction industry is the development of partnering (see Chapter Sixteen). Partnering is derived in part from recent Japanese-American experience that develops mutual commitment to common goals in an atmosphere of trust and cooperation, seeking to prevent and mitigate problems before they become unmanageable. It marks an important step in moving upstream from conflict (the result) to addressing the root cause of conflicts: lack of commitment to a common goal jointly developed in an environment where trust can be developed, so that each participant has some ownership. This integrates potentially competing interests into an approach to the project that draws deeply on the complementarity of these interests.

We are so used to paying the costs of intransigent conflict that we find stories of its demise incredible. Consider the British Columbia Hydro story. In a major project, this institutional owner in Canada got through $55 million in construction involving 119 contracts with only forty-seven disputed claims. All but twelve of these were negotiated face to face. Only two reached the "standing neutral"—the neutral engaged for the contract period—and all were settled prior to binding arbitration (Sandori, 1994).

We are so used to paying the costs of intransigent conflict that we find stories of its demise incredible.

These mechanisms have gone far toward reducing conflicts, and thus the need for litigation *and* mediation. There is, of course, much room for improvement, and this improvement is being sought by organizations and associations within the industry.

The engineers' approach to conflict prevention has been adjudicatory in nature, such as through the DRBs (Stipanowich, 1998b). The architects, however, took a different view. Mediation is now required in all AIA standard contract documents as part of the 1997 revision, "as a precondition to arbitration or any legal or equitable proceeding" (American Institute of Architects, 1997). By placing the mediation step between the rights-based architect's decision and arbitration, there is greater likelihood that mediation will occur early enough to mitigate the impact of a dispute on the project and on contractual relationships. It's a way of saying, "Hold on! Let's see what common interests there are that can show us a way out of this situation."

There is risk, of course, that this one-size-fits-all approach of mandating mediation will discourage the use of other ADR procedures that might be better for a particular case. But the parties have flexibility. These are, after all, contractual requirements, subject to modification.

BREAKING OLD-MIND THOUGHT PATTERNS

In the process of opening the construction industry to mediation, many tired assumptions have been exposed. For example, the 1994 construction industry survey found that the lawyers responding "overwhelmingly rejected yesterday's popular wisdom that proposing mediation was a sign of weakness, or that revelation of confidences or trial strategy was a serious drawback to its use." The 1991 construction industry survey had also found no perceived prerequisite for discovery prior to mediation. However, respondents appreciated the advantage that focused discovery and informal exchanges of information can provide. "While more respondents found mediation appropriate right before trial (81.7 percent), a strong majority (60.1 percent) of those responding favored mediation even in the absence of discovery. . . . A number of respondents envision a middle ground in which discovery is limited to that basic quantum of information needed to permit informed settlement" (Stipanowich, 1996, pp. 101, 103).

Staging discovery *first* to support settlement evaluation and only if necessary to prepare for trial is a wise use of resources. It depends on client awareness and permission whenever it is used, whether in construction or another field such as employment.

The survey also found that "to some extent, therefore, increasing the number of parties . . . does not appear to reduce the odds of settlement," reflecting, perhaps, a realistic assessment of the alternatives to settling. Except when large sums of money are involved, most respondents disfavored making mediation mandatory, perhaps because in construction work, mediation may readily be provided for by contract; in addition, ad hoc mediation is widely accepted in construction conflicts.

THE IMPORTANCE OF CHOICE

It is apparent that motivation is a key to success with the nonlinear process of mediation. The survey and other studies have found a statistically significant correlation between success in mediation and parties developing their own rules and procedures for the mediation process. Providing choice increases motivation, increases satisfaction, and invites quality participation. The process of litigants' developing procedures demonstrates that they can agree. This recognition builds trust, the currency of mediation.

The construction industry experience shows that experienced lawyers and sophisticated clients can use a balanced approach to resolving conflicts. With experience, they can apply the practical collaborative process skills learned

> *Providing choice increases motivation, increases satisfaction, and invites quality participation.*

in mediation in other business settings, thus reducing the need for both litigation and mediation.

THE TILT TOWARD A LAWYERED VERSION OF CONSTRUCTION MEDIATION

Construction came late within the purview of the bar. Principals in the construction business are used to resolving their own conflicts and could do so, until contracting became a multistate and multinational affair, in the view of construction industry observer, critic, and visionary Tom Stipanowich. He pegs the greater involvement of lawyers in construction conflicts to the development of the interstate highway system, which brought more and more contractors into communities away from their home base, where there were fewer personal and professional relationships encouraging informal solutions to job problems (Stipanowich, 1998b).

When construction conflicts reach lawyers today, the mediation is likely to become essentially a lawyer-driven process, focused so intently on settlement that communication, relationship, and fairness values suffer. Stipanowich tells the story of a prominent architectural-engineering firm that wanted to use mediation in part to enhance communications with the major contractor on the other side of the conflict. The lawyer-mediator allowed short presentations in joint session and then, having apparently reached his own conclusions about the merits, separated the disputants and spent the rest of the day twisting arms to achieve a settlement (Stipanowich, 1998b).

Although mediation is now widely recognized as giving the parties the greatest flexibility in structuring solutions to their own problems after taking into account the full range of issues the parties bring to the table, it remains much influenced by the model and mentality of the mediator. It is true that business relationships can be preserved, and those that have been lost can be recovered as the obvious misunderstandings are removed and each side can see more clearly that the other sides were not acting from malice or evil intent. But this is not automatic. So selecting your mediator wisely is a major part of crafting the best strategy for mediation.

The 1990s saw substantial progress in transforming an industry dedicated to disputes to one that learned to take the lessons of mediation and move them upstream to do the work of conflict management. There is a quality of community that is inescapable in the construction industry as well. It brings a sort of mutual respect closer to the surface even though emotions may be at gale force over the conflict. It's an industry that is not afraid of the expression of emotion either. The illusion of separation weakens in the face of a constant need to rely on others. Industries, organizations, and agencies that have not yet learned this lesson ignore it at their peril. What you give, you get. It's just a matter of time.

Chapter Fourteen

Turbocharging Contract Negotiations

There is nothing more likely to start disagreement among people or countries than an agreement.
E. B. WHITE, "MY DAY," IN *ONE MAN'S MEAT*

Have you ever wondered about mediating contract negotiations? Labor negotiations are mediated all the time, but historically they have been more confrontational than other business negotiations. In negotiations between businesses, communication seems easy at first. Everyone is getting along. We think, "Why raise sticky issues? We're trusting that once we build a good relationship, we'll be able to tackle the more difficult points. And, after all, there is always the chance we might miss the deal entirely if difficult issues are raised too early."

Perhaps we're the ones seemingly in the driver's seat in the negotiation. The other side will go along with what we want even if it sounds oppressive, because we have the economic power. Why use mediation?

MEDIATION AS A TOOL

The biggest reason for using mediation is that it becomes safe to raise difficult issues. We therefore can take on highly sensitive subjects like, "What will we do in the event one of us feels the contract has been breached?" We can also motivate key people on both sides not only to put their all into performance of the agreement but to address problems early, before communication breaks down.

American contract negotiations often take a long time. Drafts are prepared, then mailed or faxed back and forth. Telephone tag begins; other work intervenes. The laborious lawyering of contract negotiation can take much of the spontaneity and creativity out of devising contractual relationships. In mediation, the mediator manages the relationship while the parties work, with a word processor if need be, on revisions, which can be reviewed almost as quickly as they are proposed, providing great savings of time.

The most common problem in business relationships is frustrated expectations. When one party thinks it is buying a product and the other thinks it is selling a professional performance such as a construction job or legal services, there is bound to be trouble. The frustrations surface gradually, and unless they are addressed at the beginning, they can cause monumental problems down the road. It requires exceptional communication skills, opportunity, and a workable structure to handle these as they arise.

The most common problem in business relationships is frustrated expectations.

The power of mediation may be seen through some contract dispute resolution mediations that turned into contract negotiations.

The Redrawn Contract

The mediation involved a dispute arising out of an agreement to license and develop software for the operation of an Arizona insurer. The parties had reached agreement in rough form on the first day of mediation, through the efforts of their chief executive officers (CEOs), the technical team, and counsel. On the second day, they attempted to hammer out a memorandum of agreement. That proved extremely difficult due to personality problems between counsel. One lawyer dotted every *i* and crossed every *t*. The other lawyer was a great generalist. The two were the American lawyer versions of Menachem Begin and Anwar Sadat (see Chapter Eleven). As a result, gaining agreement on anything was very difficult. The CEOs and lawyers came to the third day of mediation six weeks later with drafts of settlement documents on which they were hopelessly polarized.

The mediator brought a mediation-trained lawyer who specialized in negotiating such agreements. This lawyer was able to provide the parties with the comfort of knowing how these types of agreements tend to work out in the geographic area where the dispute occurred. At one point, the feuding lawyers even allowed him to meet privately with their clients and the mediator in order to resolve one particular problem. His contribution enabled counsel for both sides to provide the cautionary advice their clients needed to hear without making agreement impossible. Finally, after ten hours, the parties signed eighty pages of agreements that had been prepared as the mediation went along.

The agreement resolved two arbitrations over a $5 million computer software development and licensing agreement. Trust had built to the point that the parties agreed to go forward with a modification of the original contract, which had gone astray due to incongruent expectations. The parties were willing to give each other another chance.

The Lesson

Many contract disputes keep perfectly good working relationships from realizing their potential. People get dug in, focused on conflict instead of making things work. Lack of attention to this slippage in trust often leads to escalation of the conflict. The time to deal with this is when it first appears. In contracts such as this one, where great cooperation is required on both sides, it would be wise to provide a mid- to high-level meet-and-confer team, perhaps with a neutral whose whole purpose is to detect and resolve incipient conflict. Select can-do people who are deeply committed to overall joint success. Consider training at the outset in building trust within each company's team and across teams, so that honest concerns can percolate upward without reservation or hesitation. This is where company culture makes the difference.

Keeping the Job Going

A school construction project was in trouble. The engineering firm, a subcontractor to the architect, had failed to submit some key calculations and seemed to be dragging its feet. In just a few days, work on the project would be so far behind that the project would stop and penalties would become applicable. But try as he might, the architect's principal could not get the work out of the engineering firm. A mediation set up that week revealed the problem.

The engineering firm had made a fixed-price bid on the basis of some inadequate paperwork, prepared by a partner who no longer was with the firm. At the time of bidding, the firm had no idea of the scope of work expected of it, and the language in the contract left a big hole. Small wonder its bid was low. It was so unreasonably low that the engineering firm's partner could not imagine that the architects did not know. "A mutual mistake," yelled the engineer, primed as he was by his lawyer for this mediation. "A binding agreement," responded the architect, equally well advised.

The mediation was convened at the suggestion of the carrier for both firms. Both sides could reach their lawyers if necessary, but lawyers were not present. After an extended joint session in which the mediator gathered the facts and identified the sticking points, the parties caucused. Typically the goal of the first caucus is to gather additional information the parties might want to keep confidential. In this case, the mediator learned that it was almost impossible for the engineering firm to do the needed work due to staffing problems.

It was apparent also that getting the project going was essential to the architect; clearly there was no time to litigate the matter. In subsequent caucuses, the mediator worked with the engineer to figure out how to get the job accomplished and with the architect to understand better how to get the result he needed. After several hours, the principals reconvened in joint session to work out the details. The architect agreed to lend his engineering intern with a background in mathematics for the weekend, and the principal engineer agreed to head the project work himself. They planned to get the work done and back to the architect by Monday morning, in time to head off stopping the job. An economic settlement was worked out, with variations depending on whether the work got done correctly and on time.

The Lesson

Neither side could benefit from insisting on its rights. The only possible way to help either side was to help both sides. The convening carrier was motivated by a desire not to have two companies it insured fighting each other. But the quick response of the mediator was also important: every day of delay took options away from the parties. Had the matter been litigated, the damages would have been enormous and all possibility of mutual benefit would have been lost.

Claimed Negligence

Two lawsuits over the quality of engineering work on a hydroelectric dam in the Southeast were settled by an agreement that the engineering firm buy out the owner-developer. This mediation began with a draft agreement prepared by a lawyer whom both sides respected. The problem was that negotiations had broken down.

Participating in the mediation were the local manager and a ranking officer in the company that owned the dam and the principals of the construction firm with their insurance carrier. The counsel who had drafted the original agreement was available by telephone.

The mediation lasted thirteen hours. At the conclusion, the parties started to leave, saying, "The mediator understands the agreement." "Not so fast," the mediator rejoined. She then had all parties put on tape their understanding of what had been negotiated paragraph by paragraph using the original draft agreement, together with new provisions agreed to in mediation. This tape was transcribed under the mediator's oversight and transmitted to the counsel on whom both parties agreed.

As it happened, the parties agreed on the language of one provision, but for different reasons. When that paragraph came up in the work to get a final agreement drafted, they asked the mediator for her recollection. Each had already accused the other of backing out of the agreement or trying to change the deal. The transcript showed clearly that there had never been agreement on the *meaning* of the words in question. The mediator informed them that they both were in error in this respect, and they needed to negotiate this point now. They did, and the settlement held.

The Lesson

The parties were perfectly capable of negotiating an agreement concerning the provision in question. What kept them from doing so was the perception apparently held by both that the other side was trying to "change the deal." This created a mental logjam that prevented them from seeing what needed to be done and how it could be done.

I have little doubt that a vast amount of business litigation could be avoided if, before adversarial procedures were invoked, someone could assist each side in testing the assumptions on which their apparent need for a fight rested. When things *look bad,* it is because that's the way we see them. It is us who make the value judgments. Things—events, behaviors, situations—are in themselves neutral. It is *how we see them* that turns them into a problem. We have a choice about this, but often it is not recognized. The works of David Bohm and Peter Senge are worth pondering in this regard.[1]

OTHER CONTRACT NEGOTIATION MEDIATIONS

There are many other examples of the mediation of complex contract negotiations. The accomplishments of these mediations tell the tale:

- Extended litigation over a patent was resolved when the allegedly infringing company became a marketing arm of the patent holder.
- A marital property dispute was resolved by a partnership arrangement for the operation of jointly owned commercial property.
- A silicon chip research and development contract dispute was resolved by negotiation of a new contract.

THE TRANSFORMATIVE POWER OF MEDIATION

In most of these examples, the parties went from being adversaries in or heading toward litigation to becoming business partners. There is little that can better demonstrate the transformative power of mediation. These transformations could not have happened if each party had not been willing to strive to understand the other side's situation. When they did, they saw the other's point of view, as well as the justification for their actions sufficiently to trust them with another agreement.

In business negotiations, there are often rough spots. One side might say, "Why don't we include a provision for resolving disputes?" The other side might counter quickly, "Why? What do you think might happen to this agreement?" The edginess in the voice might betray a new doubt about the wisdom of making the deal at all. "What do they know that I don't know?" one negotiator might be thinking. "What could go wrong here? Have I missed something?" In the honeymoon days of deal making, who wants to take such a chance?

This tendency to be agreeable, to make no waves, is also evident when businesspeople come together after trouble has cropped up. Lower officials or juniors may have met before and been unable to resolve differences, perhaps because of decisions by higher management. Eventually senior officials from each side will come together. They exchange pleasantries, perhaps have lunch or dinner. But there's a real reluctance to tackle difficult or sensitive subjects.

The reluctance is understandable. Each side knows that the next step is likely to be a lawsuit. Often there is high tension around the topic of concern. What do they do if the thing blows up in their faces? It could be years before there might be another chance to talk. This way, at least the door is still open.

The presence of the mediator changes all of this. A good mediator is patient and tenacious in allaying the anger that can disrupt discussions. An example is the mediation of a $30 million construction dispute that had been in litigation for a year and a half. In the mediation, a key executive on one side was so angry about what he saw as the other side's negligence that at times he could hardly speak. Finally, on the morning of the third day of this mediation, he looked up suddenly after the other side had completed an explanation on one point and said, "Oh, yes. I see what you mean." The tension in the room melted visibly. The mediator and others took a deep breath. It was time to begin. The negotiations eventually bore fruit in several major agreements.

When situations grow tense, the mediator redirects people's attention. Perhaps a comment or story allows people to laugh, or the mediator relates how this type of problem has been handled in other mediations. The mediator may simply call a break and give people a chance to stretch. Quick, informal caucusing with each side can elicit enough information to allow the mediator to change the focus so more information can be developed or to give the issue a rest. There is an infinite number of strategies; good mediators learn to pick appropriate ones for each situation.

Perhaps the best explanation for the powerful interface between contract negotiations and mediation is this: negotiation is an art form. It reaches its highest form with highly skilled, sensitive negotiators and a supportive environment. When a skilled mediator provides that environment, understands the negotiation game, and knows how to support the parties at every turn, the negotiation has a lot going for it. It is a small investment with big returns.

Chapter Fifteen

Charting Public and Private Policy

Impasse is in the eye of the beholder.
Anonymous

Are you happy about the condition of the world? Do you feel your local, state, and federal governments—employees and officials— are doing what they should be doing? How does politics strike you? Can you see someone like yourself getting involved in politics? When you hear on the news how one side is screaming at the other side in so many disputes, do you feel that progress is being made? Or do you find yourself suspicious of leaders' motives and of both governmental action and inaction?

This is the world we have made. American values supporting individuality and rights have left the equally strong historical American values of cooperation and collaboration in the dust. In my lifetime, "collaboration" came close to being synonymous with treason, as the oppression of Cold War thinking made fear a way of life in the 1950s.

Single-issue politics and the politics of confrontation have ground much of government to a halt, despite the fact that there is broad agreement that something should be done:

> Every effort by public agencies to shift priorities in response to new problems is met by fierce resistance from organizations that are content with the status quo. Media campaigns, intensive lobbying,

referendums, and similar strategies give these groups substantial leverage.

The courts find it difficult to impose their will. Groups unhappy with court decisions press their legislators to change the relevant laws. Cases come back again and again on appeal as single-minded groups seek to have things their way [Susskind and Cruikshank, 1987, p. 3].

BEYOND DISPUTING

Courts, agencies, and private organizations are finding that it is more productive to let people discuss problems in a protected environment such as mediation than merely to satisfy the obligation to hear each side out with an adversarial proceeding. In adversarial proceedings, there is no exchange of ideas, no reasoning with demands. These can take place only through discussions.

But how does one make such discussions productive? Unassisted negotiations fail for many reasons, among them that the issues are too many or too complex, the full range of stakeholders may not be obvious, and all key parties may not be willing to engage in negotiation, believing that litigation is acceptable without testing the alternatives. In the premeeting stages, mediators and facilitators can bring a change in all or any of these areas (Susskind and Cruikshank, 1987).

Another option is the consensus process. The goal of the consensus process is a decision that all group members can live with. It does not mean that everyone must be completely satisfied with the final outcome. Rather, the decision must be acceptable enough that all will agree to support the group choosing it. Although it is an ancient process, it has not been used extensively except by the Religious Society of Friends (Quakers), which has over 300 years of cumulative experience with consensus.

As we saw in Chapter Two, in the story "Vulnerability Works," consensus is a slippery concept for many people brought up on majority rule, but its promise is powerful. When everyone supports a group decision, little can stop it. When participation is broad enough, criticisms are dealt with up front, avoiding the costly arguments and litigation that often dog top-down decisions. The members' commitment to the process, which is also needed, may grow during the group process. The durability and strength of decision reached by consensus is the answer to criticism that it takes too long. This commitment need not be present at the outset, but usually grows during the group meetings. (See Avery, 1981).

When everyone supports a group decision, little can stop it.

Facilitators are often assigned a variety of prenegotiation tasks. These include working with the conveners—those who are inviting others to participate and learning more about who has an interest or stake in the situation. The conveners' lack of confidence in the process and clarity in the goals may undermine the process and add to the cynicism that may defeat subsequent collaborative efforts. So facilitators will work to build that confidence and increase clarity (Nash and Susskind, 1987). Prenegotiation tasks may well include an analysis of what the stakeholders are looking to achieve and what incentives might get them to join in a discussion.

In addition to a stakeholder analysis, the facilitator might help devise a proposed set of ground rules for the group to consider adopting. Facilitators also help to develop an agenda that will make it easier for the group to reach consensus. Sometimes facilitators provide logistical support for the discussion group, such as arranging the time and place of meetings and taking and distributing minutes. This may seem laborious and time-consuming, but as the computer generation reminds us, garbage in, garbage out. The quality of the discussion depends on a firm foundation. And the more that people invest in the process, the more they get out of it.

Mediators and facilitators may provide the additional service of conducting the meetings. Mediators are more proactive than facilitators and must develop sufficient trust to work privately with participants. Some experts recommend using a mediator whenever caucuses or confidential meetings between group sessions are likely to be necessary. Mediators may even propose mutually advantageous agreements when the participants run out of ideas, which facilitators generally would not do (Susskind and Cruikshank, 1987).

Mediators in public policy disputes do concern themselves with issues of overall fairness and the workability of agreements. It is considered legitimate for them to focus attention on the attributes of a good outcome but not legitimate to steer the negotiations toward a particular outcome. As with all other mediation, the agreement, if any, must be that of the participants.

The parties or participants in a public policy discussion also need to prepare themselves. Their preparation would include determining several things:[1]

- *What are the main issues that need to be negotiated?*
  It is no simple task to frame the issues such that when they are resolved, all participants' concerns are met.
- *What are the secondary issues within each issue that need to be negotiated?*
  There may be subissues within the primary issue that need to be identified.
- *What side agreements (not among all parties) might be needed in order to make overall negotiated agreement among all stakeholders more likely?*
  In a mediation to set priorities for a long-term statewide environmental program, for example, you might need a side agreement between a company and the enforcement agency, allowing a manufacturing facility a fixed amount of time to clean up its site on its own.
- *Are there procedural agreements that need to be reached in order to keep the group discussion progressing?* (See Figure 3.1 on page 45.)
  Consider a mediation over proposed regulation of public land grazing. Ranchers and the government might agree to postpone changes in their leases, pending the outcome of monitored tests of new approaches to grazing management, that offer the opportunity to restore the damaged land.[2]
- *What procedural agreements need to be reached first?*
  For example, in the mediation of a lawsuit over Indian fishing rights, it might be imperative to start with a joint fact-finding process in order to narrow the areas of disagreement.

These and other questions lead to the drafting of an agenda. Imagine devising that agenda so that as members of the group work through it, they are led to reach an agreement that everyone can subscribe to. It is obvious that this preparation work requires a lot of attention and a fair amount of skill, but the payoff is enormous. Those parts of the agenda and priorities that survive in the crucible of a joint process may become the agenda and priorities of your group, your community, and even your nation. (For a useful guide for citizen action, see Susskind and Cruikshank, 1987.)

Further steps in preparation for a public or quasi-public dialogue might include the following:

- *What set of ground rules for the discussion would help participants to gel as a group and be able to accomplish its goals?*
  A set of proposed ground rules might be developed during the conflict assessment and then submitted to the group for approval or amendment. Examples of such rules might be that every member must attend every meeting; that participants speak for themselves, not for their groups; that criticism be reserved for appropriate times and be constructive; or that no press comment be made except by a designated representative. Some ground rules might be worked out in advance, but it is often still desirable to allow them to develop from the group itself. There is more ownership.
- *Who should facilitate or mediate the discussion?*
  The individual needs to be neutral and also to be seen as neutral. He or she also needs to be capable of understanding the issues under discussion. Sometimes insiders, government or private officials, are used as neutrals if they are not perceived as having a political stake in the outcome of the discussions. Otherwise outsiders are preferred. Trust is always the issue.

The level of detail involved in preparing for a public policy dialogue speaks volumes about the nature of the process. The exercise of going through these preparation steps, as well as those required to make the meeting itself productive and to follow up on progress in the group meetings, invests parties in arriving at an agreement that all can subscribe to. It is the opposite of an adversarial process.

An example is the salmon mediation that took place in 1992. The Confederated Tribes of the Umatilla Indian Reservation in Oregon secured mediation over a $100 million Columbia River water management project. Involving state and federal agencies, Water Watch of Oregon, Oregon Trout and the Oregon Natural

Resources Council, several irrigation districts, and the tribes, this matter was mediated in five full-day sessions over a period of less than three months by a professional mediator and a water law expert. As a result, tribal fishing rights that had been lost through depletion of the streams were restored, and irrigators became members of the team working to replenish the salmon runs. The cost to the parties was roughly $20,000 (Harvard Project on Negotiation, 1992). Imagine how long and at what cost this might instead have been addressed through litigation. Clearly, the parties had the essential knowledge and know-how, so that when they came together in common cause, they could build an agreement. This is far from the zero-sum process that simple bargaining envisions. Through cooperation, these parties literally restored water to the streams when it was needed for salmon recovery.

BUILDING COMMUNITY

Americans at all levels of society are using mediation and facilitation to strengthen their communities and solve local problems.

Community Groups

An example is found in rural Oregon. In 1991, the Oregon Economic Development Department (OEDD) was convinced that top-down efforts to help communities face catastrophic losses in the timber industry were futile. Only efforts owned by the communities themselves could make a difference, and that meant a from-the-ground-up model.

In 1992, Rural Development Initiatives (RDI), a nonprofit organization founded by Lynn Youngbar with financial assistance from OEDD, began operating. Its facilitators are invited in by community groups or officials. After a preliminary SWOT (strengths, weaknesses, opportunities, threats) assessment, RDI staff guide a series of meetings that take members of the group through the steps of identifying what they like and do not like about the existing situation and what they would like to see happen in the future. This becomes a vision statement and forms the framework for establishing medium-term goals affecting business and workforce development, infrastructure, and quality of life to achieve this vision. From the vision, the group may develop a prioritized action plan to accomplish these goals. RDI provides information about what other communities are doing and access to other resources, such as mediation, where needed.

Most of RDI's work is for rural communities with populations of fewer than 10,000, with a special focus on those with populations under 2,500.

In many communities, leadership is deterred by unwritten rules that discourage speaking up. RDI's facilitators help free people from these self-defeating behaviors. RDI provides leadership training for some community members who have participated in the planning process and supports a network of such leaders across rural Oregon—and since 1999, rural Washington. By the end of 2000, RDI had assisted over 120 communities and provided leadership training to over 400 rural community leaders. Participating communities have completed many successful projects to create jobs, develop recreational and cultural opportunities, and attract critically needed health and safety improvements. RDI has been recognized by federal, state, and national groups for its leadership training work and the quality and uniqueness of its work—touching as it does on business development, market analysis, conflict resolution, workforce and real estate development, forestry strategic planning, and training design. Through these efforts, it is showing communities how to reverse the nationwide trend toward the decline and death of rural communities.

Through facilitation and by use of mediation as needed, communities are often turning around economic, population, and resource decline and are beginning to move back to health. In the past two years, RDI has provided leadership training for leaders from sixty-six communities and worked with eleven communities on strategic plans. Private funding is now essential in supporting this catalytic work.

Burns is a small community in southeastern Oregon. It is where my mother was born. When the lumber mill shut down for two years in 1979, the town's heart stopped. Then the mill reopened with three hundred jobs, and things began looking up. When the mill finally closed in 1989, Harney County lost fifteen hundred of its eighty-five hundred residents. Unemployment soared to 20 percent. Stores on Main Street closed; vacancy signs sprouted like flowers on the sagebrush in late summer. Many predicted ruin. But a tough-minded gathering of citizens from all walks of life refused to say die. They formed a group to talk about their mutual problems. This was a first for the town. Then they called in RDI and brought in a consultant to assess the community's strengths, weaknesses, opportunities, and threats. From there, they began a planning process.

Things started turning around. The power of people with a common goal and a vision of what might be working together is phenomenal. Stephen R. Covey (1989) calls it synergy, a supercharged, exciting adventure in creativity. Discussions take place. People stop making speeches and begin to hear what others are saying. More important, they become committed to the process because they own it. And they begin to see that only when everyone owns it do things start to happen. Today every store on Main Street is occupied, and now there is a new drug superstore. The weekly 7:00 A.M. follow-up meetings of everyone who cares to come are on track and lively.

On sensitive issues such as water, logging, grazing, and mineral extraction, mediation is often required. In this context, mediation helps people find how to live together in peace and prosperity, recognize and discard destructive patterns of interaction, and learn from experience that they personally can make a difference.

Organizations and Industry

There is no reason that community cannot be built within an organization or industry. If there were community, there would be mutual respect. There would be a sort of resilience that there can never be when individuals within a group think of themselves as entirely separate from one another. In the past, community was a kind of given in some organizations. A community may be hierarchical or egalitarian, but it presupposes mutual obligations of one to another. It would go far in relieving business relationships of the hard edge that causes so much difficulty.

There is no reason that community cannot be built within an organization or industry.

Even the economists know that the free market model is not a true representation of how our society works. Francis Fukuyama, a senior social scientist with RAND Corporation, writes compellingly of the critical role of trust in the success of Western economies:

> A society built entirely out of rational individuals who come together on the basis of a social contract for the sake of the satisfaction of their wants cannot form a society that would be viable over any length of time. . . . If individuals formed communities only on the basis of rational long-term self-interest, there would be little in the way of public spiritedness, self-sacrifice, pride, charity or any of the other virtues that make communities liveable [Fukuyama, 1995, p. 351].

Fukuyama points out that it is only in high-trust societies that Western economic liberalism has succeeded. He concludes:

> The degree to which people value work over leisure, their respect for education, attitudes toward the family, and the degree of trust they show toward their fellows all have a direct impact on economic life and yet cannot be adequately explained in terms of the economists' basic model of man [Fukuyama, 1995, p. 351].

Old mind is a product of the values of philosophers of the Enlightenment, untouched by the total revolution in that way of thinking that has occurred in the past hundred years. It is time that organizations, public and private, wake up. The tools for retooling are available.

One of the most powerful tools, the dialogue process—the art of thinking together—has the effect of creating community at a profound level. As Isaacs (1999) shows, it changes lives. The business community as a whole has not yet recognized the depth of the change of mind that must occur for meaningful change to take place in organizations.

A study of how resistant we are to change is the story of a car launch in which a whole project team within a smokestack industry, trained in the art of being a learning organization, performed miracles by comparison with past efforts—only to find its process ignored, its leaders shuffled off into early retirement, and its accomplishments discounted (Roth and Kleiner, 1999). Never underestimate the power of old mind to ignore the realities. Beck and Cowan (1996), the spiral dynamics pioneers, would say, "But, of course. One cannot take in information that conflicts with one's world view." And that is the reality with which all those who seek change must come to terms.

The problems that face people all over the world are very similar and compelling. But human nature is a resource as well as a liability. Mark Smith, executive director of the Burns Chamber of Commerce, says, "It's attitude. We started working on our attitude, with beautification projects, for example. We just changed our attitude." It might help to think of mediation and consensus as attitude adjustment tools.

In truth, it's a lot more than attitude that holds us back. It's old mind. This is the root of attitude. When it is your turn to influence how your organization does business and handles conflict, think of the potential. What people worldwide want out of life is much the same. In this new millennium, are we willing to commit our own fortunes to new mind—to building community and to collaborative processes such as consensus and mediation? Can we afford not to do so?

Chapter Sixteen

The Emerging Synthesis

*Every action taken, from the moment we switch off the
alarm clock in the morning . . . has the potential to
change the world.*
DAVID WHYTE, *THE HEART AROUSED*

As children of the argument culture, we have been accustomed to
looking for things to criticize and things that distinguish us from
others. All of this is habit, in a sense. But it's not destiny, geneti-
cally programmed into us. We have the choice. You and I together
can bring about change in how we in our culture think, how we
relate, and how we carry on social discourse including the management of conflict. Key to all of this is the rule of one: it only takes
one. When one person in the
game changes, the whole game
changes. That is because the
game of life is a system in which
what we do influences what others do, and vice versa, and if we
are not mindful of the larger pic-
ture, we will deprive ourselves of the very things we most need
(Senge, 1994). Destructive, reactive cycles are vulnerable to the
reality that it takes only one.

*When one person in the
game changes, the
whole game changes.*

Old mind rejects the rule of one. It needs an "other" to make
itself separate from. It always wants to judge. If one dominated by
old mind does something creative and new, it wants to show up
others—to make itself look good at their expense. Thus, it builds

enemies and loses the opportunity to create allies in productive endeavor. Such a one insists on control, the familiar *power over,* and so loses the immense resources that would have been available for a shared vision. An example is employers running in fear of litigation, seeking to force employees to arbitrate their employment concerns, often in unfair arrangements.

In employment as elsewhere throughout our institutional structures, old mind hangs on to judgment and control, as if death itself were the alternative. It is incongruous to have such power-based approaches spreading at a time when new-mind strategies and approaches are becoming more widely recognized and available. New mind looks to the conditions that give rise to the complaints and addresses these. It looks for ways of sharing power and seeking power with. New mind is not driven by fear. The mind is servant to the heart. When the heart is closed, it leaves the mind in control. When it is open, the heart directs the mind into channels of creativity and healing beyond imagining—what we call flow.

The form of conflict resolution in North America is changing profoundly from primarily litigation, based on confrontation, to primarily mediation, based on collaboration. These changes are evident on a grand scale—if you know where to look. We do not have the statistical tools to document it, which leads to rather humorous studies being released purporting to detect the effectiveness of mediation and other ADR processes, such as the 1996 RAND study of ADR in the federal courts (RAND Corporation, 1996). (The RAND study showed virtually no effect from resolving through mediation compared with litigation and was widely questioned.) In truth, the lack of data leaves researchers out of the water, but new categories for the collection of data require time. Even as new categories are devised, there is the question of whether every court, agency, and organization is using the same definitions. It will take years to sort this out (Galanter, 1993). Meanwhile, mediation is being integrated and absorbed into every major institution in the country, public and private, at a rate that would be the envy of the virus world.

What this is bringing with it is fresh air. We are learning that rights disputes can be resolved with an eye to the parties' emotional health, relationships, feelings, needs, goals, resources, and psychological impact of the process. We're learning that creative conflict management and resolution can promote both the healing of wounds and the desire to address the sources of the problems that keep generating the conflicts. There is a very real opportunity in conflict resolution to create value-added through vastly reduced transaction costs, far earlier resolution (particularly where mediation is used as the container for the dispute), and the intangible benefits of improved attitude and restored business relationships.

There is every reason for mediation to live up to its promise. But it may not. Mediation can fail to realize its potential if it is strapped down too tightly to a legalistic model by legislation and rules and old mind. You, however, can influence the outcome by how you approach and use the process. By looking for and working with reflective mediation, you can strengthen those forces that would explore the power of the mediation process, or you can choose to strengthen those who choose not to do so.

WELCOMING NEW MIND

Old mind is not the enemy. There is no enemy. The strength of old mind comes largely from the fact that it is embedded deeply in each one of us. When we move against it, we carry our own headwinds with us. It takes the art of inquiry to change this. When we look for the underlying assumptions and core beliefs that our thinking is based on, we're engaging in inquiry. When we offer our underlying thinking to others in negotiation and in conversation, we're inviting them to do the

Old mind is not the enemy. There is no enemy.

same. We're also building strength in little-used muscles. Old mind cannot survive the light of day. It has power only when it goes unrecognized and unexamined.

Old mind cannot see that the situations it criticizes and fights against are often created by itself. David Bohm (1994) gives the example of one who likes flattery, being taken advantage of time and time again by flatterers yet never associating the conditioning— liking flattery—with the result—being taken advantage of. He points to the way we have acted completely contrary to our long-term interests as a nation and as part of the Western alliance, by selling arms to the Middle East. A classic case within the United States is the way we deal with crime, through longer and longer sentences, at costs comparable to or exceeding the cost of a private college education, even though—as those within the system know—this perpetuates recidivism rather than reduces it. For most of us, including most of our institutions, that awareness is below consciousness, so we keep on creating the very thing we fight against (Tuchman, 1992). That's old mind.

CLARITY BROUGHT TO "THE WAY IT HAS ALWAYS BEEN DONE"

As scholar and consensus pioneer Lawrence Susskind (Susskind, McKearnan, and Thomas-Larmer, 1999) writes, we have moved way beyond a world that could be ordered by or sorted out through *Robert's Rules of Order.* The majoritarian rules that governed the conduct of business by the Congress in the nineteenth century are weak tools for fashioning a resolution that many diverse interests can wholeheartedly support; everyone must find it in their self-interest to do so and believe in the fairness and appropriateness of the process used to reach that resolution. We have become too aware of the interconnectivity of interests and relationships in too many spheres of life to ignore them. *Linear* is out as a way of organizing human affairs. *Holistic* is in (see Appendix E). We're discovering it doesn't always have to be work. There can be flow. It can be fun.

The twentieth century saw the physical sciences shaken out of their comfortable reliance on a Newtonian worldview by Einstein's theory of relativity and the many discoveries following it. Small-particle physics came to recognize the interconnectedness of all life, visible, for example, through the immense impacts of tiny perturbations on living systems such as the weather and the effects of the researcher on research. Today legal systems around the world are becoming conscious and aware that an orderly society and the vindication of rights do not depend on some form of combat, verbal or otherwise. There is a small but growing recognition that when interests are served and respect shared, rights are vindicated in ways that adversarial compulsion of strict adherence to rule, law, or mandate could never do. This is not to say these are not needed, merely that there are better ways of doing things, provided the background of protections is in place to curtail habitual overreaching.

In 1995, Australia's attorney general, also a member of Parliament, asked the Australian Law Reform Commission to "review the adversarial system of conducting civil, administrative review and family law proceedings before courts and tribunals exercising federal jurisdiction," having regard to, among other things, "the need for a simpler, cheaper and more accessible legal system" (Australian Law Reform Commission, 2000). The final report, *Managing Justice*, examines not merely the practices of courts and judges, but also judicial education, legal education, practice standards, and legal assistance. It not only speaks to the judiciary but seeks to "engage the legal profession, the academy, government and others in the task of reshaping legal practice and professional culture in aid of meaningful reform of the civil justice system." In addition to a number of advisory and working groups, the commission cosponsored two conferences in connection with its inquiry: "Beyond the Adversarial System: Changing Roles and Skills for Courts, Tribunals and Practitioners" and "The Management of Disputes Involving the Commonwealth. Is Litigation Always the Answer?"

There is movement in the European Union toward the convergence of English and continental civil procedure. The ancient split between common law and civil law blurred in many types of proceedings during the later years of the twentieth century. That will not any time soon cause wholesale displacement of traditional common law adversarial processes (trial by jury and having one's day in court), but the debate is now more subtle and nuanced, and there is evidence of a search for common ground. It seems clear that among thoughtful observers, there has been almost universal dissatisfaction with the way things have always been done, within the legal institutions of many, many countries. In the United Kingdom in 2000, the lord chancellor began an initiative to introduce mediation more broadly into what have been wholly court processes.

OUR PREFERENCES ARE SHOWING

People worldwide are discovering that what others are coerced into, they resist. Studies in the United States show that compliance rates for mediated agreements with monetary settlement were 70.6

percent, compared to 33.8 percent for adjudications, with an additional 16.5 percent of mediated settlements and 21.1 percent of adjudicated settlements partially paid (Goldberg and others, 1992). Similarly, studies of court-ordered restitution in criminal cases in the United States show that 20 to 25 percent of such orders are complied with, compared with 90 to 95 percent when victim-offender mediations result in a written agreement, which they do in the vast majority of instances.[1] There are bottom-line benefits to a more personal process, one in which everyone, even a convict with no hope of reduced sentencing, can play a meaningful part.

The remarkable move toward consensus processes for public policy issues is indicative of the direction of this enormous change in the way we do things around our differences. Consensus, after all, requires that everyone be able to live with an outcome, even if they cannot wholeheartedly subscribe to it. It gives every person involved a sort of veto power over the outcome, so it is an ideal process for low-trust situations. No one can afford to overlook someone else—to fail to take his or her concerns seriously.

THE EXPLOSION OF COLLABORATIVE PROCESSES

In 1998, the chief judge of Maryland's highest appellate court, Robert M. Bell, launched a statewide effort to develop and implement an action plan to advance the appropriate use of ADR in the courts as well as in communities, schools, state and local government agencies, criminal and juvenile justice programs, and businesses. Judge Bell appointed a forty-member commission composed of representatives of all of the stakeholder interests in the future of ADR in Maryland, including the governor's chief of staff, the attorney general, high-ranking state legislators, the president of the state bar association, the chief judges from each level of the court system, community representatives, business representatives, educators, mediators, and others. The commission used ADR techniques, such as fact-finding and collaborative problem solving, as a modus operandi for all of its work.

The commission's statewide consensus-building process ultimately involved 700 people in developing a practical action plan titled "Join the Resolution" (Maryland ADR Commission, 1999). The commission has been implementing the action plan since that time. The judiciary provided the commission's operating budget, and both the state legislature and the governor's office contributed funding to initiate the commission's projects.

Among the challenges noted by the commission was a lack of public awareness and understanding of ADR. To address this, one of the priorities was a public awareness campaign. Imagine a TV ad with Arnold Schwarzenegger stepping out of a particularly violent clip from *The Terminator* and saying to the audience, "This only happens in the movies. . . . You know, in real life, we need to mediate." Although the commission was not able to make that TV spot, it is working to develop something equally powerful.

The Maryland ADR Commission has now evolved into the Maryland Mediation and Conflict Resolution Office (MACRO), which is housed within the judiciary as a court-related agency funded as part of the judiciary's budget. A report on the status of implementation efforts submitted to the commission during its final October 2000 meeting noted many interesting projects and initiatives that are underway. A statewide public relations campaign includes marketing community mediation, developing a documentary video on the power of mediation in many areas, and conducting a statewide public awareness effort highlighting the benefits of mediation. There will be training for legal service providers and assistant attorneys general in how to represent parties in mediation. There is a school initiative to involve school superintendents and train future teachers in conflict resolution. A cultural shift is necessary to instill unfamiliar, peace-oriented behavior that involves sharing power with students in order to make the students responsible for resolving disruptions and disputes in the classroom (National Center for State Courts, 1999, pp. 16–18).

The commission supports model schools that are mentoring troubled schools. The commission also is involved in a whole school peace and tolerance initiative with feeder school mentoring components. There is a Mediator Quality Assurance Project using consensus building methods to define best practices. Community mediation programs are being funded, expanded, and promoted, with support from a commission-created non-profit community mediation association. Community mediators are evaluating several HotSpot criminal and juvenile justice teams and developing plans to integrate good conflict resolution practices. State government is incorporating mediation into environmental services, human resources, and agricultural issues. The commission also is planning to assist in the creation of a video on the use of ADR in youth and family service delivery systems. There is a business initiative spearheaded by corporate organizations that promotes a speakers' bureau and an ADR pledge program for Maryland companies and law firms. And, of course, there are pilots and programs at every level of the court system.

This is a remarkable example of using ADR to involve the public in setting public policy. It is not just a pro forma effort undertaken to satisfy a statutory requirement. Instead, it is a truly expansive, ongoing collaboration of people from all walks of life who are committed to creating a more peaceful and civil society. It shows what new mind can do.

Other examples of the application of consensus-building techniques are dialogues between prochoice and antiabortion advocates,[2] school system–community discussions around school closures and prison sitings, determining the condition of ecosystems and developing plans for their restoration and management, and sidestepping litigation among condominium owners over the division of a multimillion-dollar settlement fund (see "Vulnerability Works" in Chapter Two). The process has been used within work teams and at every level of corporate management and decision making. The old models are dying away where there is openness and responsiveness to change.

Mediation may incorporate all or some of the elements of consensus building and may involve teaching and modeling the techniques of dialogue. It is rapidly becoming the most widespread of the new processes for collaborative problem solving and decision making. It can serve equally well as a beginning of a newly defined relationship and as an ending to a conflict, depending on what the situation calls for.

Collaborative processes will be moving upstream toward the prevention of conflict in the first place. Leading the way in this is the partnering movement. Spawned by the tremendous difficulties that the construction industry faced in the 1980s, it involved the creation of "highly structured agreements between companies to cooperate to an unusually high degree to achieve their separate but complementary objectives" (Cook and Hancher, 1990). In the more common form used in the 1990s, it applies the principles of the Japanese-initiated Total Quality Management approach, by which "the contracting partners get to know one another, identify common goals and discuss specific plans and expectations, establish clear channels of communication and fail-safe mechanisms for resolving potential problems." It took off in the public works contracting arena in the early 1990s (Stipanowich, 1998a, p. 378). It is really a facilitated planning of long-term relationships, which is the essence of large construction projects.

THE TRAINING ELEMENT

A partnering session begins with training and exercises designed to enhance interpersonal communication skills, dialogue techniques, and an understanding of styles of disputing and the management of conflict. During the training and facilitated discussion following it, participants discuss the project mission, evaluate specific performance objectives and potential problems, and identify the expectations of the various companies and individuals. There is often a project charter or plan setting forth agreed-on goals and the mission statement for the members of the project team.

The shared experience of training and education in communication skills and often team-building capacities are essential elements of state-of-the-art conflict resolution design and implementation of a conflict management system. In their excellent book *Designing Conflict Management Systems* (1995), Costantino and Merchant speak compellingly of the need to recognize problems created by the culture of the organization and to address these through enhancing awareness of the contributions of self and context to the problems encountered, bringing awareness of new tools and resources and developing essential and appropriate skills. In the new paradigm, such broad-based training may become a way of life rather than something that is only skill based and otherwise outside the purview of organizational thinking.

This enlarged presence of training built into collaborative processes is part of a trend. It is happening in consensus-building processes and even in mediations. Where the parties really need more refined tools for communicating, it can happen that a brief training session plus some materials may enable a more civil discussion to take place, embodying at least the basics of inquiry, which looks behind statements, views, and positions and may lead in some instances to dialogue.

The risk in partnering, as in mediation, comes through loss of commitment to the integrity of the partnering process. By downgrading the process, making it routine or mundane, most of its potential is lost. To be effective, partnering must become not just an event, however central that might be; instead, the principles of partnering must become an integral part of project relationships. If the inaugural workshop does not reflect a commitment of the highest levels of management that is communicated to personnel at every level of the project, it is not really partnering. It's form but not substance. If the initial workshop does not draw out some mutual understanding of where the problems are likely to arise and produce some collaborative problem solving on how to avoid or manage these potential fracture points, much of the potential has been missed. If the initial workshop does not create a mutual expectation of a high level of integrity in the performance of commitments on the project, it will have failed to discourage the opportunism that so troubled the industry in the early 1980s.

THE WEAK LINK

More than ever before, what you do makes a difference. Peter Senge (1994) teaches us to think of ourselves and our problems as part of a system—that problems aren't the result of causal events, as linear thinking would dictate. Rather, they are the result of our relationship to them. As Black Elk said, everything in the world tries to be round. Senge points out that we are constantly interacting with our problems—organizational, personal, and societal—in a sort of feedback loop, that is, a kind of circle. When you no longer see conflict as an isolated event but rather as part of a system in which your relationship to it is key, the world will never look the same again.

No matter how good a process is, it is always possible to cheapen it and lose most of its benefits. That is truly the burning issue of the day. It is not whether mediation but how. It is not whether upstreaming collaborative processes but how. It is not whether to begin to share power and to experience the vast increase in real power that brings, but how we will approach it that is the most obvious step in moving away from power-based and rights-based approaches and toward interest-based approaches and beyond.

In the work of maintaining integrity and moving in flow, reflective mediation has much to offer. By letting go of the mediators' agendas, whether to solve your problem or to transform you, by mirroring to you and the others what it is that you seek, both consciously and unconsciously, by reflecting to all of you the vastness of the resources you bring with you, as well as your vision and wisdom, the reflective mediator is in service not just to your short-term interests, but to your midrange interests and long-term values, which are dearest to your heart. Conflict cannot be composted without heat. Reflective mediation allows you the opportunity to turn up the heat, so that you can get the breakthroughs your conflict experience is offering to you. The breakthroughs that conflict can offer include greater insight, better communication, renewed relationships, a resolution perceived as just and proper under the circumstances, renewed commitment to resolving intractable problems of the sort that led to the conflict in the first place—even the experience of your heart being touched and much more.

The twentieth century may go down in history as a time of ferment leading to a massive reorientation of our conflict management systems or as a time when opportunities for peaceful change were seen but ignored. Not since the Middle Ages has there been such a thorough assault on institutions of all kinds. Not for a thousand years have people been faced with such enormous change, and only in times of ecological disaster has such change come to people so suddenly as it is coming today.

Where you—as lawyer or other professional or as a consumer of conflict resolution services—choose to stand will affect the balance and influence the outcome. In a very real sense, the whole world is in your hands. Your weight will be felt through each choice you make in every conflict situation with which you come into contact. For all of us, make it a good one.

Perspective Exercise

Breathing has long been a vehicle for increasing self-awareness, something that is hard to achieve in our busy lives. Self-awareness in the context of resolving differences means recognizing our own contribution to the continued difficulty and deciding to do something about that. The body is also a great teacher, as this experience demonstrates.

Set aside a full five minutes. You may want to tape the following material for playing back or have another person read it slowly to you as you do the exercise. With a tape, you can pause it when you need more time doing the exercise. Without either of these aids, simply read the material to yourself a couple of times before beginning.

Close your eyes, and breathe slowly and deeply. Allow the breath to fill you deeply. Exhale all of the air, slowly, fully. Notice how relaxed you feel at the end of each breath, in that quiet space before the next breath begins.

Allow intruding thoughts to drift away, without any effort on your part. It is counterproductive to chastise yourself for having these thoughts. You are in a space beyond blame, a place of action and consequences rather than who is right and who is wrong.

Check your face muscles, your jaw, your shoulders, your back for tension. Allow your shoulders to fall back and down, noticing the comfortable

---

Source: This exercise is based on the work of Edith Stauffer, director of Psychosynthesis International, teacher and author of *Unconditional Love and Forgiveness.*

stretch. Wiggle your toes. Imagine the breath going to a place in your body that hurts or is tense. As you exhale, imagine that each breath carries with it a little of the pain or the tension you are feeling.

Put your hands on your belly, and breathe into it for a moment, noticing if there is any feeling of fear or anxiety there. It is said that fear lives in the belly and that it is the child in us who fears. Comfort that child in you that is anxious or afraid by thinking of all the goodness and happiness in your life. Let yourself be like a baby: warm, comfortable, breathing easily.

Now recall a dispute or a situation that causes you anxiety. Notice what happens to your body as the thought of these difficulties floods your mind. Notice your face and jaw muscles, your back, your belly. Now take the recollection of the dispute, and in your imagination put it on a little shelf just to one side of your head. Clear your mind by breathing deeply and slowly again three times.

Next, remember a time when you felt really good about yourself. Relive that experience in your imagination now, reexperiencing the sounds, sights, smells, and feelings it brings back. What a great time of your life! Revel in it, for it is part of you. Now notice how relaxed your body feels. Notice your jaw and face muscles in particular. Hold the recollection of that experience, for you will use it as a filter.

Now holding on to that good experience, gently retrieve the recollection of the events of the dispute. Keep breathing. Keeping in mind the good experience, let these events replay. Notice if the whole situation seems to have lost some of its power. Keep breathing.

Now stretch, wiggle your toes, and open your eyes when you are ready. Look at the situation with new eyes, loving yourself for the good you've done and tried to do, forgiving yourself for the errors. Look at the other person in the same way. When you can fully appreciate his or her view, including, perhaps, how unattractive what you did or failed to do appears, your perspective is in balance.

Done properly, this exercise evokes compassion and moves you beyond judgment. You can now view the situation dispassionately enough to make sound decisions in your own best interest.

Most of the time, people find that the events leading to the dispute are softened and in some way rendered more responsive by this exercise. Sometimes they realize that before doing the exercise, what happened seemed to carry a personal attack. Afterward, it becomes just another event. Sometimes, even though we know that it is we who are hurting, we're not ready yet to stop. If you find the exercise doesn't help, be patient. Do it again in a few weeks and perhaps in a few months. Imagine thinking about this person, this event, with no stress, with no emotional spin on it at all. That is within your grasp.

Writing Agreements in Mediation

Agreements reached in mediation are wisely captured in written form at the time. More and more counsel bring draft settlement agreements to the mediation. Louise LaMothe, first woman chair of the American Bar Association's Litigation Section, writes:

> It is best to document the agreement on the spot. This often requires some doing, since the session may conclude in the wee hours of the morning (in fact, that seems to be the rule). To handle those problems, I bring a notebook computer loaded with sample settlement agreements. Using the computer, we draft and plug in specific language to implement the settlement. Often this process exposes other issues that the mediator can help the parties to consider, using the goodwill developed during the mediation [LaMothe, 1993, p. 4].

Postponing such documentation to another day has many pitfalls. Most annoying, the momentum toward resolution developed during the mediation dissipates when the lawyers return days later to the task of writing the agreement. Sometimes clients (and lawyers) find ways to raise new issues or alter agreements; the process can then falter, often taking weeks to conclude and sometimes unraveling.

It is not unusual to see counsel working together, one at the keyboard and one or more standing by. Sometimes the mediator is at the keyboard. Everyone strives for agreeable language; the mediator may also propose language. Redrafts of key paragraphs are done until they are satisfactory.

The process is time-consuming but moves quickly compared to trying to negotiate such agreements by telephone and facsimile, when everyone has turned to other business. One mediation of a gender-based wrongful-termination case took sixteen hours to reach agreement and four more to conclude the settlement agreement. The lawyers brushed aside their fatigue as best they could in order to secure closure. The clients were well served and well pleased. Although the plaintiff had a week to revoke the agreement, it held.

Working up an agreement in mediation saves weeks to months of delay and significant expense. In addition, in cases with strong emotional currents, it is far easier to get a signature at the time of the mediation than later. Even if there is a statutory revocation period, such as the seven-day waiting period in age discrimination matters, the signature at the time is an important token of intent to reach finality.

INTERIM AGREEMENTS

All mediation can lead to interim agreements on procedures that, when followed, will lead to resolution. Various mediators are more or less likely to keep the parties focused long enough to get to this stage if overall agreement proves impossible at the time. As a mediation participant, make it your responsibility to request this discussion whenever you feel it appropriate.

If the mediation is early, its most productive use may be to win agreements on procedures for collecting and disseminating information that everyone now sees is needed. You may have taken a run at settling a case that seemed too small to justify much premediation effort. You may have a big case that cries for a highly effective working relationship among counsel. Mediation develops this.

If it appears that adjudication will be necessary, the parties may readily negotiate an agreement on issues to be presented for decision, stipulations to be reached, and what scope the parties will have in presenting evidence or arguments. For example, negotiating a pretrial order or an agreement for binding arbitration can save the parties an immense amount of time, effort, and expense.

FINAL AGREEMENTS

Negotiating the terms of a final agreement can be time-consuming. It is helpful not only to have a draft settlement agreement in hand, but to have considered which paragraphs need negotiation and to have some options in mind with respect to these. For example, if confidentiality of the settlement terms is required, what difficulties might be encountered in negotiating for this? What alternatives might you consider? Or if future action is to be required by the agreement, who is motivated to do it? Who will take care of the details? How will you know when it is done? What agreement might you seek to ensure needed compliance? Do you want to negotiate any fallback arrangement if it isn't done or is not done in a timely manner?

DISPUTE RESOLUTION CLAUSE

Always include a dispute resolution clause in the agreement. At the minimum, this should provide for mediation. If the mediator has been satisfactory, name him or her as mediator for any dispute relating to performance or interpretation of the agreement.

In long-term construction contracts, joint administrative committees are sometimes constituted, primarily to head off problems of differing interpretation. Sometimes a mediator is provided for should this group be unable to reach agreement. Differing expectations are often the biggest headaches in contract administration. It is best to recognize and deal with these early, before frayed tempers make productive discussions impossible.

MEMORANDUM OF AGREEMENT CHECKLIST

1. An agreement to resolve, stating each party's obligations: (a) plaintiff to provide a full release as specified and usually to dismiss the complaint with prejudice; (b) defendant(s) obligation to pay what and to whom (with employer ID numbers); who will bear fees and costs incurred.
2. A tax indemnity and hold harmless for payors where payment might be characterized as income to the recipient (optional).
3. Confidentiality of the terms of settlement (optional).
4. Mutual non-disparagement (optional).
5. Signatures for parties and counsel, with date and place of execution.

Cutting the Baby
Beyond Solomon's Solution

Lawyers and mediators use the following techniques to help parties reach agreement over the division of property.

Mutual selection: Each party places their initials next to the items they want, then they discuss contested items in terms of who selected it or uses it, and attempt to reach agreement.

Barter: Each party takes certain items of property in exchange for other items. For instance, the car and furniture in exchange for the truck and tools.

One divides, the other chooses: One divides the property into two parts and the other gets to choose between the parts. Or one chooses first and the other second, rotating until all items are divided.

One values, the other chooses: One places a value based on present fair market value on each item of property and the other gets to choose items totaling one-half the total value.

Appraisal and alternate selection: A third person such as an agreed-upon appraiser places a value on contested items of property, then the parties choose alternately.

Sale: Some or all of the items are sold and the proceeds divided equally.

Secret bid: Each party places a secret bid on each contested item of property and the one who bids highest for the item gets it. Where one party receives items that exceed their share, there will be an equalization payment to the other party.

Source: Ken Cloke, Center for Dispute Resolution, Santa Monica, Calif.

Private auction: The parties openly bid against each other on each item of community property. If one receives more than his or her share, an equalization payment will be made.

Mediation: The parties negotiate, using a mediator.

Arbitration: The parties select an arbitrator who will make the final decision about valuation and division after hearing from both parties and considering all the evidence.

The Emotional Stages of Letting Go of Conflict
Lessons from Divorce

Particularly visible in divorce situations are the emotional aspects of conflict. The emotional stages of divorce are the same as those found in any other situation where one or another side feels wronged: denial ("This can't be happening to me"), anger ("He, she, they can't do this to me"), and eventually acceptance ("It happened to me, I had a part in it, I've been hurt, but the remedy is sufficient under the circumstances").

DENIAL

As with death, the first stage in reacting to divorce is denial. Mediators work with the parties to get them to accept the fact of their separation and choose it or a return to marriage counseling to discover whether the marriage is in fact over. Divorce brings one or both parties the end of a consistent source of self-definition. Denial is triggered when a party has no sense that a better, happier self-definition may emerge from separation.

ANGER

Following denial comes anger. Mediation allows divorcing parties to experience the full range of emotions appropriate to their separation. It then becomes possible to change incrementally, evolving from one stage to another without compromising the process or detracting from its result. The expression of anger at the opposing party may help both move on to agreement. In mediation, power remains with the participants rather than with the mediator. Attachment to objects, which is so troublesome in legal proceedings, in mediation leads to better understanding of the emotional tides of divorce. For example, mediation allows a couple to use the children or the money or Aunt Mary's chest of drawers to act out their sense of abandonment, entitlement, and acceptance of loss. The object in dispute is allowed to become irrelevant (metaphorical) or practical (problem solving). Once the anger is dissipated, mediation lets them choose solutions based not on anger but on their existing needs.

ACCEPTANCE

Agreement and acceptance grow out of the progressive refinement of individual needs in the negotiation. They do not depend on objective abstract criteria as in law or subjective or internal processes as in therapy. At a certain point, it becomes obvious that anger is not working, and when a person is ready, he or she can make a choice to give the anger up, since anger is a way of maintaining a negative kind of intimacy. The surrender of anger is the first real acceptance of the fact of divorce.

EMOTIONAL STATES

There are important differences in the emotional states each party experiences during their separation. Mediation acknowledges, respects, annotates, and comments on their progression through these states. The parties' interim working compromises chronicle their resolution.

Reconciliation can be achieved in mediation—not necessarily in the sense of a return to marriage, but of creating a friendship out of intimate knowledge of the other, a common history, and a lack of compulsory attachment. For many divorcing couples, the rage is too recent to consider reconciliation. Yet the glimmerings of future friendship are often evident at the conclusion of the mediation. This parallels the pattern of processing business disputes as well, for human nature is a constant.

Appendix E

| Love of the Dance

A holistic, integrated approach embodies the essence of the sacred feminine. This missing element in our system of justice and civil process is elaborated on by writer and mystic Andrew Harvey (Harvey and Matousek, 1994). Harvey and Matousek explore what balance and wholeness mean as they delineate three powers of the sacred archetypal feminine: (1) knowledge of the interrelationship of all life, (2) the law of rhythm, and (3) the love of the dance. I've included this material to incorporate into this book some of the lyrical quality—the lightness and relatedness—of the deep feminine.

Inherent in the interrelationship of all life are "respect . . . gratitude, and natural compassion for all . . . life" (Harvey and Matousek, 1994, p. 61). With this knowledge, we diminish the power of appeals to fear based on *they* and *them.* For example, what *they* think about something or what *they* might do becomes less important when we see those others in ourselves. Fear-mongers play on our sense of separateness and isolation to whip us into conformity, cruelty, and mob behavior. If we do not feel separate, we deprive the fear-mongers of the raw material they need to do this. We come to recognize in others something of ourselves.

We come to recognize that what goes around comes around— that what we dish out, we get, one way or another, in return. When we treat others disrespectfully, we hurt ourselves, even though we cannot see how at the time.

The governor-general of New Zealand, on the occasion of the fiftieth anniversary of V.J. Day (Victory over the Japanese in World War II), read a prayer that ends this way: "In the end, we will not be

truly reconciled until you are as important to me as I am to myself."
(This reconciliation prayer is available in full at www.mediate.com/
baphillips.) In the new paradigm, using new mind, we look for
mutual benefit and mutual gain.

The law of rhythm is "the knowledge that the universe has its
own laws and harmonies that are already whole" and we must
"intuit, revere and follow them" (Harvey and Matousek, 1994, pp.
61–62). This power recognizes that "to everything there is a season
and a time to every purpose under the heaven" (Ecclesiastes 3:1).
There is a time to catch the flame of interest in resolving with
negotiation, but it is not *all* the time or *any* time. Knowing that
there are tides and seasons in human relationships and human
affairs, as there are in nature, and that they are beyond our control, our greatest success will come from patiently going with them
rather than struggling against them.

The love of the dance, in which "life itself, in all its paradoxes,
is seen as completely sacred," allows an appreciation of the intricate web of human affairs and human interactions. It allows life to
be appreciated in all its "ordeals and wonders" (Harvey and
Matousek, 1994, p. 62). This power allows us to accept the fact that
others do things that make no sense to us—for good and sufficient
reasons that just are not apparent to us at the time. We no longer
reject what we do not understand, demanding that it be served up
our way before we take cognizance of it.

Simple Mediation Confidentiality Agreement

The undersigned parties are attempting to resolve a dispute and have engaged the services of [name] as mediator. In order to promote communication among the parties and the mediator and to facilitate settlement of the dispute, we agree that the mediator has no liability for any act or omission in connection with the mediation, and further agree:

All statements made during the course of the mediation are privileged settlement discussions, are made without prejudice to any party's legal position, and are inadmissible for any purpose in any legal proceeding. Any information disclosed to the mediator by a party, or by a representative of a party, or by a witness on behalf of a party, is confidential. The mediator cannot be compelled to disclose such information unless required to by law or court order.

All disclosures made during the course of this mediation are conditioned upon this promise and agreement of confidentiality. The mediator shall act as a neutral intermediary, shall not act as an advocate for any party and is not serving as legal counsel to any party.

We will not seek, nor will we encourage or permit another, to compel the mediator to disclose any such confidential information in any legal or administrative proceeding or otherwise. We may not introduce into evidence or use for any adversarial purpose any written or oral communication of the mediator. We agree not to introduce into evidence or use for any adversarial purpose any other confidential information disclosed in this mediation, except as required by law or court order.

All privileges and the protection of attorney work product that preexisted the mediation are unaffected by the mediation, whether or not disclosure is made in the mediation.

Breach of this agreement would cause irreparable injury and monetary damages would be an inadequate remedy, since we are relying upon this agreement of confidentiality in disclosing sensitive business and/or personal information. We therefore agree and stipulate that any party to this agreement may obtain an injunction to prevent disclosure of any confidential information or mediator communication in violation of this agreement. If any party breaches this agreement, that party shall be liable for and shall indemnify the other parties and the mediator for all costs, expenses, liabilities, and fees, including attorney's fees, that may be incurred as a result of such breach.

Signed before mediation this _____ day of _____, 20__.

World-Wide Web Resources

Three key resources for information and links to the mediation field and what is going on in it are the following:

Conflict Resolution Information Source (CRInfo)
(http://www.crinfo.org)

CRInfo is a cooperative effort to strengthen the conflict resolution field's information infrastructure. Funded by the William and Flora Hewlett Foundation, it is an exhaustive collection of materials and leads concerning the conflict resolution field.

Mediation Information and Resource Center (MIRC)
(http://www.mediate.com)

MIRC is a meeting place for people dealing with conflict. At this Web site, you will find over seven hundred articles and discussions that will increase your knowledge about mediation and conflict resolution. Over five thousand mediators can be contacted through the Conflict Resolution Practitioner Directory and Referral Program.

Association for Conflict Resolution (ACR)
(http://www.ACResolution.org)

ACR's interactive Web site serves a large membership of neutrals as well as the public. Visitors have access to a learning center, an ACR product catalogue, on-line conference information and registration, mediator referral, and a calendar of current events and training opportunities in the field.

For information on restorative justice, see the following:

Victim-Offender Reconciliation Program (http://www.vorp.com)

Center for Restorative Justice and Peacemaking
(http://www.che.umn.edu/rjp)

Victim-Offender Mediation Association (http://www.voma.org)

For information on government ADR programs and policies, see the following:

Policy Consensus Initiative (PCI) (http://www.policyconsensus.org)
PCI is a national nonprofit program working with leaders at the state level—governors, legislators, attorneys general, and others—to establish and strengthen the use of collaborative practices in states to bring about more effective governance.

Other useful and informative Web sites include the following:

International Alliance of Holistic Lawyers (IAHL)
(http://www.iahl.org)
The IAHL Web site includes essays, a directory of holistic lawyers, and a calendar of events.

Convenor Dispute Resolution Consulting
(http://www.convenor.com)
Christopher Honeyman's Web site contains an enormous amount of information on theory and practice, quality, qualification standards, and ethics in mediation.

DIAlogos (http://www.dialogos-inc.com/home.html)
Founded by William Isaacs, DIAlogos provides high-level training and consulting on the dialogue process.

Public Conversations Project (http://www.publicconversations.org)
The Public Conversations Project promotes constructive conversations and relationships among those who have differing values, worldviews, and positions related to divisive public issues.

Notes

Introduction
1. Judicial settlement conferences historically have excluded parties from active participation, at best allowing them an opportunity to listen rather than speak. In 1989, the Rand Corporation's Institute for Civil Justice studied the perception of justice of 286 personal injury tort litigants; the study indicated that parties whose cases had been tried or arbitrated reported higher degrees of satisfaction with the outcome and perceived greater fairness in the process than did litigants whose cases had been handled through judicial settlement conferences (Lind and others, 1989).

   Contrast a 1999 study of 1,229 users of mediation in Nebraska. Eighty-three percent were satisfied or extremely satisfied with mediation, and 84 percent said they would rather use mediation than go to court (Nebraska Office of Dispute Resolution, 1999).
2. Particularly in informal courts, judges vary greatly in styles and approaches to the law. For insight into the complex reasons why, see Menkel-Meadow (1996).
3. Restorative justice reduces crime and violence with community-based peacemaking circles and victim-offender mediation.
4. See Luban (1995, p. 2639): "To the extent out-of-court settlements are based on bargaining power and negotiation skills, facts lose their importance to the outcome, and the outcome will resemble legal justice only coincidentally."
5. This is the message of leading business advisors in this country. See Stephen R. Covey, *Principle-Centered Leadership* (1991) and *The Seven Habits of Highly Effective People* (1989); Tom Peters, *Liberation Management: Necessary Disorganization for the Nanosecond Nineties* (1992); and Thomas J. Peters and Robert H. Waterman, Jr., *In Search of Excellence: Lessons from America's Best-Run Companies* (1982).
6. See Menkel-Meadow (1996) for a laser-eyed walk through the structural, epistemological, remedial, and behavioral aspects of the

adversary system in the context of a profoundly changing society, with suggestions for developing alternatives.

7. Peter Garrett is founder of a program designed to create dialogue between convicts and prison staff in England. He is a partner in DIAlogos. Further information may be found at http://www.dialogos-inc.com.

Chapter One

1. The federal courts' business is tied to legislation (for example, Age Discrimination in Employment Act cases), enforcement activity (student loan collection cases), and at times decisions that bar or limit access to the federal courts (prisoner petitions; mass tort actions). In the federal courts in 2000, the case load was 479 filed cases per judge, 402 of them civil filings (*U.S. District Court—Judicial Caseload Profile*). It is little wonder that judges have become fanatical about calendar management.

2. See the article "PTA: The Psychologically-Minded Lawyer," by Steven Keeva at http://www.transformingpractices.com/qa/qa5.html.

3. In 1976, Frank E. Sander delivered an address in which he posited what was to become of the concept of the "Courthouse of Many Doors" (Sander, 1976).

4. In an address at the Colorado Judicial Institute's 2001 Dispute Resolution in Colorado conference, Chief Judge Mary Mullarkey of the Colorado Supreme Court observed, "I'm still trying to bring the courts into the twentieth century—and you know what century this is!"

5. Not a few voices have been raised to challenge the ethics of lawyers who offer only litigation to resolve clients' problems (see Burkhardt and Conover, 1990).

6. See Los Angeles County Bar Association. "Financing Legal Expenses of Another's Lawsuit." Formal Ethics Opinion No. 500, May 10, 1999. See also two commercial Web sites: http://www.lawmall.com/lm-finan.html and http://www.oakfinancial.net

7. Alschuler (1986); Church, Carlson, Lee, and Tan (1978), describing findings of a national research project on inefficiency in the courts.

8. Summers and Atiyah (1987) examine the underpinnings of English and American decision-making and legal institutions. It is comforting to see how much of the burden of transforming the law that has fallen to the American courts is structural rather than merely temperamental. Those who would reduce the law-making function of American courts may find guidance here.

9. Mary Rowe, special assistant to the president at Massachusetts Institute of Technology and a founder of the corporate ombuds move-

ment, reports that there is some reluctance in many quarters to use the term *ombuds*. *Ombudsman* is the original term, used in Scandinavia where ombudsmanry originated. *Ombudswoman* is occasionally used. *Ombudsperson* is much more common. *Ombuds practitioner* is widely used in print, though not as a title.

Chapter Two

1. In David Kantor's four-player system of discussions in family settings identifies four categories of roles: mover, follower, opposer, and bystander. For details of this model, see Kantor, 1975 (cited in Isaacs, 1999).

Chapter Three

1. *Warm okayness* is discussed by John de Ruiter on page 72 of his book *Unveiling Reality*.

Chapter Four

1. Unfortunately, it often comes down to a resource issue. There is so much money tied up in the criminal and civil justice systems—systems that largely are not working—that resources for meaningful alternatives are often scarce. This is not to say that courts have the resources they need to do what the legislatures require of them; some do, and some clearly do not.

2. In an advanced family mediation workshop, West Virginia mediator Michael John Aloi presented the topic of "Sacred Space" as follows: "[T]he opportunities for growth and healing in the midst of conflict are sacred opportunities. Once we acknowledge that the mediation space is sacred, we are both empowered and comforted: empowered in that we are intentional about the healing and growth that can take place, and comforted by the knowledge that if we are successful in creating sacred space, we are no longer burdened with the outcome." Aloi is vice president of the West Virginia State Bar, and will be president in 2002–2003. He has been mediating cases for over fourteen years.

Chapter Five

1. The list of common rationalizations was compiled by Ken Cloke of the Center for Dispute Resolution in Santa Monica, California, and Jerry Murase.

2. For an interesting vignette about resolving youth gang disputes by recognizing and working with the motivator, fear, see Edelman and Crain (1993).

3. For a critique of needs as an interpretive tool for analyzing conflict as developed in Burton (1987), see Avruch and Black (1990).

Chapter Six

1. Thanks to John de Ruiter for this metaphor.
2. For an excellent exposition of the transformative power of using story in conflict resolution, see Cloke and Goldsmith (2000).
3. "Rosen, Hers," *New York Times* story, Nov. 25, 1982, p. 16. This story is reprinted in a thoughtful textbook for law students on alternative dispute resolution (Riskin and Westbrook, 1987).

Chapter Seven

1. The Society for Dispute Resolution Professionals (SPIDR), headquartered in Washington, D.C., is a nationwide organization of neutrals, particularly arbitrators and mediators. Since the beginning of the 1980s, SPIDR has been informing efforts around the country that would define and restrict what mediators can do. Its charter is the protection of this infant profession so that it may evolve unencumbered by narrow or misinformed regulation. SPIDR is now part of the Association for Conflict Resolution (ACR), which was formed in 2001 as the result of a merger of SPIDR, the Academy of Family Mediators (AFM), and the Conflict Resolution Education Network (CREnet).
2. ABA Model Rule provides, "A lawyer shall explain a matter to the extent reasonably necessary to make informed decisions regarding the representation." See also Burkhardt and Conover(1990); "Ethical Considerations in ADR," *Arbitration Journal* 45 (Mar. 1990): 21; "Colorado Adopts Ethics Rule," *Alternatives to the High Cost of Litigation* (May 1992): 70, 71.

Chapter Eight

1. See Forester (1989, pp. 82–106), for a comparable model of mediating land use planning issues. See also McCreary, Gamman, and Tietke (1992) for a similar approach in that arena.
2. This example is drawn in part from the training work of William F. Lincoln, Conflict Resolution Research and Resource Institute, Tacoma, Washington, my first mediation teacher and mentor.
3. See Introduction, n. 3.
4. For a comprehensive treatise, see Rogers and McEwen (1989). See also Kovach (1999).

Chapter Nine

1. See Honoroff, Matz, and O'Connor (1988); Honeyman and others (1995); Honeyman (1988).

2. The Convenor Web site (http://www.convenor.com) is an excellent resource for learning more about this entire effort. Many in the mediation field are reluctant to see so-called objective testing (such as most state bar examinations) used for a performance-oriented profession like mediation. Such tests by their nature examine only the ability to recall information the candidates have memorized, not their ability to mediate.

3. For further discussion on evaluating mediators, see Menkel-Meadow (1993) and Matz (1993).

4. For a justification of an expert level of substantive knowledge, see Friedman and Silberman (1993). What the authors overlook in their enthusiasm for subject area expertise (such as lawyers and engineers rather than mediators, for example, might have) is that traditional mediators who are process experts are able to move much more rapidly to what the parties see as critical, because they are not encumbered by their own professional opinions.

5. Actually, initially it was referred to as *early neutral evaluation,* but the test of time has shown it to be inappropriate when used really early, since the expert's ability to evaluate is dependent on the development of adequate information beforehand. It would make a lot more sense to call a neutral evaluation *process neutral evaluation,* rather than calling it mediation. You may find it useful to be aware of this potential for confusion when it comes time to select a mediator.

6. They may take comfort in the history of the evolution of the profession of surgery from that of the barber. In 1540, in the reign of Henry VIII, the formation of the Company of Barber Surgeons of London marked the beginning of some control in qualifications for the performance of operations on humans. This guild, which lasted 200 years, was the precursor of the Royal College of Surgeons in London.

7. An excellent discussion of this is contained in "Preserving the Integrity of Mediation Through the Adoption of Ethical Rules for Lawyer-Mediators," Maureen E. Laflin, *Notre Dame Journal of Law, Ethics & Public Policy,* 14:479 (2000).

8. See Michael Moffitt, "Loyalty, Confidentiality and Attorney-Mediators: Professional Responsibility in Cross-Professional Practice," *Harvard Journal Negotiation Law Review* 1 (1996), p. 203. See also Nancy H. Rogers and Craig McEwen, *Mediation: Law, Policy and Practice,* 2nd ed. (1994), Sec. 10.02.

9. See Introduction (page xxiv) for a definition of "spiritual."

10. Those trainers included William F. Lincoln, National Center Associates; Tom Colosi, American Arbitration Association's vice president for national affairs; Edith B. Primm, Justice Center in Atlanta;

Michael Lewis, Center for Dispute Settlement in Washington, D.C.;
and Christopher W. Moore, CDR Associates in Denver.

11. See Aaron (1996); Kovach and Love (1996). See also Bickerman
(1996) and Alfini and Clay (1994). For a somewhat contrary view,
see Stempel (1996). Stempel's approach, which is to validate evaluative techniques—with which Love does not disagree as long as they
are used to help the parties do their own evaluation—reminds me
of the discovery of fractals, in which a measurable line becomes infi-
nitely long depending on the degree of resolution one is using. I
prefer the practice of separating evaluation into an ENE program,
as the U.S. district court in San Francisco has done. A key question
for me is whether, by spreading the net of mediation to include
processes in which the neutral renders an opinion, we confuse consumers of the services. A more important question is whether a mediator's willingness to render an opinion helps or hinders a mediator's
functioning in harmony with the rule that says, "It is the parties who
decide." I believe it hinders, and so steer clear of rendering opinions. The best summary of the reasons not to include mediator evaluation in the term *mediation* is Love (1997).

This debate, while often conducted in black-and-white terms, has
many subtleties and nuances once we move past putting a number
on a case or telling the parties what we think they ought to do. Many
disagreements would disappear if we could define clearly what it
means to render an opinion.

Chapter Eleven

1. I am grateful to Ken Cloke for much of this material.

Chapter Fourteen

1. This lesson does not address situations in which true evil is involved.

Chapter Fifteen

1. This checklist is adapted from a 1992 teaching note developed by
Scott T. McCreary and John Gamman of CONCUR, a nationwide
environmental and public policy training and mediation firm with
offices in Berkeley and Santa Cruz, California.

2. Allan Savory, author, wildlife biologist, and consultant, has sparked a
movement to restore holistic management practices to the land. He
argues that with the loss of vast herds of wild animals, we must use live-
stock to restore the land to fruitfulness. He celebrates the interrelationship of all life, from microorganisms to predators, and is teaching

ranchers and government officials how to use animals to heal the land. His approach centers on the creation of a common goal, much as consensus and mediation do. Rejecting purely economic approaches, he teaches how to improve the quality of life, reduce debt, and live again in harmony with the land. See Savory (1988).

Chapter Sixteen

1. See Introduction, n. 3.
2. See the Public Conversations Project Web site: http://www.publicconversations.org.

Bibliography

Aaron, Marjorie C. "ADR Toolbox: The Highwire Act of Evaluation." *Fourteen Alternatives to the High Cost of Litigation,* 1996.

Alfini, James, and Clay, Gerald S. "Should Lawyer-Mediators Be Prohibited from Providing Legal Advice or Evaluations?" *Dispute Resolution Magazine* 1:1 (Spring 1994).

Alpert, Steve. "ADR Forum of Choice for Harassment Claims.*" Recorder,* San Francisco, February 23, 1994, pp. 1, 16.

Alschuler, Albert W. "Mediation with a Mugger: The Shortage of Adjudicative Services and the Need for a Two Tier Trial System in Civil Cases." *Harvard Law Review* 99 (1986): 1808–1830.

American Bar Association. *Model Rules of Professional Conduct.* Chicago: American Bar Association, 1983.

American Bar Association. *Standards of Practice for Lawyer Mediators in Family Disputes.* Chicago: American Bar Association, 1984.

American Bar Association. *The State of the Legal Profession 1990.* Chicago: American Bar Association, 1991a.

American Bar Association. *At the Breaking Point: A National Conference on the Emerging Crisis in the Quality of Lawyer's Health and Lives, Its Impact on Law Firms and Client Services.* Chicago: American Bar Association, 1991b.

American Bar Association—Section of Dispute Resolution and SPIDR. *Model Standards of Conduct for Mediators,* 1994.

American Bar Association. *Career Satisfaction.* Chicago: American Bar Association, 1995.

American Bar Association. "Improving Profits and Client Relationships through Alternative Fee Arrangements." *Counselor's Computer and Management Report Newsletter* (Winter 1996).

American Bar Association. *ADR Statistics Report, 1997.* Chicago: American Bar Association, 1998.

American Bar Association. "Proposed Model Rules for Mediation of Client-Lawyer Disputes." August 1998. Available at: http://www.abanet.org/dispute/clilaw.html

American Bar Association. *Model Rules of Professional Conduct,* 2001. http://www.abanet.org/cpr/ethics2k.html

American Institute of Architects. Doc. A201, Sec. 4.5.2 and Doc. 3141, Sec. 1.4.3.4.1, 1997.

Andrew, G., and others. "Comprehensive Lawyer Assistance Programs: Justification and Model." *Law and Psychology Review* 16 (1992).

Antes, James R., Hudson, Donna Turner, Jorgensen, Erling O., and Moen, Janet Kelly. "Is a Stage Model of Mediation Necessary?" *Mediation Quarterly* 16:3 (Spring 1999): 287–301.

Australian Law Reform Commission. *Managing Justice: Continuity and Change in the Federal Civil Justice System, The Terms of Reference.* Sydney: Australian Law Reform Commission, June 29, 2000.

Avery, Michel. *Building United Judgment: A Handbook for Consensus Decision-Making.* Madison, Wis.: Center for Conflict Resolution, 1981.

Avruch, Kevin, and Black, Peter W. "Ideas of Human Nature in Contemporary Conflict Resolution Theory." *Negotiation Journal* (July 1990).

Barrett, Jerome T. "In Search of the Rosetta Stone of the Mediation Profession." *Negotiation Journal* 15:3 (July 1999): 219–227.

Beck, Don Edward, and Cowan, Christopher, C. *Spiral Dynamics.* Cambridge, Mass.: Blackwell Publishers, 1996.

Bickerman, John. "An Evaluative Mediator Responds." *Fourteen Alternatives to the High Cost of Litigation,* 70 (1996).

Bingham, Lisa B. "Mediation's Impact on Formal Discrimination Complaint Filing: Before and After: The REDRESS Program at the United States Postal Service." Paper presented at the International Association for Conflict Management, St. Louis, Mo., June 20, 2000.

Bohm, David. *Thought as a System.* New York: Routledge, 1994.

Bohm, David. *Wholeness and the Implicate Order.* New York: Routledge, 1995.

Boskey, James B. "The Proper Role of the Mediator: Rational Assessment, Not Pressure." *Negotiation Journal* 10 (1994).

Boulle, Lawrence, and Kelly, Kathleen J. *Mediation, Principles, Process, Practice.* Markham, Ont.: Butterworths, 1998.

Bowling, Daniel, and Hoffman, David. "Bringing Peace into the Room: The Personal Qualities of the Mediator and Their Impact on the Mediation." *Negotiation Journal* 16:1 (Jan. 2000): 5–28.

Brazil, Wayne D. "Institutionalizing Court ADR Programs." In American Bar Association, *Emerging ADR Issues in State and Federal Courts.* Chicago: Litigation Section of the American Bar Association, 1991.

Brazil, Wayne, D. *Olam vs. Congress Mortgage Co.* (N.D. Cal.) 199999 WL 909731, 1999.

Brazil, Wayne D. "ADR and the Courts, Now and in the Future." *Alternatives* 17:5 (May 1999).

Brill, Steven. "Headnotes: The New Leverage." *American Lawyer* (July–Aug. 1993).

Burkhardt, Donald, A., and Conover II, Frederic K. "The Ethical Duty to Consider Alternatives to Litigation." *Colorado Lawyer* (Feb. 1990).

Burton, John W. *Resolving Deep-Rooted Conflict: A Handbook.* Lanham, Md.: University Press of America, 1987.

Bush, Robert A. Baruch. "Mixed Messages in the *Interim Guidelines.*" *Negotiation Journal* 9:4 (Oct. 1993).

Bush, Robert A. Baruch, and Folger, Joseph P. *The Promise of Mediation.* San Francisco: Jossey-Bass, 1994.

California Judicial Council. *Justice in the Balance: Report of the Commission on the Future of the California Courts.* San Francisco: California Judicial Council, Feb. 1994.

California Judicial Council. *Court Statistics Report.* San Francisco: California Judicial Council, 2000a.

California Judicial Council. *Foundations for a New Century: 2000 Judicial Council Annual Report.* San Francisco: California Judicial Council, 2000b.

Carse, James P. *Finite and Infinite Games.* New York: Free Press, 1986.

Center for Public Resources–Georgetown Commission on Ethics and Standards in ADR. *ADR Ethics Project.* (Proposed draft), 1999.

Chapman, Roger. "The Role of Lawyers in Mediation." *New Zealand Law Journal* (May 1996).

Chopra, Deepak. *Quantum Healing.* New York: Bantam Books, 1989.

Church, Jr., T., Carlson, A., Lee, J., and Tan, T. *Justice Delayed: The Pace of Litigation in Urban Trial Courts.* Williamsburg, Va.: National Center for State Courts, 1978.

Cloke, Kenneth, and Goldsmith, Joan. *Resolving Personal and Organizational Conflict: Stories of Transformation and Forgiveness.* San Francisco: Jossey-Bass, 2000.

"Colorado Adopts Ethics Rule." In *Alternatives to the High Cost of Litigation.* New York: Center for Public Resources, May 1992.

Conley, John M., and O'Barr, William M. "Fundamentals of Jurisprudence: An Ethnography of Judicial Decision Making in Informal Courts." *Northern California Law Review* 66 (1988).

Cook, E. Lynn, and Hancher, Donn E. "Partnering: Contracting for the Future." *Journal of Management in Engineering* 6 (1990): 431, 432.

Cooley, John W. "Mediation Magic: Its Use and Abuse." *Loyola University Chicago Law Journal* 29 (1997).

Costantino, Cathy A., and Merchant, Christina Sickles. *Designing Conflict Management Systems.* San Francisco: Jossey-Bass, 1995.

Covey, Stephen R. *The Seven Habits of Highly Effective People.* New York: Simon & Schuster, 1989.

Covey, Stephen R. *Principle-Centered Leadership.* Orangeville, Ont.: Summit Books, 1991.

CPR Institute for Dispute Resolution. "Proposed Model Rule of Conduct for the Lawyer as Third Party Neutral." April 1999. Available at: www.cpradr.org/cpr-george.html

Daicoff, Susan. "Lawyer, Know Thyself: A Review of Empirical Research on Attorney Attributes Bearing on Professionalism." *American University Law Review 1337* (1997).

Daicoff, Susan. "The Lawyer Attributes." (1999). Available at: http://users.law.capital.edu/sdaicoff/schma.html

Daicoff, Susan. Afterword to David B. Wexler, Dennis Stolle, and Bruce J. Winick, *Practicing Therapeutic Jurisprudence Law as a Helping Profession*. Durham, N.C.: Carolina Academic Press, 2000.

Daily Labour Report (BNA). No. 182, Sept. 20, 1988.

Della Noce, Dorothy J. "Seeing Theory in Practice: An Analysis of Empathy in Mediation." *Negotiation Journal* 15:3 (July 1999).

Denenberg, Tia Schneider, Denenberg, Richard V., and Braverman, Mark. "Reducing Violence in U.S. Schools." *Dispute Resolution Journal* (Nov. 1998): 28–35.

Denenberg, Tia Schneider, Denenberg, Richard V., Braverman, Mark, and Braverman, Susan. "Dispute Resolution and Workplace Violence." *Dispute Resolution Journal* (Jan.–Mar. 1996): 6–16.

de Ruiter, John. *Unveiling Reality. Edmonton, AB.:* Oasis Edmonton Publishing, 2000.

Edelman, Joel, and Crain, Mary Beth. *The Tao of Negotiation*. New York: HarperCollins, 1993.

Eisler, Raine. "The Goddess of Nature and Spirituality—An Ecomanifesto." In Joseph Campbell and Charles Muses, eds., *In All Her Names*. San Francisco: HarperCollins, 1991.

Equal Employment Opportunities Commission. "Best Practices Presented by Companies in Alternative Dispute Resolution." EEOC Report. (1997). Available at: http://www.ilr.cornell.edu/ICR/best.html

Equal Employment Opportunities Commission. Section 9 in "Best Practices of Private Sector Employees." (1997). Available at: http://www.ilr.cornell.edu/ICR/best.html

Erickson, William H., and Savage, Cynthia A. "Alternative Dispute Resolution in Colorado." *Colorado Lawyer* 28:9 (Sept. 1999): 67–71.

Federal Judicial Center's Summary of Findings on the Court's ADR Program, U.S. District Court for the Northern District of California, 1997. Available at: http://www.adr.cand.uscourts.gov/adr/Jan152001

Fisher, Roger. "Negotiating Power: Getting and Using Influence." *American Behavioral Scientist* 27:2 (1983).

Fisher, Roger, and Ury, William. *Getting to Yes*. Boston: Houghton Mifflin, 1981.

Fiss, Owen. "Against Settlement." *Yale Law Journal* 93 (1984): 1073–1090.

Fontana, David. *The Secret Language of Symbols: A Visual Key to Symbols and Their Meanings.* San Francisco: Chronicle Books, 1993.

Forester, John. "Planning in the Face of Conflict: Mediated Negotiation Strategies in Practice." In J. Forester, *Planning in the Face of Power.* Berkeley: University of California Press, 1989.

Freedman, Lawrence. *Confidentiality in Mediation: A Practitioner's Guide.* Chicago: American Bar Association, 1985.

Friedman, George H., and Silberman, Allan D. "A Useful Tool for Evaluating Potential Mediators." *Negotiation Journal* 9:4 (Oct. 1993).

Fukushima, Susan. "What You Bring to the Table: Transference and Countertransference in the Negotiation Process." *Negotiation Journal* 15:2 (Apr. 1999).

Fukuyama, Francis. *The End of History and the Last Man.* New York: Avon, 1992.

Fukuyama, Francis. *Trust: The Social Virtues and the Creation of Prosperity.* New York: Free Press, 1995.

Fuller, Lon. "Mediation—Its Forms and Functions." *South California Law Review* 44 (1971).

Galanter, M. "News from Nowhere: The Debased Debate on Civil Justice." *Denver University Law Review* 71 (1993).

Gerard, Glenna. *Dialogue: Rediscovering the Transforming Power of Conversation.* New York: Wiley, 1998.

Gimbutas, Marija A. *The Language of the Goddess.* New York: HarperCollins, 1989.

Gleick, James. *Chaos: Life Is Non-Linear.* New York: Penguin, 1988.

Goldberg, S., and others. *Dispute Resolution: Negotiation, Mediation and Other Processes.* 2nd ed. Boston: Little, Brown, 1992.

Goleman, Daniel. *Emotional Intelligence.* New York: Bantam Books, 1995.

Greenberg, Hindi. "Career Satisfaction in the Law." *Complete Lawyer* (Spring 1996).

Grillo, Trina. "The Mediation Alternative: Process Dangers for Women." *Yale Law Journal* 100 (1991): 1545.

Hale, Katherine. "The Language of Cooperation: Negotiation Frames." *Mediation Quarterly* 16:2 (Winter 1998): 147–162.

Harvey, Andrew, and Matousek, Mark. *Dialogues with a Modern Mystic.* Wheaton, Ill.: Quest Books, 1994.

Haynes, John. "Power Balancing." In Jay Folberg and Ann Milne, eds., *Divorce Mediation: Theory and Practice.* New York: Guilford Press, 1988.

Henry, James F., and Lieberman, Jethro K. *The Manager's Guide to Resolving Legal Disputes: Better Results Without Litigation.* 1985.

Hill, Norma Jeanne. "Qualification Requirements of Mediators." *Journal of Dispute Resolution,* no. 1 (1998): 37–51.

Hill, Richard. "Non-adversarial Mediation." (1995). Available at: http://www.batnet.com/oikoumene/arbmed3.html

Honeyman, Christopher. "Five Elements of Mediation." *Negotiation Journal* 4 (1988): 149–158.

Honeyman, Christopher, and others. *Test Design Project: Interim Guidelines for Selecting Mediators.* Washington, D.C.: National Institute for Dispute Resolution, 1993.

Honeyman, Christopher, and others. "Performance Based Assessment: A Methodology for Use in Selecting, Training and Evaluating Mediators," 1995. Available at: http://www.convenor.com/madison/performa.html

Honrohoff, B., Matz, D., and O'Connor, D. "Putting Mediation Skills to the Test." *Negotiation Journal* 6 (1988): 37–46.

Huber, Peter W. *Liability.* New York: Basic Books, 1988.

Huff, Marilyn. "Fast Track Reduces Court Delay." *Journal of Contemporary Legal Issues* 2 (1989): 138140.

Huppauf, Bernd. "The Violence Among Us." *New York Times,* Nov. 21, 1993, p. E17.

Interagency Alternative Dispute Resolution Working Group. "Report to the President on Federal ADR Programs." Interagency Alternative Dispute Resolution Working Group, 2001.

International Alliance of Holistic Lawyers. "Mission Statement," 2000. Available at: http://www.iahl.org

Isaacs, William. *Dialogue and the Art of Thinking Together.* New York: Doubleday, 1999.

Jaffe, Josef. "America the Inescapable." *New York Times Magazine,* June 8, 1997.

Jorgensen, Erling O. "Relational Transformation in Mediation: Following Constitutive and Regulative Rules." *Mediation Quarterly* 17:3 (Spring 2000): 295–312.

Judicial Council of California. *1999 Judicial Council Annual Report.* St. Paul, Minn.: WestGroup, 2000.

Judicial Council of California. *2000 Judicial Council Annual Report.* St. Paul, Minn.: WestGroup, 2001.

Kahn, Lynn, S. *Peacemaking, a Systems Approach to Conflict Management.* Case Study 27: Camp David, September 1978. Lanham, Md.: University of America Press, 1988.

Kantor, David. *Inside the Family.* San Francisco: Jossey-Bass, 1975.

Katzeff, Paul. "Master Mediator Makes Masterly Use of Doubt—Tom Colossi: VEEP of AAA." *Consensus,* Oct. 1996.

Keeva, Stephen. *Transforming Practices.* Chicago: Contemporary Books, 1999.

Keilitz, Susan. "Civil Dispute Resolution Processes." Working paper for the National Symposium on Court Connected Dispute Resolution Research, State Justice Institute, Oct. 1993.

Kelly, Justin. "ABA House of Delegates Votes Down MDP Recommendations," 2000a. Available at: http://www.adrworld.com

Kelly, Justin. "Broad Input Sought for Federal ADR Confidentiality Effort." 2000b. Available at: http://www.adrworld.com

Kirtley, Alan. "The Mediation Privilege's Transition from Theory to Implementation: Designing a Mediation Privilege Standard to Protect Mediation Participants, the Process and the Public Interest." *Journal of Dispute Resolution* 1 (1995).

Kolb, Deborah M. *The Mediators*. Cambridge, Mass.: Massachusetts Institute of Technology, 1983.

Kolb, Deborah M. *When Talk Works: Profiles of Mediators*. San Francisco: Jossey-Bass, 1994.

Kovach, Kimberlee K. "Good Faith in Mediation—Requested, Recommended, or Required? A New Ethic." *Texas Law Review* 38:2 (1997): 100–145.

Kovach, Kimberlee. *Mediation: Principles and Practice*. 2nd ed. St. Paul, Minn.: West/Wadsworth, 2000.

Kovach, Kimberlee, and Love, Lela. "Evaluative Mediation Is an Oxymoron." *Alternatives to High Cost Litigation* 14 (1996): 31.

Kovach, Kimberlee, and Love, Lela. "Mapping Mediation: The Risks of Riskins' Grid." *Harvard Negotiation Law Review* 71 (1998): 3.

Krishnamurti, Jutta. *Talks and Dialogues*. New York: Avon Books, 1968.

Laflin, Maureen E. "Preserving the Integrity of Mediation Through the Adoption of Ethical Rules for Lawyer-Mediators." *Notre Dame Journal of Law, Ethics and Public Policy* 14:1 (2000).

Lambert, Wade. "Calls for Guidelines on Mediation." *Wall Street Journal*, Oct. 22, 1993.

LaMothe, Louise. "Opening Statement: Thinking of Mediation." *Litigation Journal* 19:4 (Summer 1993).

Lang, Michael D., and Taylor, Alison. *The Making of a Mediator: Developing Artistry in Practice*. San Francisco: Jossey-Bass, 2000.

Lewis, Michael. "Advocacy in Mediation: One Mediator's View." *Dispute Resolution Magazine* (Fall 1995).

Lind, E. Allan, and others. *The Perception of Justice: Tort Litigants' Views of Trial, Court-Annexed Arbitration, and Judicial Settlement Conferences*. Santa Monica, Calif.: RAND Corporation, 1989.

Lipsky, David B., and Seeber, Ronald L. "The Use of ADR in U.S. Corporations: Executive Summary." Available at: http://www.ilr.cornell.edu/ICR/NEW/execsum.html

Los Angeles County Bar Association. "Financing Legal Expenses of Another's Lawsuit." Formal Ethics Opinion No. 500, May 10, 1999. Available at: http://www.lacba.org/opinions/eth500.html

Love, Lela P. "The Top Ten Reasons Why Mediators Should Not Evaluate." *Florida State University Law Review* 24 (1997): 937, 939–948.

Lovenheim, Peter. *Mediate, Don't Litigate.* New York: McGraw-Hill, 1989.

Luban, David. "Settlements and the Erosion of the Public Realm." *Georgetown Law Journal* 83 (1995).

Macfarlane, Julie. *Rethinking Disputes: The Mediation Alternative.* London, England: Cavendish Publishing, 1997.

Maryland ADR Commission. *Practical Action Plan.* Baltimore: Maryland ADR Commission, 1999.

Maryland ADR Commission. *Status Report, Action Plan Implementation Efforts.* Baltimore: Maryland ADR Commission, Sept. 8, 2000.

Matz, David E. "Some Advice for Mediator Evaluators." *Negotiation Journal* 9 (1993).

Matz, David E. "Mediator Pressure and Party Autonomy: Are They Consistent with Each Other?" *Negotiation Journal* 10 (1994).

McCreary, Scott T., Gamman, John K., and Tietke, Cornelia. *Using Joint Fact-Finding Techniques to Resolve Complex Environmental Policy Disputes.* CONCUR working paper 92–02. 1992.

McEwen, Craig A., and Maiman, Richard J. "Mediation in Small Claims Court: Achieving Compliance Through Consent." *Law and Society Review* 18 (1984).

McGovern, Francis E. "Beyond Efficiency: A Bevy of ADR Justifications." *Dispute Resolution Magazine* (Summer 1997).

McKay, Robert B. "Ethical Consideration in ADR." *Arbitration Journal* 45 (Mar. 1990): 21.

MacNaughton, Ann L. "Expanding Your ADR Practice: Creating Value Through Conflict Management and Dispute Resolution Processes." Paper presented to Minnesota's Third Annual ADR Institute, Oct. 2000a.

MacNaughton, Ann L., ed. *Multidisciplinary Practice: Staying Competitive and Adapting to Change.* Chicago: American Bar Association, 2000b.

Melamed, James C. "Mediation: A Fascinating Endeavour," 1999. Available at: http://www.to-agree.com/intro.htm

Menkel-Meadow, Carrie. "Toward Another View of Legal Negotiation: The Structure of Problem-Solving." *UCLA Law Review* 31 (1984).

Menkel-Meadow, Carrie. "For and Against Settlement: Uses and Abuses of the Mandatory Settlement Conference." *UCLA Law Review* 33 (1985).

Menkel-Meadow, Carrie. "Measuring Both the Art and Science of Mediation." *Negotiation Journal* 9:4 (Oct. 1993).

Menkel-Meadow, Carrie. "Whose Dispute Is It Anyway? A Philosophical and Democratic Defense of Settlement (In Some Cases)." *Georgetown Law Journal* 83 (1995).

Menkel-Meadow, Carrie. "The Trouble with the Adversary System in a Postmodern, Multicultural World." *William and Mary Law Review* 5 (1996).

Moffitt, Michael. "Loyalty, Confidentiality and Attorney-Mediators: Professional Responsibility in Cross-Professional Practice." *Harvard Journal Negotiation Law Review* 1 (1996).

Moore, Christopher. *The Mediation Process: Practical Strategies for Resolving Conflict.* San Francisco: Jossey-Bass, 1996.

Mullarkey, Mary J. "ADR in Colorado: A Vision for Restoring Community." *Colorado Lawyer* 29:6 (June 1999): 17–20.

Nash, Jennifer, and Susskind, Lawrence. "Mediating Conflict over Dioxin Risks of Resource Recycling: Lessons from a Flawed Process." *Environmental Impact Assessment Review* 7 (1987): 79–83.

National Center for State Courts, Policy Consensus Initiative and Cardozo Online Journal of Dispute Resolution. Transcript of symposium "State of the States," Sept. 1999. Available at: http://www.cardozo.yu.edu/cojcr/state.html

National Conference of Commissioners on Uniform State Laws. *Uniform Mediation Act—February 2001 Draft.* Available at: http://www.law.upenn.edu/bll/ulcl/ulc.htm umediat

Neihardt, John G. *Black Elk Speaks.* Lincoln, Nebr.: University of Nebraska Press, 2000.

Nicolau, George. "Ill-Considered Criteria Endanger Mediation, SPIDR President Warns." *Alternative Dispute Resolution Report* 2 (1988): 244, 245.

Nolan-Haley, Jacqueline M. "Informed Consent in Mediation: A Guiding Principle for Truly Educated Decisionmaking." *Notre Dame Law Review* 74 (1999).

Novich, Lee. "What to Do When a Claim Strikes." Speech to the Association of Engineering Firms Practicing in the Geosciences, National Meeting, Apr. 8, 1991.

Ogawa, Naomi. "The Concept of Facework: Its Functions in the Hawaii Model of Mediation." *Mediation Quarterly* 17:1 (Fall 1999): 5–20.

Ornstein, Robert E., and Ehrlich, Paul R., *New World, New Mind: Moving Towards Conscious Evolution.* New York: Simon & Schuster, 1989.

Ostrom, Brian J., Kauder, Neal B., eds. "Examining the Work of State Courts, 1998." Williamsburg, Va.: National Center for State Courts, 1998.

Palmer, Helen. *The Enneagram: Understanding Yourself and Others in Your Life.* San Francisco: Harper San Francisco, 1991.

Peters, Thomas J. *Liberation Management: Necessary Disorganization for the Nanosecond Nineties.* New York: Knopf, 1992.

Peters, Thomas J., and Waterman, Robert H., Jr. *In Search of Excellence: Lessons from America's Best-Run Companies.* New York: Warner Books, 1982.

Phillips, Bruce. "Reformulating Dispute Narratives Through Active Listening." *Mediation Quarterly* 17:2 (Winter 1999): 161–180.

Policy Consensus Initiative. "States Mediating Solutions to Environmental Disputes." Santa Fe, Calif.: Policy Consensus Initiative, Summer, 1999.

Pollock, Ellen Joan. "Victim-Perpetrator Reconciliations Grow in Popularity." *Wall Street Journal,* Oct. 28, 1993.

Press, Sharon. "Institutionalization: Savior or Saboteur of Mediation?" *Florida State University Law Review* 24 (1997).

Program on Negotiation. *Consensus: Helping Public Officials Resolve Stubborn Policy Disputes.* Cambridge, Mass.: Program on Negotiation, July 1992.

"Protecting Confidentiality in Mediation." *Harvard Law Review* 98 (1984): 441.

RAND Corporation. "Institute for Civil Justice Report." *Daily Labor Report,* Bureau of National Affairs, No. 182, Sept. 20, 1988.

RAND Corporation. *RAND Report on the Civil Justice Reform Act: Just, Speedy, and Inexpensive? An Evaluation of Judicial Case Management Under the Civil Justice Reform Act.* Santa Monica, Calif.: RAND Corporation, 1996.

Ray, Paul H. *The Integral Culture Survey: A Study of the Emergence of Transformational Values in America.* Sausalito, Calif.: Institute of Noetic Sciences, 1996.

Reavley, Thomas M. "Consider Our Consumers." *Pepperdine Law Review* 14 (1987).

Reed, Richard C., ed. *Beyond the Billable Hour.* Chicago: American Bar Association, 1989.

Renfrew, Charles B. "ADR in the 21st Century: A Forecast for Delivery Changes." *Alternatives* 17:4 (April 1999).

Resnik, Judith. "Due Process: A Public Dimension." *University of Florida Law Review* 39 (Sept. 1987).

Resnik, Judith. "Many Doors? Closing Doors? Alternative Dispute Resolution." *Ohio State Journal on Dispute Resolution,* 10 (1995): 211.

Reuben, Richard C. "The Lawyer Turns Peacemaker." *American Bar Association Journal* (Aug. 1996).

Ricker, Darlene. "The Vanishing Hourly Fee." *American Bar Association Journal* (Mar. 1994).

Riskin, Leonard L. "Mediation and Lawyers." *Ohio State Law Journal* 43 (1982): 29, 43–48, 57–59.

Riskin, Leonard L., and Westbrook, James E. *Dispute Resolution and Lawyers.* St. Paul, Minn.: West, 1987.

Rogers, Nancy H., and McEwen, Craig. *Mediation: Law, Policy and Practice.* San Francisco: Bancroft-Whitney, 1989.

Ross, Lee, and Stillinger, Constance. "Barriers to Conflict Resolution." *Negotiation Journal* (Oct. 1991).

Roth, George, and Kleiner, Art. *Car Launch—The Human Side of Managing Change*. New York: Oxford University Press, 1999.

Rothman, Jay. *Resolving Identity-Based Conflict*. San Francisco: Jossey-Bass, 1997.

Rottman, David B., and Tomkins, Alan J. "Public Trust and Confidence in the Courts." *Court Review* (Fall 1999): 24–41.

Russell, Richard A. "Economic Mediation Is on the Horizon." *New Jersey Law Journal*, Aug. 23, 1999.

Salem, Richard A. "The *Interim Guidelines* Need a Broader Perspective." *Negotiation Journal* 9:4 (Oct. 1993).

Sanchez, Valerie A. "Towards a History of ADR: The Dispute Processing Continuum in Anglo-Saxon England and Today." *Ohio State Journal on Dispute Resolution* 11 (1996): 1.

Sander, Frank E. A. "Varieties of Dispute Resolution." Address delivered at the National Conference on the Causes of Popular Dissatisfaction with the Admnistration of Justice, April 7–9, 1976.

Sandori, Paul. "ADR in Canadian Construction Contracts." Address at the Dallas Construction Industry Conference Charting a Course to the Year 2000 Together!, 1994.

San Mateo Superior Court. "Multi-Option ADR Project (MAP), Evaluation Highlights—July 1999–March 2000." San Mateo, Calif.: San Mateo Superior Court, 2000.

Savory, Allan. *Holistic Resource Management*. Washington, D.C.: Island Press, 1988.

Scheider, Carl D. "What It Means to Be Sorry: The Power of Apology in Mediation." *Mediation Quarterly* 17:3 (Spring 2000): 265–279.

Schrader, Charles R. "Construction Mediation Booms." *Oregon State Bar Bulletin* (Feb.–Mar. 1992): 36.

Scorza, John. "EEOC Plans to Expand Voluntary Mediation Program." June 9, 2000. Available at: http://csi.toolkit.cch.com

Semas, Judith Markham. "Is Mandatory Arbitration a Fair Way to Resolve Workplace Disputes?" *High Technology Careers Magazine*, 1998. Available at: http://www.hightechcareers.com/doc498/ethics498.html

Senge, Peter M. *The Fifth Discipline: The Art and Practice of the Learning Organization*. New York: Currency Doubleday, 1994.

Singer, Linda. *Settling Disputes*. Boulder, Colo.: Westview Press, 1990.

Slobogin, Christopher. "Therapeutic Jurisprudence: Five Dilemmas to Ponder." *Psychology, Public Policy and Law* 1, 1995.

Society for Professionals in Dispute Resolution. *Report: Qualifying Neutrals: The Basic Principles*. Washington, D.C.: National Institute for Dispute Resolution, 1989.

Society for Professionals in Dispute Resolution. *Report 1, Mandated Participation and Settlement Coercion: Dispute Resolution as It Relates to the Courts.* Washington, D.C.: Society for Professionals in Dispute Resolution, 1990.

Staletovich, Jenny. "Black Farmers Finally Reap Benefits." *Denver Rocky Mountain News,* June 20, 1999.

Stauffer, Edith. *Unconditional Love and Forgiveness.* Whittier, Calif.: Triangle Publishers, 1987.

Stempl, Jeffrey W. "Reflections on Judicial ADR and the Multi-Door Courthouse at Twenty: Fait Accompli, Failed Overture or Fledgling Adulthood?" *Ohio State Journal of Dispute Resolution,* 11 (1996).

Stillinger, Constance, Epelbaum, Michael, Keltner, Dacher, and Ross, Lee. "The Reactive Devaluation Barrier to Conflict Resolution." Working Paper No. 3. Stanford Center on Conflict and Negotiation, December 1988.

Stillinger, Constance, and Ross, Lee. "Barriers to Conflict Resolution." *Negotiation Journal,* Oct. 1991.

Stipanowich, Thomas J. "Beyond Arbitration: Innovation and Evolution in the United States Construction Industry." *Wake Forest Law Review* 31 (1996).

Stipanowich, Thomas J. "The Multi-Door Contract and Other Possibilities." *Ohio State Journal on Dispute Resolution,* 13:2 (1998a).

Stipanowich, Thomas J. "Reconstructing Construction Law: Reality and Reform in a Transactional System." *Wisconsin Law Review* 2 (1998b).

Stipanowich, Thomas, and O'Neal, Leslie K. "Charting the Course: The 1994 Construction Industry Survey on Dispute Avoidance and Resolution, Part I. The Construction Lawyer," Nov. 1995.

Stipanowich, Thomas, and O'Neal, Leslie K. "Charting the Course: The 1994 Construction Industry Survey on Dispute Avoidance and Resolution, Part II. The Construction Lawyer," April 1996.

Stone, Douglas, and others. *Difficult Conversations.* New York: Penguin, 2000.

Stuart, Barry D. "Circle Sentencing in Canada: A Partnership of the Community and the Criminal Justice System." *International Journal of Comparative and Applied Criminal Justice* 20:2 (Fall 1996).

Stuart, Barry D. "Key Differences: Courts and Community Circles." *Justice Professional* 11 (1998).

Sub, Mori Irvine. "Serving Two Masters: The Obligation Under the Rules of Professional Conduct to Report Attorney Misconduct in a Confidential Mediation." *Rutgers Law Journal* 26 (1994): 155.

Summers, Robert, and Atiyah, Patrick. *Form and Substance in Anglo-American Law.* Oxford: Clarendon Press, 1987.

Susskind, Lawrence, and Cruikshank, Jeffrey L. *Breaking the Impasse: Consensual Approaches to Resolving Public Dispute.* New York: Basic Books, 1987.

Susskind, Lawrence, McKearnan, Sarah, and Thomas-Larmer, Jennifer, eds. *The Consensus Building Handbook: A Comprehensive Guide to Reaching Agreement.* Thousand Oaks, Calif.: Sage, 1999.

Tannen, Deborah. *The Argument Culture: Stopping America's War of Words.* New York: Random House, 1998.

Toben, Steven. "The Future of the Conflict Resolution Field." *NIDR News* (Jan.–Feb. 1996).

Tuchman, Barbara. *March of Folly.* New York: Ballantine Books, 1992.

Tutu, Desmond. *No Future Without Forgiveness.* New York: Doubleday, 1999.

Umbreit, Mark S. *Mediating Interpersonal Conflicts: A Pathway to Peace.* Cpi Pub., 1995.

United Nations Educational, Scientific, and Cultural Organization. *Constitution.* New York: United Nations, 1945.

Ury, William L. *Getting to Peace: Transforming Conflict at Home, at Work and in the World.* New York: Viking Press, 1999.

Ury, William L., Brett, Jeanne M., and Goldberg, Stephen B. "Three Approaches to Resolving Disputes, Interests, Rights and Power." In William L. Ury, Jeanne M. Brett, and Stephen B. Goldberg, *Getting Disputes Resolved.* San Francisco: Jossey-Bass, 1988.

van der Post, Sir Laurens. *A Mythic Journey with Sir Laurens van der Post.* (Audiotape). New Dimensions Foundation, 1994. Available at: http://www.newdimensions.org

Van Duch, Darryl. "Assault on Mandatory Arbitration." *National Law Journal,* Aug. 25, 1997. Available at: http://www.ljx.com/practice/laboremployment/0825mandar6.html

Wexler, David B. "Therapeutic Jurisprudence and the Culture of Critique." *Journal of Contemporary Legal Issues* 10 (1999).

Wilkinson, John H., ed. *Donovan, Leisure, Newton and Irvine ADR Practice Book.* New York: Wiley, 1990.

Williams, Michael. "Can't I Get No Satisfaction?" *Mediation Quarterly* 15:2 (Winter 1997): 143–154.

Wondolleck, Julia M., and Ryan, Clare M. "What Hat Do I Wear Now?" *Negotiation Journal* 15:2 (Apr. 1999): 117–133.

Wulff, Randall. "A Mediation Primer." In John Wilkinson, ed., *Donovan, Leisure, Newton and Irvine ADR Practice Book.* New York: Wiley, 1990.

Zariski, Archie. "Lawyers and Dispute Resolution: What Do They Think and Know (And Think They Know)?" June, 1997. Available at: http://www.murdoch.edu.au/elaw/issues/v4n2/zaris422.html

About the Author

BARBARA ASHLEY PHILLIPS has twenty years' experience as a mediator specializing in complex, technical, and highly sensitive matters. A graduate of Yale Law School, Phillips served as an assistant United States attorney and practiced primarily federal civil trial law in Oregon and California prior to becoming a mediator. She provides mediation, training, dialogue, coaching, and facilitation services through American West Institute for Conflict Resolution.

Phillips offers public and private training in reflective mediation practice and the art of presence through the nonprofit North American Institute for Conflict Resolution. She also provides coaching on fruitful conflict management. She is the author of *Finding Common Ground: A Field Guide to Mediation* (1994) and "Mediation: Did We Get It Wrong?," which was published by the *Willamette Law Review* (1998) and is available on her Web site.

Phillips brings compassionate presence along with a quick mind, solid litigation experience, and insight to sensitive situations. She mediates in many fields, including medical and legal malpractice; employment issues; intellectual property, insurance coverage, construction and disaster, computer software development and licensing agreement disputes; lender liability and collection matters; agricultural issues; family business and marital property disputes; and aviation cases, among others.

For more information on the offerings of Barbara Ashley Phillips, the North American Institute for Conflict Resolution, and American West Institute for Conflict Resolution, call (780) 465–1721, fax to (780) 433-4163, or visit the Web site http://www.mediate.com/baphillips.

Index